Corra Harris and the Divided Mind of the New South

UNIVERSITY PRESS OF FLORIDA

Florida A&M University, Tallahassee
Florida Atlantic University, Boca Raton
Florida Gulf Coast University, Ft. Myers
Florida International University, Miami
Florida State University, Tallahassee
New College of Florida, Sarasota
University of Central Florida, Orlando
University of Florida, Gainesville
University of North Florida, Jacksonville
University of South Florida, Tampa
University of West Florida, Pensacola

Corra Harris and
the Divided Mind
of the New South

Catherine Oglesby

University Press of Florida
Gainesville/Tallahassee/Tampa/Boca Raton
Pensacola/Orlando/Miami/Jacksonville/Ft. Myers/Sarasota

Copyright 2008 by Catherine Oglesby
Printed in the United States of America on acid-free paper
All rights reserved

12   11   10   09   08   6   5   4   3   2   1

Library of Congress Cataloging-in-Publication Data
Oglesby, Catherine.
Corra Harris and the divided mind of the new south / Catherine
Oglesby.
p. cm.
Includes bibliographical references and index.
ISBN 978-0-8130-3247-4 (acid-free paper)
1. Harris, Corra, 1869-1935. 2. American literature—Southern
States—History and criticism. 3. Literature and society—South-
ern States. 4. Progressivism (United States politics) 5. Southern
States—Intellectual life—1865- I. Title.
PS3515.A725Z78 2008   2008011030
813.52—dc22

The University Press of Florida is the scholarly publishing agency
for the State University System of Florida, comprising Florida
A&M University, Florida Atlantic University, Florida Gulf
Coast University, Florida International University, Florida State
University, New College of Florida, University of Central Florida,
University of Florida, University of North Florida, University of
South Florida, and University of West Florida.

University Press of Florida
15 Northwest 15th Street
Gainesville, FL 32611-2079
www.upf.com

Parts of chapters 1 and 2 were published previously as "The 'Seem-
ingly Contradictory' Life and Legacy of Georgia Novelist Corra
White Harris" in *Georgia Historical Quarterly* 87, no. 2 (Summer
2003): 200–244. Parts of chapter 4 were published as "Reluctant
Suffragist/Unwitting Feminist: The Ambivalent Political Voice of
Georgia Novelist Corra White Harris" in *Southeastern Political
Review* 28, no. 3 (2000): 397–426.

For my namesakes,
Chelsea Catherine Ricks-Wait
Olivia Catherine Olsen
and
Chloe Catherine Paulk

Contents

Illustrations

Preface and Acknowledgments

For a book whose operative theme is contradiction, it seems fitting to begin with a statement of what is *not* its intended purpose. An observation borrowed from Bettie Rains Upshaw, a close caretaker of Corra Harris, helps. In 1969, shortly after reading John Talmadge's recently published biography *Corra Harris, Lady of Purpose*, Upshaw wrote in a letter, "I don't think it a great book and I doubt if it will sell, but I do think it is the truth. And that is what a biography is supposed to be."[1] Most academics would take issue with Upshaw's suggestion that a narrative could reveal the "truth." And both defenders and critics of the genre of biography would have a field day with her assertion of what a biography is supposed to be.

The present volume's interpretation of Corra Harris makes no claim to be the "truth," and none for what a biography is supposed to be. Its goal has evolved since the project began several years ago when I proposed, through comparing the ideas of Corra Harris with those of Charlotte Perkins Gilman, to determine the role of gender identity in the development of social consciousness. After an initial revision, I grew simultaneously exasperated and intrigued with the contradictions and inconsistencies that filled Harris's life, behavior, and actions as well as with the ideas and beliefs that informed her writings. Contradiction became the lens through which I focused on this exceptional woman. Increasingly, I came to see her against the backdrop of the New South, a time, place, and culture historians also characterize as contradictory. My purpose then became to write a micro-history of time and place through the life of a once-famous individual.

An alternative purpose evolved, however, as I recalled Emerson's observation that "foolish consistency" is "the hobgoblin of little minds." Although Emerson did not make explicit what he meant by "foolish," one finds that Harris developed distinct ideas about the difference between wisdom and foolishness with regard to consistency. She grew to equate consistency with obstinacy, rigidity, and legalism; conversely, the ability to admit error, to change one's mind, she equated with wisdom, humility, and a "clean heart."

My developing understanding of Harris's contradictory nature suggested the need for a more flexible interpretation. Harris was not merely a bundle of contradictions, which some might dismiss as a character flaw, but an extremely complicated person, as most who think deeply are. When complexity of character intersects with circumstances that include personal tragedy within and a rapidly changing culture without, contradiction could be interpreted as a normal outcome that invites a variety of viewpoints, be they from one mind or many. Consistency of belief or action may be the luxury of those who can be satisfied with oversimplified thinking. If Harris was nothing if not a contradiction, she was also anything but simple-minded.

Moreover, Harris engaged in intense self-scrutiny throughout her mature years. Her ability to critique herself and to admit her own contradictions led her in a perpetual effort—sometimes successful, sometimes not—to overcome self-admitted prejudices. Through such candid self-scrutiny she disarmed many critics. She also thereby became greater than the sum of her oftentimes distasteful politics, or of any particular belief system.

Harris would have wanted readers to know up front how to say her first name. It was pronounced as if spelled Carra, and she never missed a chance to set anyone straight who mispronounced it. "Corra is spelled with two 'r's,'" she wrote. "I always feel as if I had a peg leg when I see it printed with one or hear it pronounced as if it was 'Cora.'"[2]

A project fifteen years in the making accrues many debts. To those who supplied material support over the years, I am grateful. In 1995 and 1996, thanks to recommendations from the Department of History at Michigan State University, the College of Arts and Letters granted two semester-long fellowships. Since 1996, Joseph Tomberlin, David Williams, and Paul Riggs, successive heads of the Department of History at Valdosta State University, have generously funded or recommended my project for funding through course releases, travel money, research and professional development grants, and finally a leave with pay during fall semester 2006. Al Jacobs, director of the Wiregrass History Consortium, funded travel and supplies for research in 2006.

Librarians at the University of Georgia, at Valdosta State University, and at Emory University have been tremendously helpful. The longevity of the staff at the University of Georgia's Hargrett Library simplified my work there over the years. Melissa Bush at Hargrett responded promptly with a much appreciated patience and courtesy. Denise Montgomery at Valdosta State's Odum Library surpasses anything I have known to date with regard to thoroughness. Deborah Davis in the Odum Archives has bent the rules and allowed me to check out special collection books by and about Corra Harris. Emily Rogers at Odum helped with final editing.

Several organizations, associations, and individuals provided venues for me to present my work, including the Georgia Association of Historians, Milledgeville, Georgia, 2007; the Western Association of Women's Historians, Santa Barbara, California, 2004; the Georgia Women of Achievement Conference, Rome, Georgia, 1999; and the Valdosta State University Women's Studies Conference, 1997. It felt like homecoming to present my work in Bartow County, Harris's residence during the last two decades of her life, where I shared reflections on her religious ideas at the Center for Regional History and Culture of Bartow County in Cartersville, Georgia, in April 2000. I am honored as well to have received from the Georgia Historical Society the E. Merton Coulter award in 2004 for my article on Harris published in the *Georgia Historical Quarterly* in 2003.

Colleagues and mentors have inspired insights that moved the project along. Norman Pollack persuaded me to avoid polemics. No one did more to help tighten the prose than Lamar Pearson. John Crowley read the chapter on Harris's religious development and offered sympathy for the task of trying to figure out Methodists of Harris's day. Others who have read parts of the work over the years and offered valuable insights include Susan Wehling, Linda Bennett-Elder, Viki Soady, Helen Wishart, and Ann Lawson. John Heirs read the first chapter and suggested ways to contextualize Harris with the Southern Agrarians. Linda Calendrillo read the work in its entirety, asked relevant questions, and suggested ways to integrate some of the notes into the text. James Cobb read parts of the manuscript and suggested ways to deal with Harris's complex identity; his encouragement at a pivotal time made a difference. I especially thank Hutch Johnson and Gardner Rogers for their thorough reading of the text. For their guidance, suggestions, patience, and tolerance, I would like to thank the staff at the University Press of Florida, especially Susan Albury, Meredith Morris-Babb, Dennis Lloyd, Nevil Parker, and Stephanie Williams.

Students, friends, and other non-academics have helped in essential ways from research to copy-editing. April Renfroe, Lisa Marie Browning, Luwana Burke, Jennifer Dutkowsky, and Shelby Calloway contributed to the research, and Ashley Herrington devoted more time than anyone else helping edit the notes and bibliography. Dottye Ricks helped with copy-editing. Kathy Johnson proved a valuable research assistant and copy-editor and a competent organizer during the months I spent in her home in Athens in 2006. Jodie Hill, current owner of Corra Harris's home in Bartow County, Georgia, shared his time and exhaustive collection of Harris memorabilia on a number of occasions.

For her infinite patience and moral support I want to thank Patricia Mincy, who has helped over the past ten years as much as any co-worker or friend possibly could. She has read, typed, photocopied, printed, mailed, faxed, phoned, celebrated, commiserated, but more importantly, she has been available in so many ways beyond those required of an administrative assistant. She has been a dear friend whose recent well-deserved retirement has left a void in our collective life as a department. Everyone misses Trish, but I know I miss her most.

I would feel negligent if I did not mention some who have been especially supportive the past couple of years. Sheri Gravett housed me several times on trips from Athens to Valdosta. Countless meals at the home of Mouyyed Hassouna and Susan Wehling have nurtured the soul.

My family's support has made the most difference. Paul Badura deserves more than a byline. His wit and perseverance went most of the distance. Sandra, Ira (now deceased), and the extended Paulk family have rewarded me in a big way by including me as one of their own and making Ocilla my second home. My siblings, Lamar, Wade, and Sherri, anchor me with their support, love, pride, and confidence in me. My mother, Sara, proves over and over again that only mothers (and possibly canine friends) can love unconditionally. My son-in-law, Wesley Paulk, enriches my life in many ways, not least by providing and caring for our mutual beloveds. My daughter, Hope, continues to inspire me as she has all her life. For the past eight years my grandson, Owen, has controlled my heartstrings. And for the past three, so has his sister, Chloe Catherine. They bring joy no matter when or where we visit, which is never often enough. And they make me laugh from deep in the heart. Besides myself, none more than Wesley, Hope, Owen, and Chloe are happier to see this project finally come to its end.

A deeply felt thanks to all who have patiently endured life with me and Corra Harris as my shadow all these years. May she finally rest in peace—that is, until someone else destined for the challenge finds her and enters the gauntlet.

Chronology

1900	Lundy accepts position teaching at Young Harris College in north Georgia; supply preacher in churches in Groveton and College Park, Georgia; December, Corra begins reviewing books for the *Independent*
1901–3	Paul Elmer More works as literary editor for the *Independent;* he and Corra correspond and work together on the *Jessica Letters*
1902	Lundy becomes assistant secretary of Methodist Church's Board of Education, Nashville, Tennessee
1903–4	*The Jessica Letters* serialized in the *Critic,* October–April; published as novel by Putnam
1903–5	Corra publishes in the *Critic*
1905	Summer and fall, Corra has surgeries for "abscesses" in her side
1905–9	Publishes in the *American*
1906	October, publishes debate on the home with Charlotte Perkins Gilman in the *Independent*
1907	Publishes in *Uncle Remus*
1907–1932	Publishes in *Saturday Evening Post*
1908	January, Lundy takes leave of absence from Board of Education in Nashville; attempts suicide
1909	June, Faith graduates from Woman's College in Baltimore; Corra meets *Saturday Evening Post* editor, George Horace Lorimer
1910	January–February, *A Circuit Rider's Wife* serialized in *Saturday Evening Post,* published as novel by Henry Altemus Company, Philadelphia; March, Corra has surgery for gallstones; spring, Faith Harris meets Harry Leech; July 17, Lundy resigns from Board of Education in Nashville; September 19, Lundy dies from self-induced drug overdose while visiting friends at Pine Log, Georgia; December 24, Faith marries Harry in Nashville
1911	Faith and Harry move from Nashville to Texas, then back to Nashville following the first of a number of job disappointments for Harry; Corra publishes *Eve's Second Husband;* travels to Europe to report on woman suffrage movement; William H. Everett, a London press, reprints *A Circuit Rider's Wife*
1912	Publishes *The Recording Angel;* publishes short story "Jeff" in the *Independent;* April, Corra visits Pine Log where Lundy died and decides to purchase a cabin she sees on the property not far from where Lundy spent his last days; writes *Co-Citizens,* then spends over two years finding an interested publisher

1913	January, purchases two hundred acres surrounding cabin in Pine Log and soon begins construction on her farm home she would eventually name In the Valley; publishes *In Search of a Husband*
1913–14	Publishes in *Harper's* and *Harper's Weekly*
1913–18	Publishes in *Good Housekeeping*
1914	Publishes in *Metropolitan;* September–December, travels to Europe to report on effect of World War I on women and children
1914–26	Publishes in *Pictorial Review*
1915	March, Faith and Harry move to the Valley to manage farm while Corra travels and writes; publishes *Justice* and *Co-Citizens*
1916	July, Faith has surgery for undisclosed illness; increasingly strained relations between Corra and Harry; August, Faith and Harry move from the Valley to Atlanta; Corra publishes *A Circuit Rider's Widow*
1916–18	Corra and Harry estranged
1917	Faith's writing career picks up as she begins publishing in *Country Gentlemen*
1918	Winter, Corra and Faith begin collaboration on *From Sun-up to Sun-down;* Corra publishes *Making Her His Wife;* December, rapprochement between Corra and Harry
1919	Corra and Faith publish *From Sun-up to Sun-down;* May 3, Faith dies at a hospital in Nashville
1920–29	Publishes in *Ladies Home Journal*
1920	Publishes *Happily Married;* August, publishes "The Widow Ambrose"
1921	May, Corra's sister, Hope, dies; sisters Bettie and Trannie Rains move in with Corra to help manage and maintain the Valley; Corra publishes *My Son*
1922	Publishes *The Eyes of Love* and *A Daughter of Adam*
1923–31	Publishes in *Country Gentleman*
1923	Begins writing her first autobiography, *My Book and Heart,* serialized in *Saturday Evening Post,* September–October; publishes *The House of Helen*
1924	Meets Marjorie McClain, the close friend with Corra at her death at Emory; Houghton Mifflin publishes in book form *My Book and Heart*
1925	Publishes *As a Woman Thinks* serially in *Saturday Evening Post,* August–October; Houghton Mifflin publishes it in book form

later in the year; travels to California to report on experiences for her final autobiography, *Happy Pilgrimage*

1926 May–October, writes *Happy Pilgrimage,* serialized in *Saturday Evening Post,* December 1926–January 1927; publishes *Flapper Ann*

1927 Houghton Mifflin publishes *Happy Pilgrimage;* January–March, travels to Winter Park, Florida, to visit with and receive an honorary doctorate from Hamilton Holt, new president of Rollins College

1929 Publishes in *Woman's Home Companion;* Hamilton Holt proposes visiting professorship

1930 Begins lecturing as Professor of Evil at Rollins College; April, Tinsley Rucker White dies at Confederate Home in Atlanta; December, Charles Dobbins secures permission from Corra to write a biography of her for his master's thesis at Columbia University

1931 June, *Atlanta Journal* buys Dobbins's thesis; Harris and Medora Perkerson edit Dobbins's thesis before the *Journal* publishes it; November 15, first "Candlelit" column published

1931–35 Publishes "Candlelit" column in *Atlanta Journal*

1932 Travels to Washington, D.C., on assignment for *Atlanta Journal;* receives the George Fort Milton Award for outstanding southern writers

1933 Addresses Georgia Press Association with reflections titled "Editors"; Houghton Mifflin reprints *A Circuit Rider's Wife;* December, visits Winter Park for the last time (stays from December through March)

1934 Health declines; May, diagnosed with "cardiac asthma"; heart attacks in July and November; against doctor's orders, she continues to write

1935 January 27, collapses at home in the Valley from congestive heart failure; January 28, taken to Emory Hospital; Saturday, February 9, Corra Harris dies shortly after 4 P.M. at Emory Hospital

1936 June 6, Hamilton Holt, John Paschall, and Al Harris conduct memorial service and dedication of chapel built over Corra Harris's grave in the Valley

1951   Twentieth Century Fox makes *A Circuit Rider's Wife* into the feature-length motion picture *I'd Climb the Highest Mountain* (released on video, spring 1995)

1988   Bristol Books, Wilmore, Kentucky, reprints *A Circuit Rider's Wife*

1998   University of Georgia Press reprints *A Circuit Rider's Wife*

I

Introduction: The "Contradictory" Legacy of Corra Harris

In 1931, *Good Housekeeping* editor W. F. Bigelow predicted that Georgia novelist Corra Harris's reputation would outlive that of Nebraska's Willa Cather, stating that Harris's novel *A Circuit Rider's Wife* was "far more important than Cather's *Death Comes for the Archbishop.*" Attesting to her continued national popularity, Bigelow informed Harris that she had held her own in *Good Housekeeping*'s contest that year to find the nation's twelve greatest living women.[1] Bigelow was wrong, of course, in his ranking of Cather's and Harris's works. Harris may have been disappointed at the outcome, but she would not have been surprised to find Cather's works remembered and her own forgotten. In a 1903 review comparing fiction in the North and South, she noted that when the country's "great fiction is written, it will come out of the West."[2] Harris was under no illusions about the merits of her own work.[3]

Whatever her legacy, Corra Harris (1869–1935) was the most widely published and nationally popular woman writer from Georgia in the early twentieth century. Critics during her day and since have had a difficult time categorizing Harris's works, many either dismissing them as part of the lightweight genre of domestic fiction or unable to categorize them at all. Indeed, little about Harris's life or writing fits neatly into any category. Whether the subject is her work or herself, she was a person who dependably, as her nephew said in a memorial speech, "defied characterization."[4] Interest in her works has revived over the past couple of decades, as indicated by the 1998 reissue of her most famous novel, *A Circuit Rider's Wife* (1910), but since 1968, when John Talmadge published *Corra Harris, Lady of Purpose*, no one has revisited her life or works in depth.

Harris's popularity during her lifetime and her legacy since then derive from her identification with *A Circuit Rider's Wife* and its heroine, Mary Thompson. Even though the book was only marginally autobiographical, Harris was ever after remembered as "the circuit rider's wife." Contemporary readers who admired Harris and her work ranked her with various literary icons, from George Eliot to Shakespeare; regionally, one reviewer compared her with Ellen Glasgow.[5] Hamilton Holt, one of her earliest editors, and John Paschall, her last, captured something of her reputation in eulogies they delivered in 1936, the year after she died, at the dedication service of a memorial chapel built over her grave. Holt was one of Harris's most distinguished and sustained admirers, and their professional association and friendship lasted from 1899 until her death.

Holt edited and for a time owned the *Independent*, which grew under his direction from a religious journal of limited reach to one focused on political issues with a much wider national circulation. He later served as president at Rollins College in Winter Park, Florida, from where he and Harris continued to correspond and visit. Politically, the two could not have been further apart.[6] Holt was known for his liberal politics, most notably peace activism, and Harris for her "extreme reactionary conservative" opinions.[7] Holt was well known for his work in journalism, politics, and education. Harris admired and respected him and valued highly his opinion. The regard was mutual.

In his speech in 1936 at the chapel dedication, Holt reiterated what he had written in 1924 in a review of Harris's first autobiography, *My Book and Heart*: "As I look back now I recall but one red-letter day like it in *The Independent* office—the day when Robert Frost—a stripling of eighteen—sent in his first poem." Or perhaps "that day when Sydney Lanier's first poem came in . . . when the whole staff gathered round [Dr. Ward's] desk . . . to listen while he read it aloud." In Holt's opinion, Harris's first autobiography, *My Book and Heart*, put her in the company of four of the Western world's most renowned autobiographers: "I know of only two living Americans who seem . . . to have the courage, candor and literary ability . . . to emulate these four immortals [Benvenuto Cellini, Jean-Jacques Rousseau, Herbert Spencer, and Benjamin Franklin]. One is E. W. Howe. . . . The other is Corra Harris." To him, however, her genius transcended her writing ability. "Corra Harris knows the human heart as does, in my judgment, no contemporary writer in America," he wrote, careful to add, "certainly no woman writer."[8]

The last editor with whom Harris worked, John Paschall of the *Atlanta Journal*, enjoyed as close a relationship with Harris as perhaps anyone in her final years. She wrote extensively for him during the last four years of her life. In his speech at the chapel dedication in 1936, he said that she had "the virility of a man, the deftness and intuition of a woman, and the wit and brilliancy of both. She is Walter Lippmann, Arthur Brisbane, Will Rogers, Helen Rowland or Dorothy Dix, as the mood strikes her."[9]

There are several reasons why Harris has not been revisited as a historical subject. Most problematic by far are the contradictions that fill her works, fiction and nonfiction, from the beginning of her writing career to the end of her life. To the frustration of anyone attempting to analyze Harris, she contradicted herself at pivotal turns as she tried to come to terms with vital social and political issues. Her contemporary readers from disparate backgrounds noticed contradiction as a defining trait.

In her mature years, Harris wrote in *My Book and Heart* about asking a reader and trusted friend (unnamed) for a candid opinion of her. After a long pause, the friend responded, "I think that you are the most enigmatical woman I have ever known." After an interview with Harris, a journalist called her "the most . . . uncatalogueable person I have met in many a day's work." Jack London, one of her "socialistic" contemporaries whom Harris loved to hate and whom she delighted in abusing, called Harris's a "curious" mind that was foremost "all complexity." A reader and longtime fan wrote Harris in 1926 that she was "frequently self-contradictory and stubbornly sad." Another wrote, "to me you are an interesting paradox."[10] Discussing primarily her eclectic religious philosophy, Charles Dobbins wrote in 1931 that one could read everything Harris had written and yet find oneself "at the end more confused than at the beginning." She was, to Dobbins, "inconsistent with amazing consistency."[11]

Indeed, Harris saw herself as a contradiction, writing in *My Book and Heart*: "I do not know what God could have been thinking about when he made me,—such a lie! A being whose outside is an absolute contradiction to her inside. Whose every action is a concealment of truth, who can never be veracious except when she is writing fiction."[12] After reflecting on the fleeting nature of fame and how she had taught herself not to "hunger" for it, she wrote Holt that she had just finished "getting the stone blasted out for the little chapel" she was preparing to have built as her memorial. She admitted the incongruousness of disclaiming fame and providing for one's own memorial but wrote that "we cannot be consistent, my dear friend, only aim pathetically at consistency."[13]

Educator, historian, and critic of southern culture Edwin Mims captured succinctly Harris's most salient trait as a person and a writer: "It is in a certain balance of seemingly contradictory elements in her personality and in her novels that her chief distinction lies among contemporary writers."[14] It is at times the "seeming"—and at other times the outright—contradictions that make Harris difficult to interpret. But it proves worthwhile to examine how she tried to achieve the balance Mims found in her life and fiction. Something in her contradictory reasoning and conclusions appealed to her readers, nationally and locally. One noted interpreter of southern identity, Wilbur Cash, considered contradiction "the very stuff of Southern psychology."[15]

Among other explanations for why Harris has been "something of an orphan in historical scholarship," one is that she held what strikes many readers today as distasteful politics.[16] She was notorious for holding poorly informed and often naively argued political positions found in much of her nonfiction. As Talmadge notes, she rarely let facts get in the way of making a point or expressing herself, and her spelling and grammar were atrocious.[17] Most of the staff at the *Independent* shared Holt's opinion about Harris's "reactionary conservative politics," albeit one they paid well and encouraged, a point worth noting since the *Independent* was reputedly a progressive periodical and considered by some "the best weekly in the country."[18]

Harris could be reactionary and conservative. She wrote contemptuously about modernization and industrialization decades before the Southern Agrarians took their stand in 1930 and legitimized the genre. On gender she could be stridently antifeminist, even misogynist. About race, she believed in white supremacy and condoned lynching. With regard to class division, she held relentlessly to a belief in meritocracy and a level playing field. On the other hand, she could be astutely insightful about issues on which she took otherwise rigidly conservative positions or was indifferent. Such was the case with gender and race, about which she revealed theoretical insights even if they were not followed by similarly insightful practices. If she expressed antimodernist rhetoric in places, she also saw the need to move forward. She believed it a mockery to expect patriotism from Native Americans, who had been "deprived" "of [their] liberties and pensioned . . . to a life of ignominy."[19]

Of particular note is Harris's legacy to histories of the New South, namely, her mocking critique of the Lost Cause, of southern literature for its blind hold on a "defunct ideal" and a Dixie that "never existed" well before such criticism was an accepted genre.[20] In *The Promise of the New South* (1995), Edward Ayers used Harris's 1912 novel *The Recording Angel* as an example of such regional self-awareness, and in 2005 Peter Schmidt recommended revisiting the same novel for that and other reasons.[21] But her sharp criticism began at least a decade before that novel was published, a significant point since such insight is chiefly reserved for the Fugitives and Agrarians, who did not surface until many years later.

On the issue of women's status, Harris catered obsequiously to the domestic ideal in most of her fiction and prescriptive essays. However, over the course of her writing career she made a startling discovery about women, namely, that whatever biology was—and in her early career she held assiduously to the notion that biology was destiny—gender was a social construct. She waged war with herself over how much the "ancient fate of women" was biology and how much social. Even though she spent her professional life promoting traditional roles for women, over time she came to do so more tentatively, awkwardly, and self-consciously. Moreover, in interviews and in much of her fiction she challenged women's secondary status by exposing the contradictions between constitutional liberty and women's reality. The subtle and obvious ways she did so are a focus of this volume.

Regarding race and race relations, Harris was never able to let go of her belief in white superiority. She maintained to the end of her life that the black race as a whole was "of a lower order," incapable of "ever attaining coucasion [*sic*] standards of morals or civilization."[22] But she reveals at times as much curiosity as antipathy in her thinking about race, as well as an effort, albeit failed, to rise above prejudice.

Locating Harris among contemporary writers is essential. Neither her conservative values nor her contradictory nature sets her apart. Both reflect the experience of a thinking woman in a time and place of devastation—the South struggling to recover from the wholesale destruction of the Civil War by simultaneously inviting and resisting modernization. Whether the subject is political ideals, class background, racial views, gender ideals, southern identity, or writing style, Harris differs from her contemporaries in degree—not in kind—of reaction and response to the dramatic changes through which they were living.

Her reputation, as was the case for writers decades before and since then, depended for its survival on the writer's relationship to the Southern Renaissance, a defining movement in the South's literary history and legacy. In *Renaissance in the South: A Critical History of the Literature, 1920–1960*, John M. Bradbury lists nearly 800 contributors to the Southern Renaissance, nearly a third of whom are women. Harris is not among them. He dismisses her (along with Mary Johnston and others) as writers of "sentimental fiction."[23] A closer look at much of Harris's work, however, reveals sentiment as a facade.

Perspectives on the Southern Renaissance differ according to academic training. Historians interpret the relevance and influence of the Renaissance differently from literary scholars, a difference consequential to understanding any of the authors' lives and writings. In a lengthy historiographical introduction to a collection of overlooked essays on the New Deal by the Southern Agrarians, Emily Bingham and Thomas Underwood write: "By the 1980s, the literature examining Agrarianism had grown into two labyrinths: one negotiated by English professors and the other by historians. The gulf . . . continues to prevent a meaningful synthesis of the literature." Historians have generally been more concerned with the political implications of the writers' works, while literary scholars, at least until recently, more often demonstrated a "willful lack of interest in the Agrarians' political commentary," focusing rather on the aesthetic value of their works.[24]

Briefly, the Southern Renaissance was a movement coalesced if not started by "Twelve Southerners" at Vanderbilt University. Four of the twelve—Donald Davidson, John Crowe Ransom, Allen Tate, and Robert Penn Warren—had gained a reputation in the mid-1920s publishing poetry as "Fugitives" in exile from two parallel constructs: a New South creed, committed to its own plan of reconstructing the South through industrialization; and the Lost Cause, a mythologized past.[25] The four later joined with eight more in somewhat of an about-face. Provoked originally by attacks on the South from critic H. L. Mencken beginning in the 1910s to portray the region infamously as an intellectual and artistic wasteland, the Fugitives turned outward in their reaction, trying to distance themselves from association with such a reputation. However, when widespread publicity from the Scopes trial in 1925 seemed to affirm Mencken's assessment, the Fugitives regrouped and took defensive action. With a revitalized sense of regional pride they hoped to rescue the region and the country from what they determined were the evils of modernization. In 1930 they published the manifesto *I'll Take My Stand*, promoting Southern Agrarian values as the only hope of saving the nation from self-destruction.[26]

Historians writing about the Agrarians often implicitly question their centrality to and influence on the Southern Renaissance. James Cobb, a historian of southern identity more concerned with the Agrarians' historical setting than with the literary value of their works, writes that the Agrarians' "true attitude toward the use of history," namely, "as propaganda," exposed the limitations of their vision for what they believed was a more legitimate New South. With little use for the "facts," Agrarians offered "no practical alternatives other than a romanticized historical vision of the country life that

Depression-era southerners were then fleeing by the thousands."[27] More-over, with the exception of a few whose racial views progressed in time, Agrarians' visions of the South excluded African Americans. By linking the Southern Renaissance with the Harlem Renaissance, Cobb further decen-ters the Agrarians' role in the South's literary revival.[28]

By collecting and publishing rarely consulted works of the Agrarians, Bingham and Underwood hoped to make these works available as "an op-portunity to examine closely one permutation of the American right."[29] As historical figures representing conservative, reactionary, or regressive values, Harris and the Agrarians offer students of history something that reformers and activists cannot. Although their works are often more dispir-iting than they are inspiring, they help explain what informs reaction.

Anne Goodwyn Jones suggests the value of studying those on the right, the "orphans" or "dark horses" of history. Writing about Louisa McCord, a slave mistress known for holding extremely conservative views in the midst of a slaveholding South, Jones explains that although McCord was "never willing to critique the myth" of southern womanhood, she "nonetheless re-veals that its roots are planted in fear."[30] To expose fear as a root cause of people's reactions and attempts to hold on to regressive values helps explain why some people choose to look forward while others look behind for ways to live in the present.

Women scholars from many disciplines have recently questioned and challenged the validity of attributing the beginning of the Southern Renais-sance to the Fugitives and Agrarians.[31] If one defines *renaissance* as "a sense of challenge that stirs the minds of men [individuals] simultaneously and stimulates a new awareness of the values by which they have been living," then, according to many scholars the beginning of the Southern Renais-sance can be pushed back two or three decades from its traditional date of the mid-1920s.[32]

Carol Manning argues that if we extend the "intellectual field" or the "larger regionalist impulse" of the Southern Renaissance back in time, southern women writers of the late nineteenth century were its "real be-ginning."[33] "If one looks objectively for first signs of a modern southern literature," she states, "one will discover that the Southern Renaissance did not wait for World War I and the Fugitives and Agrarians at Nashville but dawned instead with scattered individuals, chiefly women, writing alone in the last decades of the nineteenth century."[34] That southern women were grappling with similar cultural experiences, creating similar characters in their fiction, and discovering and revealing similar cause and effect in their works, largely "scattered" and "writing alone," demonstrates the influence of time and place. Both perception and perspective explain the differences between the writings of women and those of men writing at the same time.[35]

For critics who examine these works for their literary merit, Manning explains, the caliber of the writing is not the issue: "While much of this writing does not merit resurrection, some of it, along with their more personal writing, is of historical, cultural, and artistic interest, as revisionists are even now discovering."[36] Manning finds that themes of ambivalence, ambiguity, and contradiction characterize the works of these "scattered" women writers.[37] Significantly, their writings reveal how women began to question and challenge, if from behind a mask, the conventions handed down to them as southern ladies.

That southern women especially "exploited the possibilities of fiction as a mask" is the topic of Anne Jones's *Tomorrow Is Another Day: The Woman Writer in the South, 1859–1936*, which examines the works of seven writers whose careers overlap with Harris's: Augusta Jane Evans, Grace King, Kate Chopin, Mary Johnston, Ellen Glasgow, Frances Newman, and Margaret Mitchell. These women demonstrate the influence of the suffrage movement as it reemerged in the late nineteenth century. It helped make women aware, if for most in inarticulate ways, of the constraints of southern ladyhood. Denied a public voice to express a curiosity about liberty and what it ought to mean to them, some southern women found a voice in writing. Trained to keep silent, however, they had to conceal any message of questioning and certainly outright defiance. "Anything that felt radical," Jones writes, "was suppressed, masked, or transformed into the familiar paradox of the strong southern woman arguing for her own fragility."[38] Southern women in general and southern women writers in particular were vulnerable to the conflict that resulted from trying to reconcile the myth of the southern lady with the reality of being a southern woman. The distance between myth and reality—between social expectation and lived experience—motivated writers who were acculturated to defer, submit, and suffer in silence rather than question the culture that entrapped them.

Jones found that these writers managed through fictional characters to express rebellion while also masking it. But there were consequences for questioning, even from behind the protection of a mask. Even with the outlet of writing, they never escaped the divided psyche that resulted from "the dual life" Kate Chopin wrote about: "that outward existence which conforms, the inward life which questions."[39] Each writer experienced the ambiguity, ambivalence, and contradiction that characterize Harris's works. Jones explains the phenomenon: "Here may be located another thread in the curious paradox of southern women, conservative as an ideal and often radical in feeling, soft and gentle in manner with a vein of iron within. . . . [O]ne can suggest the outlines of a tradition of liberalism—often veiled rather than direct—in southern women's writings."[40]

One reviewer's caustic words about Ellen Glasgow and Frances Newman explain why southern women might have been reluctant to be direct in their writing. According to Elmer Davis, "the South must begin to realize that its only salvation lies in taking the girl babies of good family who look as if they have brains, and drowning them as soon as possible after birth."[41] It is little wonder that women writers had difficulty finding their voice. Such sentiments illustrate how challenging it could be for southern women who happened to be bright, such as Glasgow, Newman, and Harris.

Harris's experiences were similar to those of other southern women writers. Harris could be called, as Clara Juncker called New Orleans writer and local historian Grace King, an "inadvertent" feminist. Like King, Harris criticized women who sought and gained public roles. However, each "expressed feminist sentiments in her fiction through her exposure of women's limited choices."[42] To the extent that one can attribute feminism to Harris, it can be described as one critic described Ellen Glasgow's feminism: "temporary, 'spiritual,' and apolitical."[43]

Harris's works shared with Georgia writer Frances Newman's what reviewers called a masculine voice.[44] Although Harris admitted cultivating one, Newman "paradoxically assert[ed] that her own literary value rested in her distinctly female voice."[45] Harris and Newman felt like misfits because they chose to be writers, and both thought that writing undermined charm and femininity because it required a developed intellect. Each suffered from the effects of the "split between lady and mind." If Harris went out of her way in her writing to mask her discontent with the constraints of ladyhood, the titles of two of Newman's novels, if not the books themselves—*The Hard-Boiled Virgin* (1926) and *Dead Lovers Are Faithful Lovers* (1928)—demonstrate her willingness to challenge the norm more openly.

But Newman and Harris held similar views about women: both were averse to any notion of a common bond of sisterhood, and each felt that women should not be involved in public life. They both satirized and valorized women. About men they were equivocal. Harris shared with Newman a "terrible insecurity in her letters to men" and, like Newman, experienced a "dependence upon male encouragement and approval for her writing." On the other hand, both women showed "surprising cockiness" at times.[46] Each struggled with, feared, and suffered from her defiance of internalized ideals, which explains their reticence to drop the mask and more directly confront the constraints of southern ladyhood.

A brief comparison of Harris with Virginia writer Ellen Glasgow, the most famous southern woman writer of their generation, helps further set Harris in context. Called by Julius Rowan Raper the "enigmatic woman who cleared the ground for the South's literary rebirth," Glasgow was four years Harris's junior.[47] The two writers reveal in their autobiographies foundational similarities as well as crucial differences.[48] In 1904, a time when few southern critics were willing to applaud writers who consciously broke from the past, Harris credited Glasgow with being a writer ahead of her time and commended her ability to see beyond the "flower-decked past" that had trapped other southern novelists.[49]

Harris and Glasgow were both shaped by lives marked with tragedy and loss. They shared the experience of having no formal education and of being self-taught. Each had an appreciation for evolution (though Glasgow developed a more sophisticated understanding of evolution earlier in life than did Harris) and a desire to find a way to move beyond the constraints of the past without disavowing their southern identity and its agrarian roots. They shared a lukewarm commitment to woman suffrage, and neither believed legislation would have a significant influence on the innate double standard. They held similarly negative ideas about human nature. Each wrote about having mystical experiences and a deep appreciation of the natural order. They shared a passionate commitment to the life of the mind. Finally, as did most other southern women writers, they endured an "unresolved struggle . . . between the desire for official approval and 'a normal life' on the one hand and for a release from the demands of conformity on the other."[50] Each was known in her day as "a bundle of contradictions."[51]

However, Harris and Glasgow differed in crucial ways. Harris came from an agrarian background and grew up in genteel poverty, while Glasgow's father was a successful businessman, allowing Glasgow to live with a degree of financial security throughout her life. Glasgow had nine siblings; Harris, two. Harris married and had children; Glasgow did not. Beyond the material differences and domestic circumstances, however, the most significant difference between the two writers related to gender identity. Glasgow was far more at home in her female skin than was Harris. Harris's struggle with gender identity was a constant refrain in *As a Woman Thinks*, the second of her three autobiographies, published in the mid-1920s, during a time when she wrestled most intensely with the contradictions in her thinking about gender. If she knew she had made her living glorifying traditional domesticity, Harris admitted her strong conviction that women were "not normal as men are normal" and was forever struggling against "a futile instinct to escape from" being a woman, from not ever being "contented and at home" in herself.[52]

In contrast, "a determining element in Ellen Glasgow's mind," Anne Jones writes, "was her own femaleness."[53] Merrill Skaggs attributes part of Glasgow's success as a writer to her ability to hold on to her female identity in spite of the pressure at the time to find a masculine voice: "Glasgow proved in her lifetime of professional work that a woman could earn the applause of her friends and the respect of her peers without sacrificing her 'femininity' or bowing her will."[54] Even if Glasgow was not able, as was common for women in her day, to reconcile the "tension between romanticism and realism," or the clash between expectations from the myth of the southern lady and the reality of being human, the evidence that it did not rob her of her female identity comes through clearly in *The Woman Within*.[55] Harris reveals the opposite in many writings, but most especially in *As a Woman Thinks*. Chapters 3 through 6 explore some of the reasons why Harris felt first compelled to assume a masculine voice, and then her deep ambivalence later in life at having done so.

Arguably, Glasgow's relative satisfaction with her gender identity and the fact that Harris considered her gender an "accident" that she needed to "overcome" explain another essential difference between the two women.[56] Glasgow's writings reveal someone made deeply empathic by her own suffering, a person who related intuitively to the suffering of others, whether human or animal. Two passages from her autobiography capture the point. "What did individual pain [her own] matter in the midst of a world's misery?" Glasgow asked. "A sensitive mind," she wrote, "would always remain an exile on earth." Known for her acute sensitivity to suffering, whether in human beings or animals, Glasgow "decided that it was easier to suffer than to make suffer." And again she claimed to have "always felt the vast impersonal anguish of life more deeply than I had felt my own small—yet vast—personal misery."[57] In her poem "The Freeman," published at the turn of the century, Glasgow wrote that she found freedom by surrendering to despair: "Hope is a slave. Despair is a freeman."[58] Dorinda Oakley, the central protagonist in Glasgow's most acclaimed novel, *Barren Ground*, "was able to take risks" because "she had the courage of desperation and that had saved her from failure."[59]

Harris could understand human suffering on an individual level, and she certainly lived in desperate straits at a point in her life, but the general suffering of humanity was likely something she did not feel until the last years of her life. Her writing until then was void of genuine empathy for those beyond her immediate family, friends, and in some cases, neighbors. Dispassion, antipathy, and a judging attitude rather than compassion and empathy characterize her writings about human suffering. Possible reasons are examined primarily in chapters 2 and 3 of this book. In part, a negative view of human nature explains her reactive ideas. Harris believed that the downward pull of human nature both directly and indirectly caused suffering.

Harris and Glasgow held similarly negative views about human nature, although they thought differently about the cause-and-effect relationship between human nature and cultural circumstance. Glasgow believed that circumstances brought out the worst in humans, while Harris believed volition to be the chief culprit, and individual responsibility the deciding factor, in people's fate. Because she believed herself to be a self-made woman, Harris defaulted most often to meritocracy. Her life proved to her satisfaction that there was nothing hard work, thrift, courage, and patience could not overcome. The fundamental difference in the way Harris and Glasgow viewed human nature may explain why Glasgow's understanding provoked empathy and a sense of kinship, while Harris's provoked fear and aversion.

Harris never let go of the belief that she was a self-made woman, that the hard-won liberty she gained from making her own money and bringing her family out of destitution in 1899 (when her writing career began) was the result of a Providence provoked to action by her driven spirit. She had, she believed, developed an "instinct for personal liberty," which explained to her why she gained and kept it.[60] Letters to her daughter especially are filled with determination never to be compromised again by any man or circumstance, always to have and hold on to the personal liberty she acquired from that pivotal experience in 1899.

Harris demonstrates how precarious the struggle to claim personal liberty was for women who felt ambivalent about aligning themselves actively with the feminist cause. For many women writers who came of age in the late nineteenth century or were born to the generation that came of age then, their works reveal a common experience of paradox, ambiguity, ambivalence, and contradiction. Whether or not works of any of the women writers merit "resurrecting" for their literary value, their messages of defiance, however veiled, make their writings valuable for further investigation.

"In rhetorical and aesthetic theory," writes Joan Scott, "paradox is a sign of the capacity to balance complexly contrary thoughts and feelings and, by extension, poetic creativity."[61] If the contradictions and equivocations in Harris's works make her a challenging subject, her defiance, as it waxed and waned over time, makes the challenge worthwhile.

The historical context also helps to explain some of the contradictions in Harris's thinking. Harris was not alone in her confusion, stark as it could be at times, as it was a mark of the New South. C. Vann Woodward devoted an entire chapter of *Origins of the New South* to "the divided mind of the South."[62] Harris came of age as a writer during an era deemed Progressive but which was, in the South more than anywhere, as much a reaction to potential progress as anything else.[63] The strongest motive in progressive reforms in the South resulted from determination to retain race, class, and gender hierarchy, whatever the cost. Harris was part of a generation whose "fate" it was, Daniel Singal writes, "to be trapped in an intellectual no-man's land between the thought of two centuries, a position that sometimes augmented, but more often crippled, their final accomplishments."[64]

Born shortly after the end of the Civil War to parents of the Old South, Harris was forced to find a way of being in the New South, itself a time and place marked by contradiction. She shared a "common dilemma" with others Singal calls "post-Victorians," or the generation of southerners who came of age in the decades after the Civil War. Singal examines historian U. B. Phillips, economist Broadus Mitchell, and writer Ellen Glasgow to illustrate a point about the time in which they lived. The changes modernization brought inevitably resulted in contradictory thinking for any coming of age in its path, but it was especially so for southerners after the war, where defeat and devastation brought challenges not faced elsewhere in the country.

The changes required to modernize the South threatened everything southerners held sacred. Was it possible to industrialize while holding on to agrarian values? New South proponents took up the challenge, trying awkwardly, and ultimately failing, to pull the region out of the field and into the factory. They focused on the benefits of industrialization, namely, the material wealth to muscle the region back into a central role in the country's development, while catering to those who needed a Lost Cause as a means of holding on to a past that never existed.[65] Veneration and glorification of the past was a safe outlet for a defeated people who needed something of the past to hold on to while they were being pushed toward a future that appeared frighteningly void of values. For people like Harris who questioned both the inevitability and rightness of industrialization as well as the empty sentimentality of the Lost Cause, there was no alternative. They had to make it up as they went along.

Harris's works reflect someone borrowing eclectically from one mentor and then another, as did, in many ways, the "post-Victorians" whose legacies, unlike hers, have survived. Their legacies survive not because their proposed solutions to the ill effects of modernization and to the banal culture of the Lost Cause worked, and certainly not because they addressed race relations as the region and eventually the nation's most urgent problem, but rather because each of them has been considered among the first from the region to offer something new to their particular fields: Phillips, a new historical methodology; Mitchell, a class interpretation of the region's past; Glasgow, a Darwinian approach to the region's history. Harris offers another example of how her generation faced and tried to reconcile the dilemmas of modernity.

Telling the story of a person's life is a daunting task under any circumstances.[66] "Actual lives are messy, often boring, and always plotless," writes biographer Jay Parini.[67] According to Mark Twain, biography is merely a facade. "What a wee little part of a person's life are his acts and his words," he wrote. "His real life is led in his head, and it is known to none but himself. . . . Biographies are but the clothes and buttons of the man—the biography of the man himself cannot be written."[68] Nonetheless, this interpretation of Harris represents an effort to examine what Twain called her "real life," the one she "led in [her] head." Unlike Talmadge's fairly conventional biography of Harris, which covered her life chronologically, this one interprets chiefly her intellectual development.

Not generally sentimental, Harris could be so about her legacy. Among other evidences, she left explicit instructions for a memorial chapel to be built and maintained in her honor. But she hoped more than anything that her writings would safeguard her legacy. She wanted to be remembered as one whose words lived on to inspire, console, or enlighten—to be remembered, she told a reader, by "the effulgence of some sentence I have written, by which the very lonely, lost, and undone might find their way in the dark."[69] She discovered from readers' response to her first autobiography "how exactly alike we all are inside," and although this realization did not fully undermine her prejudices, the seed of the insight that people are "exactly alike inside" fueled her questioning mind.[70] The discovery from reader response that so much of her experience resonated with readers all over the country and beyond made Harris examine what it was that all humans

shared. That and extraordinarily eclectic, unorthodox religious ideals challenged her otherwise "extreme reactionary" opinions and help to explain
many of the contradictions in her writing and her personality. Clearly, Harris hoped that her legacy would be her having conveyed with words the
archetypal "human heart." To the extent that she has one, her actual legacy
beyond a few local admirers is as irresolute and contradictory as she was.[71]

A few years before her death, Harris wrote to Hamilton Holt that she
wanted "to be remembered and loved a little" for providing an outlet for
readers, for allowing them to "speak their hearts through me." That was all
she wanted in her "last years . . . and nothing at all afterwards—[except] to
escape the brilliant damnation of modern biographers!"[72] After a close call
with Charles Dobbins, a biographer writing during her lifetime, who was
not as careful with her story as she would have liked, it is not surprising that
she expressed appreciation for biographers who protected "the feelings of
the dead."[73]

But Harris, in any case, did not care for flattery. "She despised flattery
but loved praise," a nephew said. "And she had a sixth sense that separated
the two!"[74] She was her own harshest critic, whether it was her work or her
motives she critiqued. Harris could be disarmingly candid about both, and
self-revealing, some might argue, to a fault. She had a passionate devotion
to her family, to her friends, to words and ideas, to her beloved home, to
Georgia, to the South, and to the country. More than a subject of history,
she was in very many ways a "woman remarkable in her own right."[75]

This interpretation of Harris's life seeks the balance suggested by Jacquelyn Hall, who wrote about "the importance of leavening politics with
poetics. Politics demand that we choose a side, take a stand. Poetics demand that we hold seemingly contradictory beliefs at the same time, that we
embrace multiple levels of meaning, that we think metaphorically . . . that
we acknowledge the ways in which beauty and tragedy, good and evil are
entwined." Inviting us to consider the value of paradox, Hall writes: "The
politics of history usually entail an Olympian stance toward our subjects,
who cannot talk back, who are dead and gone. Poetics require a different
stance, one that . . . implicates us in the history we write."[76] Or, one that
requires the historical biographer to grapple with paradox, complication,
and complexities of character—not to solve a riddle, but rather to gain an
understanding of the processes people utilize in the effort to achieve meaning in their lives.

Finally, with regard to the book's organization, to borrow again from
Mark Twain, not only is it impossible to tell more than a "wee little part" of

a life story, but there is no seamless way to tell even that small part. Readers who prefer chronological coverage will be disappointed with this book's thematic structure. A chronology that identifies pivotal events and publications is included. Chapter 2 examines traditional biographical details, family relationships, and events relevant to Harris's intellectual development and political ideology. The crucial role and abiding influence of editor Paul Elmer More, one of her first mentors, is the topic of chapter 3. Chapters 4, 5, and 6 address the role of culture, especially gender, but also race, class, and other variables, in shaping Harris's political and social ideology and her strong sense of personal identity. Chapter 7 examines the role a writing career played in molding Harris, and chapter 8 examines religion as a central and cohesive force in Harris's development.

Family and Tragedy in
the Development of Corra Harris

In the spring of 1923, Corra Harris was working on the sixth installment of *My Book and Heart*, her first autobiography serialized in the *Saturday Evening Post*. She wrote editor and friend George Horace Lorimer to ask that he edit the fifth installment as he saw fit. It was about a time and events in her life that he, without "knowing or feeling" the weight of the "facts" as she did, could "cut more wisely." She had taken pains to tell as discreetly as she could the story of the most pivotal decade in her life, the one leading up to the suicide of her husband, Lundy Howard Harris, in 1910. She mentioned in the letter the suicide attempts she left out of the narrative to be published, as well as the successful one to which she only alluded in the text. She had struggled with the story—how much to tell, how much to withhold. She felt compelled to be as forthcoming with him as possible because she expected Lorimer to hear from readers who had been around at the time and who would most likely write him to "set the record straight" as they recalled it. Then she concluded: "It is impossible to write my record without some reference to these dark tragedies, because upon them my own life turned and was changed and made. . . . They had everything to do with the developement [*sic*] of my character as a human being and with my worth as a writer. I was forced by fearful anguish of mind to escape into this work."[1]

Harris's struggle with loss and personal hardship did not end with her husband's suicide. The decade from 1910 to 1920 was also marked with tragedy and heartache, including family estrangement and the deaths of Harris's daughter, Faith, and sister, Hope. But there were also many significant accomplishments. Harris traveled frequently to New York and other parts of the Northeast. She went twice to Europe on assignment for the *Saturday Evening Post*, once in 1911 to investigate European women's attitudes on and progress toward woman suffrage, and in 1914 to report on the war's effect on women. She published eight novels, continued prolific publishing of articles and short fiction in the *Independent* and the *Saturday Evening Post*, and added other noted magazines of the day, including *Good Housekeeping, Pictorial Review,* and *Harper's.*

The details of Harris's early life as she told the story read much as though they had evolved from the pages of classical southern myth—that in which the South's gallant and heroic gentry overcame the ill effects of war and Reconstruction and emerged poor but proud, ennobled more than ever through defeat.[2] Corra Harris was born Corra Mae White on March 17, 1869, on Farmhill Plantation in the northeast mountains of Elbert County, Georgia, to Tinsley Rucker White and Mary Elizabeth Mathews White.[3] Corra had two younger siblings, a sister, Hope, and a brother, Albert.

Corra's career began in 1899 when she started writing for the *Independent,* a well-known New York periodical. She responded to an editorial written by its editor, William Hayes Ward, condemning the lynching in Newnan, Georgia, on April 23, 1899, of Thomas Wilkes, alias Sam Hose. Wilkes, a black man, was accused of killing his employer, Alfred Cranford, a white farmer, and raping Cranford's wife.[4] Harris's perspective on lynching was typical for the time.[5] She defended it by focusing on the presumed and highly exaggerated threat of the rape of innocent white women by lawless, primitive black men. It provoked the ire of many of the periodical's readers and contrasted sharply with opinions of the editorial staff, who believed that she "failed to see . . . the implications" of what she had written. Nonetheless, because there was such "an air of sincerity" in her writing, the editors wrote back immediately asking for more homespun reflections on race, and later gender relations from a southern woman's viewpoint.[6] Her career was launched. Over the next twenty years she published more than a thousand book reviews and dozens of articles and short fiction in the *Independent.* Additionally, Harris wrote for *Good Housekeeping, Harper's, Ladies Home Journal, Pictorial Review, Saturday Evening Post,* and others. She published nineteen books, including three autobiographies and sixteen novels, two of which became films.[7] Purportedly the first woman war correspondent to go abroad in World War I, Harris maintained a national audience from the turn of the century through most of the 1920s. From 1931 until her death in 1935, she wrote "A Candlelit Column" for the *Atlanta Journal.*[8]

Harris wrote with affectionate humor about her father and with more reserve about her mother. Tinsley White was a colorful and proud Confederate veteran, known throughout his life for his wit, oratory, and love of strong drink. Mary White had a profound, steadfast commitment to evangelical Christianity and had "an Old Testament mind." According to Harris, her mother would have "died at the stake for a doctrine." Her religious fervor explained in part why Harris claimed that she "formed no apron string at-tachment" to her mother.[9] Her description of her parents suggests they were models for the archetypes in some of her early publications.[10] The family's two-thousand-acre plantation, Farmhill, was "mortgaged to the last cotton bloom." At the time of her birth, Corra was the fourth and last generation born under the debt. Not until later in life did she discover "how anguish-ingly poor" her family was.[11] But theirs was, she believed, a genteel poverty, respectable and redemptive.

In her autobiographies, Harris writes with mixed feelings about her mother. She writes with reserved understanding as well as misgivings and regret that she never escaped the hold her mother's religion had on her. Harris praises her mother for her steadfast faith, her resulting "power to endure," and especially the long-suffering patience she practiced in watch-ing out for her father's salvation. Harris believed her mother was one of those women who was genuinely good, one who represented a "generation where grace and virtue were the ordinary attributes of women, nothing to make a fuss about."[12] Mary White was "literally a religious woman," with a "stern . . . rigidly orthodox" character. Whether it was the orthodoxy of the Baptist faith of her youth or that of the Methodism to which Mary and her husband converted at some point is not entirely clear, but Harris describes her mother's religion as unemotional.[13] "She would perform her spiritual duties on a cold collar and keep the Commandments without praying or fasting. I have always thought," Harris wrote, "she might have been a trifle short on the Beatitudes, because she practiced them with less emotion than any other person I have ever known."[14]

Mary ruled her household with a kind of "order and righteousness" that affected all who entered. "Nothing could be changed in it," Harris remem-bered, "least of all mother." Harris's sense in coming home, wherever she had been, was always as that of the "prodigal son." Mary "kept a good little house. . . . Everything in it was clean, white where it should be white, glis-tening where it should shine. If by chance an unworthy person crossed her threshold, he brought his former virtues with him and practiced them. She demanded at least noble deceit of goodness."[15] But that sort of godly inten-sity came with a price. This mother was a proud woman. "She had resigna-tion and endurance to a remarkable degree, but she was sublimely deficient in humility."[16] Harris remembered her having had a "brilliant temper," the sort of woman Harris would never have thought of disobeying. Worse than the temper, though, Mary could also be aloof, keeping an emotional dis-tance between herself and those around her, even her children. When she

Fig 1. Corra Harris. Courtesy of Hargrett Rare Book and Manuscript
Library, University of Georgia Libraries.

Fig 2. Lundy Harris. Courtesy of Hargrett Rare Book and Manuscript Library, University of Georgia Libraries.

Fig 3. Portrait of Faith Harris Leech, 1920, by Ella Sophonisba Hergesheimer (1873–1943). Courtesy of The Parthenon, Metro Board of Parks and Recreations, Nashville, Tennessee.

became preoccupied with her husband's sins, "she would be wrestling in prayer with that particular angel whose business it was to look after father," and then especially she "would pass into silence," become "inaccessible," and "retire far beyond our reach into some dim land of sorrows where even we were unknown."[17] Harris writes that neither she nor her sister, Hope, ever "attempted to penetrate into the mystic regions of her gentle spirit," a "gentle spirit" they nonetheless had to admire from afar.[18] This kind of detachment led Harris to write that she could never "remember crying for" her mother as a child.[19]

Neither did she recall crying for her father, but she did recall having with him a "certain silent intimacy." "Nothing," Harris writes, "could cure me of a dangerous likeness" to her father, with whom she was "closer kin" in "mind and spirit" than her mother. Both she and her father "were highly sensitized emotionally, but not morally."[20] Mary's stern character was tempered and even overshadowed at times by the colorful and quick-witted Tinsley, who loved strong drink a lot more than planting cotton and who took Shakespeare as seriously as the Bible. He "was spiritually minded, but only intermittently religious, during which periods he far outstripped mother in the bloom and beauty of his virtues," Harris recalled. "But he frequently fell back into original sin, where he seemed to belong." "Give him a full glass, a roistering companion, and he could race with the devil himself." Just as quickly, however, "Give him the noblest words of penitence and he could produce the accompanying remorseful emotions." He was a man as readily "moved to the left or the right in the moral world."[21]

Tinsley was never more animated than when he was under the influence of liquid spirits and pontificating on the war (he was a faithful Confederate veteran) or when repenting at Mary's knee for his sins of indulgence. Harris most often writes of her father with humor, especially when a bout of hard drinking was followed by "operatic" acts of repentance before the open family Bible. These episodes were dramatic, "grand," and "invariably the same"; the "methodical routine" followed the classic pattern of sin, fall, repentance, redemption, restoration. The sin and fall always took place elsewhere; the repentance, redemption, and restoration always occurred at home, where Harris was "quarantined by the tightening ligaments of my mother's virtues and obliged to practice my rectitudes more scrupulously than usual. No escape to the terrace outside. And the house felt like a church—terribly hallowed." Every member of the family had a role to play. "When the hero of the house fell from grace," she writes, "he disappeared." It never failed, though, that Tinsley would "emerge from the dark pit of his transgression" with a "moral grandeur" that made Harris "behold him with awe and speechless admiration."[22] Tinsley would begin each occasion of repentance in abject contrition, "staring with pale composure at the open Bible," and end with a "histrionic" prayer so eloquent that it must have been an "honor [for God] to forgive him."[23] Never mind that in his heart he "dreaded the blasphemy demanded of him"; that was something Mary never knew, and something Harris only figured out much later in life.[24]

Mary bore Tinsley's transgressions as her culture demanded, with long-suffering. She loved him even "more than she could have loved a better man." Harris believed it was the quality of truly good women like her mother to be able to love especially men who were moral rogues like her father. No matter what he did or how often he fell from grace, Mary "could not be made to forsake him." Actually, she needed him as much as he needed her. Her good-ness depended upon his sinfulness, which made the pain and suffering of remaining righteous worthwhile. His falls from grace were her redemption. She looked at them each time "as if she gazed upon her cross and knew she could bear it." "She loved him with a shrewd tenderness," Harris explained, "but let him break his traveling gait toward Heaven and she was the most adroit persecutor of the damned and fallen I have ever known."[25] Having taken her mission in life seriously, however, Mary could do no other. From beginning to end of each of these incidents, Mary would move from some inner state of anguished distress to one with "an expression of crucified joy upon her countenance."[26]

Until her father's process from fall to restoration ran its course, it was Corra's responsibility to sit quietly and observe reverently. It was not easy, but she sensed it was necessary. Even when she was "bursting with emotion" over the "wind of sorrow blowing from the eloquent lips of my father," she was restrained by her mother's "inscrutable face." Sometimes, however, she simply could not take it, and once "her lid came off in this mysteriously electric atmosphere." She had listened with solemn restraint as he prayed passionately the words of the psalmist, "Hear my prayer, O Lord, give ear to my supplication," and she had managed to "repress" her anguished empathy when he prayed "woefully," "Hear me speedily, O Lord: my spirit faileth," but her resolve broke after "casting a watery glance through my fingers, I saw father wiping his face on the blue curtains. This was too much. I keened my nose and let out a wail that steadied the great mourner and ended his petition."[27] Similar episodes happened at least as often as there was cotton to take to market. Tinsley would leave with fifty bales of cotton and return with "fifty cents in his pocket and never be able to tell what he had done with the cotton."[28]

The episodes finally ended when Tinsley became the hero of a temperance drive to vote Elbert County dry. He supported Anne Scott's claim that although "temperance as a cause dated back to the 1830s, temperance as a practice was not widespread among antebellum men."[29] At his wife's request, Tinsley rounded up the local freedmen, whose vote would determine the outcome. While Mary intended to persuade the recently enfranchised "negroes" with the best food feast she and their wives and mothers could provide, Tinsley had a surer plan in mind. With his connections he was able to provide more liquid incentive than the liquor proponents on the other side of the county. At the end of a week of debauchery, as well as a successful campaign to make Elbert County dry, Tinsley was carried home "recumbent." Nevertheless, he had grown so impressed with his role as the hero of a righteous cause that he forswore strong drink—a promise he managed to keep at least for the rest of Mary's life.[30]

Harris recalls her father's drinking, as painful as it obviously was to her mother, with amusement ostensibly because when he was drinking the change he underwent was, at least to her and her sister's minds, for the better. When sober he was "the most taciturn and unapproachable of men"; when drinking he became a loving and frolicking playmate carrying them on his back and tossing them to the ceiling. He briefly went from being "our paternal sovereign," a man to behold in awe from a distance, to being an accessible parent. Neither Corra nor Hope would understand for years the financial price they were all paying for her father's indiscretions. Nor would they be able until then to appreciate their mother's long-suffering in dealing with their father.[31] Once she married a man of equally destructive excesses, Harris grew to appreciate her mother's role as wife of a profligate.

Harris knew she was a "human hybrid" composed of the "natures" of both her parents. Some of the gender confusion one finds in Harris's works (explored in chapters 4, 5, and 6) may be traced to having grown up with parents who embodied a good deal of gender confusion. Mary's stern reserve and absence of emotion reflected traditional male traits, while Tinsley's volatility and emotionalism were traditional feminine traits. Although Harris knew she inherited traits from both parents, she believed it was her mother's stern moral training and not her father's emotional nature that had the most troubling effect. As much as she felt an affinity with her father in "mind and spirit," she "inherited some invincible stamina from mother, a capacity for standards and principles" that remained with her all her life. It was her mother's "stamina" and penchant for "standards and principles" Harris became convinced, that had shaped her own moral ethos, resulting in a rigid moralism that warred against her innate spirit of personal liberty. The tension between a moralism that strangled liberty and a passion to gain that liberty whatever the cost exacted a price, Harris discovered later in life. "The burden of being obedient to mother's God, and later on to the God of a still more drastic saint [her husband], has wearied me," she wrote. The scriptures as interpreted by her mother and then her husband required "too much submission, too much bondage to sacrifice."[32] She was sure she would have been a different person if she had spent her formative years under less austere circumstances. "I have no idea," she reflects in As a Woman Thinks, "what kind of mind and life I might have had if I had enjoyed the same religious freedom in my youth that I had in choosing the texts I studied."[33]

Both sides of Harris's family were from Virginia. Her paternal ancestors migrated to Georgia in the early nineteenth century and made their livelihood banking and serving in state politics; the Ruckers farmed large Georgia plantations, but they had a local reputation for good humor and grandiloquence, traits her father inherited in abundance. Harris's maternal grandparents also migrated from Virginia. Harris noted that she and her younger sister, Hope, had shared a moderately carefree existence.[34] There was a much younger brother, Albert, but he figured little in the memories Corra shared in autobiographical accounts of her life. Corra and Hope became sisters-in-law as well when they married brothers, Lundy and Al Harris, respectively, and so shared married names.

Education was to fit Corra for the classroom. Although she lacked a passion for teaching, she did have an aptitude. Her family needed money, and it was one of the few opportunities open to women.[35] She attended Elberton Female Academy until she turned fifteen, in 1883, when her mother sent her to live with Albert Mathews, Mary's brother, to prepare for a career in teaching. Mathews was principal of a school in nearby Banks County. After a year Harris returned to the Female Academy in Elberton, though she never graduated.

In 1885 Corra met and fell in love with Lundy Howard Harris (1858–1910). Lundy Harris was almost the opposite of Corra in temperament and general outlook. Like Corra's parents, Lundy exhibited many traits associated with the opposite sex. He was volatile, emotional, deferential, at times diffident. Brilliant and handsome, he embodied the excesses of both her parents and the strengths of neither. Lundy shared his mother-in-law's zealous commitment to faith, but unlike Mary, whose stoic reserve likely resulted from a kind of certitude that marks the unquestioning, he was haunted by religious doubts. He shared with Tinsley a penchant for strong drink and public oratory, but he lacked his father-in-law's carefree temperament, sense of humor, and constitutional tolerance for strong drink to balance the excesses. This no doubt caused the deep and painful knowing look etched on her mother's face that Corra wrote about in the story of her wedding day, February 8, 1887. In spite of all the activity at the time, Corra caught a glimpse of her mother, "somehow seeming to stand alone, and apart from every one else . . . regarding me with a strange foretelling look . . . through me and past me beyond all the years to come."[36] Her mother's discerning look was prophetic. Protracted hardship marked Corra's twenty-three-year marriage to Lundy Harris from beginning to tragic end, when he took his life in 1910.[37] Among the hardships, the couple lost two sons, one at birth and Lundy Jr. at age two in December 1898. A daughter, Faith, born December 24, 1887, survived to adulthood.

In some ways Lundy embodied within his own mind the struggles of the Methodist Church in the decade or so before his death. The struggles likely facilitated his despair as well as Corra's eventual alienation from the church after his death. In a study of Methodism and society in nineteenth-century Georgia, Christopher Owen discusses how the political and social changes taking place in Georgia in the 1880s and 1890s both reflected and influenced parallel changes taking place within the Methodist Church, and how those changes eventually led to "ideological disintegration" and denominational discord. "Deep fissures appeared in regard to basic social and ecclesiastical issues," Owen writes.[38] Owen identifies two "main camps" in the Methodist Church by the late nineteenth century: modernizers, who made up most of the church leadership and elite worshippers, and traditionalists, among whom were many of the rural preachers and lay members. Within each of the two main camps, further divisions facilitated discord.

Lundy had something in common with members of both main groups and divisions within the two. His educational background and humanitarian impulse led him to identify with the modernizers and their "rational theology," but his zeal for piety, his mystical bent, and his association of the traditional Wesleyan conversion experience with the piety he believed essential for salvation made him equally at home with some of the professional evangelists and Holiness advocates of the traditionalist camp. Moreover, he was friends with both Atticus Haygood, a progressive in the modernizing camp, and Warren Candler, a neoconservative within that group. Just as

the various ideological differences undermined unity within the Methodist denomination, they simultaneously undermined a perpetually tenuous
emotional balance within Lundy's own mind.[39]

Although his religious sensibilities caused the problems he suffered in
his adult life, Lundy came by his ecclesiastical leanings honestly. He had
grown up a minister's son in north-central Georgia during the Civil War
and Reconstruction and was descended from a long line of itinerant Methodist ministers, the earliest of whom was ordained by John Wesley.[40] As a
young man he possessed enviable personal traits. Besides good looks, he
had a sharp intellect and bore an aristocratic manner fabled as the envy of
the southern elite. But he had a morbidly pensive nature that finally undid
him in the end. Corra was one among many who believed he "was not only
a learned man; he had an original mind, [was] brilliant and charming," traits
that somewhat compensated for the sacrifices she made as a wife.[41] Corra,
not naturally the submissive or obedient wife her mother and southern culture taught her to be, managed to sidestep those expectations while keeping
the facade of deference intact.[42] Besides, as Talmadge noted, Lundy was
likely drawn to Corra's marked self-confidence, since "troubled, indecisive
men are often drawn to strong women."[43] Moreover, Corra was well aware
of the influence she had on Lundy: "Strange as it may seem," considering he
was the one with the reputation of intense spiritual devotion, "I had great
influence over him spiritually."[44]

Lundy entered Emory College at Oxford, Georgia, at the age of fourteen
and graduated four years later, in 1876, with bachelor's and master's degrees.
He trained there to preach the gospel according to evangelical Methodism,
or to teach Greek to others who would become preachers. Lundy announced
in 1886, the year before he and Corra married, that he felt called to the pul-
pit rather than the classroom. His forefathers' legacy likely influenced him,
and he may also have been encouraged by the example of fellow Georgian
Samuel P. Jones, a contemporary Methodist minister. Jones's popularity and
success as an itinerant led him to considerable financial success, a marked
exception to the norm, as most "circuit riders" and their families lived on or
close to the edge of poverty. Unfortunately, though he may have surpassed
Jones in spiritual devotion, Lundy had neither Jones's business sense nor his
unquestioning mind. There were many differences between the two ministers, but likely the one of most consequence in explaining the success of one
and the failure of the other on the circuit is captured in Jones's observation,
"I despise theology and botany, but I love religion and flowers."[45]

Lundy's interests were largely the opposite. He would agonize over theological debates Jones apparently never gave a second thought. Jones's religious conversion seemed to have delivered him once and for all from a serious drinking problem, and made him as zealous against every other sin of the flesh as he became against use of alcohol. In contrast, Lundy had no such luck, and once he was consumed by spiritual doubts he fell victim often to the litany of sins Jones denounced in every sermon.

Lundy joined the ministry as an itinerant, a life for which neither he nor Corra was temperamentally suited. The clerical vow of poverty was merely one of the things that made the life of an itinerant and his family unbearable. The austere existence tested the faith of the most devoted and likely ruined the faith of lesser inclined. Thankfully for the Harris family, Lundy's tenure on the circuit in the mountains of north Georgia was a short one. It provided experience for Corra's first and most popular novel, *A Circuit Rider's Wife* (1910). The book established her reputation in the literary world, and though popularly regarded as autobiographical, the novel was at most a spiritual autobiography but otherwise largely fiction.[46] Much to his bride's relief, in 1888 Lundy accepted a position teaching Greek at Emory College, where they lived until 1898, when indiscretions by Lundy set the family on another course. After temporarily abandoning his family, then publicly confessing affairs with other women, Lundy lost his job at Emory College. From 1898 until 1902 he held several teaching and preaching positions beneath his training and credentials before being appointed assistant secretary of the Methodist Church's Board of Education housed at Vanderbilt University in Nashville, Tennessee, where he remained until shortly before his death in 1910.

Lundy Harris was a complex, often tortured individual who never reconciled the tensions between orthodox Christian theology and the higher criticism at its apex when he came of age. Writing after his death, a journalist eulogized: "Scholar though he was—a great linguist, and a thorough scientist—his faith was as simple as a little child's, and the advocates of the 'new theology' drove him to despair. This vision was being destroyed by iconoclasts and he knew not how to replace the picture."[47] He had the intellect of a scholar, the temperament of an artist, the longings of a mystic, and the soul of an early Christian martyr—a combination likely to bring personal turmoil anytime, but especially at a time when the whole country was in the throes of what one historian called a "spiritual crisis."[48]

Commonly regarded as a man for whom zeal on the one hand and despair on the other knew no bounds, Lundy may have been clinically manic-depressive. His friends thought him generally "mad" and considered his wife simply "mad on the subject of religion."[49] Left to himself, Lundy interpreted his zealous moods as evidence of God's approval and indwelling Spirit, and saw his despair and depression as evidence that he had lost them. For years many of his friends and relatives tried to explain away his behavior and mood swings by attributing them to overwork and his "tendency to brood." He was simply, they decided, a person who thought "too much and too deeply."[50]

Many people, especially his students, recalled Lundy fondly, but they always pointed out that he was a man governed by a temperament of foreboding. "He was a great professor, and he made his classes fond of Greek, but even in the classroom the vision of a world to be won for Christ, and so little being done, would come over him and he would drop into fits of deepest gloom."[51] Corra believed his pessimism came from having "mixed the fatalism of the Greeks with his Christian faith."[52] She wondered after his death if "he might have fared better in the spirit if he had been free as a monk to seek his sacrifices and renunciations."[53] Growing up in a region mired in evangelical Christianity and hostile to the religious climate elsewhere in the world made coexistence a hellish martyrdom for him and other sensitive spirits who had conflicting values and beliefs. Corra grieved most over the fact that although he was "trusted with the most delicate spiritual disorders of other people," he was the classic "great physician who could not heal himself."[54]

Unlike many of his colleagues, Lundy's otherworldliness did not preclude a social consciousness.[55] His genuine "capacity for pity" led him sometimes to do things "beyond the comprehension of his devoted friends," such as fraternizing with the dispossessed; seeking out, finding, and "attach[ing] himself to the least significant person present"; and spending "his spare time visiting the sick, the poor, and the totally lost and damned."[56] He lived, worked, and prayed for "a world where justice and love reigned," and he did everything an individual with a tortured psyche could do to bring about that vision.

Whether in spite of or because of his spiritual intensity, Lundy periodically did backslide. In the summer of 1898, convinced that he had lost the "witness of the Spirit," he lost whatever restraint rational faculties would have exercised on less intense individuals. At these times his indiscretions typically resulted in the abuse of alcohol, and in 1898 it included sexual liaisons with women of color (he insisted that he had never "been intimate" with another white woman).[57] And while his wife, his two brothers, and his Methodist friends forgave him, believing that the women's race "lessened the gravity of his sins," Lundy wrote his friend Warren Candler, president of Emory College, that he believed his "conduct was as criminal before God as if a white woman had been" involved.[58]

If his racial views were progressive by comparison with those of family and most colleagues, Lundy may have been influenced by his close friend and mentor Atticus Haygood, onetime president of Emory College and bishop of the Methodist Church in Georgia. Haygood was known for his opposition to the violence that was associated with racial oppression in the South and for sympathizing with the cause of racial justice.[59] He was respected even by people who did not share his racial opinions and by church leaders who disagreed with his liberal ideas.

Lundy's excesses in 1898 may be explained in part by his relationship with Haygood. In addition to having progressive racial views, Haygood also embraced liberal theology and the social gospel and could be as irresponsible with money as Lundy was. He and Lundy frequently talked about the conflict between Wesleyan theology and the higher criticism. Failing to reconcile science and theology, Haygood died an agnostic. He and Lundy discussed common spiritual and intellectual dilemmas and spent much time together in the last three years of Haygood's life when he moved with his wife back to Oxford, ill and in debt, where he died in January 1896. For Lundy to witness Haygood's doubts, his "flagging faith," his turning to alcohol in his last years to relieve pain from illness, and his generally reduced state compared with the celebrated man he had been throughout his professional life may have weighed on Lundy and contributed to the extreme measures he took in 1898.[60]

Corra and Lundy spent most of their married life struggling financially. The experience influenced her attitudes toward poverty throughout her adult life, attitudes that reveal typical contradiction. On the one hand, she feared living without material sources, a theme in much of her private correspondence. On the other hand, she had a reputation for "endeavoring" to "glorify" poverty.[61] She wrote that poverty instilled virtue, and she often blamed the poor who complained about their plight. Her attitudes toward poverty and the politics surrounding it likely stemmed from the excesses Lundy exercised in expressing his "complete indifference to social distinctions." The religious intensity that led Lundy to extremes shaped Corra's conservative ideas about poverty and charity and confirmed what she had already decided from her mother's religious excesses, namely, to find a less exacting God. Lundy's reputation wherever he went for "attach[ing] himself to the least significant person present" troubled Corra. Just a few years into their marriage she discovered that she lived much closer to reality than her husband. She had to seek out and make the "strong, effective, influential friends" to secure his career. While Lundy was "temperamentally deficient" in "this kind of wisdom"—that is, finding socially influential friends—she had "always been particularly flush" with it.[62] Social prestige aside, a very real problem for Corra was what Lundy's big heart cost not just him but his family. She recalled his "touching charities, the rage he used to fall in toward Christmas time when the worthy poor were hawked about for funds to feed them, and how he denied himself to bestow little personal blessings upon the unworthy poor."[63] Corra was convinced that Lundy's charities had led them to the poor house, and despite what she wrote in some of her published essays about the benefits of poverty, it was something she did not want to experience herself.

Corra revealed some of the frustration she felt over Lundy's handling of finances in a letter to W. F. Hunt, one of the authorities in Nashville, who wrote to insist that she "furnish an inventory of the estate of" her late husband. She wrote Hunt that her husband died with "$52.35 in his purse" and $116 in the Union Bank and Trust, while "the major part of his estate was invested in heavenly securities." She went on to detail the nature of these securities:

> He invested every year something over twelve hundred dollars in charity, so secretly, so inoffensively and so honestly that he was never suspected of being a philanthropist and never praised for his generosity. He pensioned an old outcast woman in Bartow County, and an old soldier in Nashville. He sent two little negro boys to school here and supported for three years a family of six persons who were unable to support themselves. He contributed to every charity in Nashville anonymously. Every old maid with a "benevolent" object received his aid. Every child he knew exacted and was paid penny tolls from his tenderness. He supported the heart of every man he knew who confided in him with encouragement and kindness. He literally did forgive his enemies and suffered martyrdom.[64]

Out of necessity, Corra developed a distinctly different sense about her family's well-being. Fiscally responsible herself, she believed even God was practical-minded where finances were concerned. Years later in her autobiography she wrote, "Our God is a sensible God." It was always her "impression," for instance, that "the blessing Jacob wrestled for" was most likely "a few more sheep or a better pasture" rather than greater spiritual insight or a closer walk with the Almighty.[65] But Lundy remained confused about the practical needs of life, and he and Corra were worlds apart in interpretation of their Christian duties. Not until after his death did Lundy's friends know that "his philanthropy somewhat outran discretion and caused him to leave nothing for his widow."[66] Lundy's extremes likely had something to do with Corra's attitude toward the "unworthy" poor. She experienced poverty throughout her married life, much of the time because of Lundy's misguided efforts to remedy the poverty of those she deemed less worthy.

In June 1898, however, it was "complete indifference" to his family, not social distinctions, that changed the direction of their lives. Lost in one of his dreaded spiritual funks and convinced that he had lost God, Lundy abandoned his family and headed for Texas in search of someone who, he believed, had the ability to help him find God again. Afterward, Al Harris concluded with relief that his brother was not the irresponsible reprobate his behavior suggested but rather simply insane: "I feel more and more the lifting of a load as my conviction deepens that he is insane."[67]

Corra, however, refused to dismiss her husband or his state of mind that simply. He might be overzealous on occasion, she conceded, but he was not insane. If she did not share his particular kind of spiritual intensity, she always took him seriously. He was a complicated person who was torn by the conflicts modernity brought to the church. He was by no means alone in his inability to reconcile orthodoxy and the higher criticism of biblical texts, which was the primary issue in religious seminaries of his day. Talmadge noted the way Corra captured Lundy's dilemma in a letter to Paul More when she pointed out that "the dichotomy in his character was made evident in his desire to write two books: a Greek grammar and a life of Christ."[68] Corra dealt with Lundy's deep doubts by trying to persuade him that divine displeasure was not the cause of his bewilderment and angst. He found her counsel especially comforting when he returned to Georgia late in the summer of 1898 in the throes of despair.

Corra understood the relationship between Lundy's spiritual life and his mental health, and she regarded it as simply a precarious and fragile balance for her husband. When Lundy kept "company as usual with the apostles and certain Old Testament saints like Isaiah," she wrote, he was fine. "He belonged to the Scriptures as truly as ever David did"; however, "when he got out of them he was not sane."[69] Unlike his brothers and friends, she did not think him insane when, in 1898, he abandoned his family and job in Georgia and headed for Texas to find a man who could put him back in touch with God. He merely sought "God with the same idea of repentance that drove the old monks into the desert."[70] After this incident Lundy lost his teaching job at Emory College, and over the next few years the family lived in various stages of destitution. The gravity of the situation led Corra to the most pivotal event in her personal life—the awakening she writes about in her autobiographies and most famously in her novel *A Circuit Rider's Wife*.

Corra's epiphany took place in the last two years of the nineteenth century. The months between the summer of 1898 and that of 1899 were the most trying of her life. The "Austin debauch," as Lundy's brothers called his escapades in Texas, unleashed an unrelenting spell of adversity. Not only did Lundy abandon her, which was humiliating enough, but to her embarrassment he felt compelled to confess his sins publicly. His public confession left Corra especially vulnerable. She detailed the scar of that public confession in a letter to her daughter, Faith, many years later, alluding to the "sorrows" she had suffered, the "imminent danger" she constantly felt, and the "poignant humiliation" and "public disgrace" Lundy's misguided disclosures cost her. After those public confessions, anything she faced paled in comparison: "I endured that and lived through it, until years before your father died nothing he could do really hurt or humiliated me, and I could not feel disgrace."[71]

Corra did not escape this vulnerability, however, before suffering a good deal more in those long months ahead.[72] Because of the financial and emotional strain, Corra sent Faith to live with Lundy's sister Mary in Cuthbert, Georgia. The family's crisis had already taken a toll on Faith, and Corra wanted to protect her from further stress. Corra wrote Warren Candler's wife, Nettie Candler, during the time Faith was living away from home, "I did not know before that a child could stay sad like an old person."[73] In December, Lundy Jr. died from undisclosed causes.

The family lost their social position and reputation and practically all their material possessions, and for a time they became dependent on charity from their extended family. After living a few months in conditions "reducing to the soul," where poverty was no longer genteel but dehumanizing, Corra's perspective changed, and so did her relationships with everyone, including herself.[74] She began to develop what one editor who knew her well called a "fearless mind."[75] For one immersed in evangelical religion, she understood the experience and explained it in religious discourse. "Until this time," she wrote, "I had trusted him [Lundy] implicitly to do our praying. I had been, you may say, no more than the copy-cat amen of these petitions for twelve years. Now it came to me suddenly like a revelation that he was not the one to represent us in this emergency before the Lord. He was still seeking holy visions and the kingdom of Heaven, when we were by nature far from that place and in need of better fortunes here. He did not have the faith or the spiritual sense to ask for what we had to have now before we died."[76] But she did have the sense, so she asked. And she remained convinced throughout her life that the literary opportunity that opened up to her after that "interview with the Almighty" was as providential as any event in history. Moreover, she considered her budding literary career evidence that being born again—not in the "Scriptural sense" but in the "worldly sense"—was a "grand thing," one to be celebrated.[77]

The experience was pivotal in affirming for Corra that God was not confined to the church, that the world itself was sacred, and that creeds and doctrines, which for her had always been suspect, choked the life of the spirit. Afterward, she came increasingly to see religion without experience as a waste of time. She learned these things and more all at once, even if she spent the rest of her life learning what it meant to be "free indeed." The experience liberated her from the legalisms embedded in evangelical religion. Even if the moral constraints of her mother's God haunted her at times, the spiritual liberation she experienced early in 1899 prevailed in the end and gave her a lasting confidence. "This was how I felt in the tail end of that bad year [1898]," she writes. "I was no longer under Lundy's spiritual thumb. His God was still my God, but never again was I to be controlled by a long-distance prayer-dimmed view of heaven. I had got the witness of my own spirit by some power in myself to achieve life here with joy and courage."[78] "My attitude to the Lord began to change [then]," she wrote, "and it has never been the same since."[79]

Laying aside the belief that "two people are one when they are married," Corra started thinking for herself and began consciously to "maintain my own individuality heroically."[80] She gained a new respect for selfhood and a liberating awareness that the concept of a husband as head of the household had its limits. In fact, even though she gave the notion lip service—to the point of making a career out of it—she discovered that her household ran much better with a shared headship. Lundy was the de jure head of the family, but to herself and before God, she was the de facto head. She believed her decision was sanctioned by God. Moreover, the sense of affirmation she felt made the difference that lasted a lifetime.[81]

Learning to think for herself, however, did not undermine her commitment to her husband. Although she lost her sense of blind devotion, Corra remained loyal to Lundy throughout his life, and she never remarried. Granted, that decision had much to do with her conviction that widowhood was the only genuinely free status for women, but nonetheless she kept his memory hallowed. Living with him had brought her the "terrible wisdom of love." "I cannot doubt," she wrote fourteen years after his death, "that I have received the best of my life and nearly every gift that prospered in me from my association with Lundy."[82] True love was not, after all, dependent upon a particular hierarchy.

But true love did not save Lundy from himself. After his death, an undisclosed Methodist minister told a reporter, "Lundy Harris killed himself because he began his ministry with a vision, and in a moment of black despair he doubted if the vision would ever be realized." He anguished most over the way the "new theology" continually questioned the divinity of Christ.[83] Lundy had been seized by the "black idea" of suicide more than once in his life, but circumstances had always redeemed him, at least until that last year when they seemed instead to conspire against him. Ever vulnerable to the politics on the church board, in his last year there he had become embroiled in the internal dissension between the board and Vanderbilt trustees for control of the university.

Lundy's suicide was a controversial subject. Talmadge, who shared Cor- ra's interpretation of Lundy's mental imbalance as a crisis of faith rather than as mental illness, believed Lundy had come particularly to question the divinity of Christ, a fundamental belief without which he felt left with a cruel and impersonal God. Talmadge cited a poem Lundy wrote the year before he died, "In the Far Forgotten Lands," in which Lundy seems to be struggling to hold on to an orthodox belief in Christ. The poem is a query of forlorn lost souls, "screaming for a God that cares," and a "cross-stained Nazarene," portrayed as equally forlorn, fighting what seems a losing battle to "drag bleeding souls from hell," and convince them that "God does care."[84] Talmadge quoted Jung on the lengths to which disillusioned believers would go to restore their faith.[85]

The role of *A Circuit Rider's Wife* in the suicide was at the time a matter of speculation. In 1968, the same year Talmadge's biography was published, the *Atlanta Journal and Constitution* reported that Lundy's suicide was "not because of anything in the book."[86] Shortly after Lundy's death, however, one newspaper reported, "Those who knew, say that Dr. Harris fell into profound melancholy after the publication of 'A Circuit Rider's Wife.' He seemed to think that it was a story of a vision unrealized, and that his life had been a failure."[87] The note Lundy left provides no direct evidence of a connection between the publication of the novel and his last depressive episode, but there is reason to believe that the publication and popularity of the novel could have had a negative impact. A closer analysis of the novel suggests reasons why, as does a passage from Corra's second autobiography. Writing about how happiness had eluded her throughout her life, Corra wrote that the closest she ever came to being happy was "shortly after 'A Circuit Rider's Wife' was published." "It seemed to me I saw it [happiness], as you look a long way down the road and see a wider brighter place where you turn in through a gate and enter your own house. I remember saying something to Lundy about this. We would get away presently from all the cares we had ever had, take a little house in the country and begin to live happy ever after. I remember his silence, the look he gave me. If in the last day when we are called there is one who hears, but cannot rise from his dust, he will have just that look of terrible comprehension."[88] According to her autobiography, the publication and success of *A Circuit Rider's Wife* brought Corra as close to happiness as she would come in her life. What it brought Lundy is impossible to know, but that "look of terrible comprehension" that followed shortly after publication preceded just by weeks his final decision to take his own life.

Within two years after Lundy's death, Corra bought two hundred acres of property in Bartow County in northwest Georgia, including the place where Lundy had taken his life. She claimed to have felt his presence there; in any case, she had an affinity for the property. She named the home and farm "In the Valley" and spent the remaining twenty-three years of her life committed in varying degrees to making it a safe haven and refuge for Faith, a haven for friends and family after Faith's death in 1919, and always a retreat for herself from the rest of the world. After Faith died, the Valley became Corra's obsession.[89]

Corra had not been able to rescue her husband from his beliefs, but she determined to keep their daughter from a similar fate. She vowed early in her married life that Faith would not grow up worshipping the same God as her father. Shielding her daughter became Corra's primary function in her role as a mother. "If it was the last thing I ever did," Corra wrote, she was determined that Faith "should inherit the normal distant sky-line God of my family. I did my best to make her a spunky little human first." It seemed successful—at least as long as Faith was a child, when she and Corra "enjoyed many cheerful blessings in a normal way without discussing divine sources."[90]

Faith grew up as sheltered as her mother could keep her from her parents' problems. Corra protected her from Lundy's humorless and unpredictable God; however, she could do nothing about his genes. Corra discovered from Faith that "Lundy's God" had not been the source of his volatile and vulnerable temperament but rather a manifestation of it.[91] Corra had suspected as much but hoped that Faith, who was a "feminine facsimile" of her father, would learn better ways of coping.[92] They sent her to camp in her teen years to toughen her temperamentally as well as physically. When Faith returned from a five-week trip to the Tennessee mountains, Corra was pleased to discover that her daughter had conquered many of her obsessive fears and become one of the camp's daredevils. For her courage her father gave her a "pretty watch," but her mother, hoping that a sound body made for a sound mind, gave her daughter "a set of golf sticks and a tennis racket and balls."[93] But even though Faith overcame her fears of "bugs, thunder and especially darkness" by going away to camp, she still had despairing moods that troubled Corra. Hoping Faith would learn some better way of coping at college, they sent her to the Woman's College in Baltimore, later Goucher College, where she graduated in 1909.

While in college, Faith wrote home regularly furnishing ample evidence in letters that she was her father's daughter and, despite all her mother's efforts, had learned to face life's problems much the way her father had, with anguish and despair. She wrote her father in 1909 exasperated because he had "scolded" her for worrying when she should have prayed instead. "Perhaps I was wrong not to pray," she wrote, "but I save that as my last refuge.—Besides—I wanted human tenderness. I clutch at the skirts of God only when I have reached the last ditch and when human kindness is ineffective." She found "this matter of learning to live serenely is hard work."[94]

Corra spent a great deal of time in Faith's adult life counseling her daughter on how to handle her brooding moods. Her counsel included everything from behavioral therapy—act as happy as a child and eventually feel happy—to various forms of resignation and acceptance. Corra often advised Faith to "practice indifference," the surest way to cheat the otherwise relentless fate of being her father's daughter. Corra equated personal liberty and hence power with achieving a feeling of indifference, and she urged Faith time and again to make it her life's goal. Unlike her mother, who came close, Faith never perfected the art of indifference to life's precariousness.[95] Faith spent her life battling on and off the same kind of melancholia that troubled her father. Gynecological and digestive disorders also impaired her physical health. The former were especially onerous given the stigma Faith believed attached to "distinctly female" problems.[96]

Corra's relationship with her daughter was arguably the most fulfilling of her life.[97] In 1916 Corra wrote Faith to take care of herself for "your mother who loves you more than she does all else in this world or the next."[98] She wrote about the contrast between her roles as wife and mother. In keeping with the modern trend that was moving away from the Victorian principle of sacralizing motherhood above the role of wife, Corra privileged the role of wife over mother in her writings. In her private life, however, her role as mother had proved the most gratifying possibly because she considered it more successful.[99] It was not that she was any less devoted as a wife.[100] She was confident that she was faithful in her devotion to Lundy, but in spite of all of her devotion to him she had failed to save him from himself.[101] By comparison, her devotion to her daughter brought her not only a sense of affirmation in her role as mother but also brought her a best friend. Her role as mother proved "more stimulating and informing," and more effective at bringing out the "best" in her.[102]

Likewise, in the balance, devotion was reciprocal between mother and daughter.[103] Corra admired and loved her husband, but their relationship was not reciprocal. He bled himself spiritually to save a fallen world, and had little left for his family. His own needs were chronic and undermined whatever capacity he had to give of himself to his wife. He loved Corra, but his needs far exceeded his love, and he took from her more than he gave in return. Her emotional support empowered him to empower the dispossessed and damned. In essence, she partially underwrote his goodwill. But little of her investment came back to her, certainly not in the form of emotional support and availability.

Such was not the case with Faith. She returned her mother's love and devotion in kind. In time the two women became closest friends and confidantes while retaining the mother-daughter relationship that deepened the bond. Faith was Corra's closest friend.[104] By comparison with Faith, Corra seemed a rock of stability, physically and otherwise, a factor that influenced the nature of their relationship. If at times their differences brought tension, more often than not they complemented each other. Whatever their temperamental differences, they had much in common. After meeting Faith, Hamilton Holt wrote Corra, "She certainly is a second 'you.'"[105] They shared a strong tendency to be loners and, as did many women writers, to remain as private as possible, with a particular antipathy to women's clubs.[106]

Living such private lives meant that they played numerous roles in each other's lives. Corra counseled, advised, inspired, motivated, and commiserated with Faith much as a close friend would. She also confided in her daughter. Faith was Corra's closest confidante, and they grew even closer once Faith began to write and publish. Faith listened, understood, tolerated her mother's eccentricities, empathized when needed, and genuinely celebrated, like a true friend, her mother's accomplishments. They wrote each other practically daily, even when other demands made it difficult to do so. Aware of those demands, they wrote to encourage each other that an occasional day without a letter would be forgiven. Faith wrote her mother in 1918, "A day would not be complete to me if I did not write you."[107] Likewise, Corra wrote, "Darling, I love to write you letters, and it is easier sometimes to write than to talk."[108]

Although their relationship was rewarding, it taxed them both for many reasons, including differences in natural temperament; but also, Corra remained disappointed that Faith had chosen marriage over a writing career. The choice may not have challenged her mother as it did—Corra's chief strength, after all, was in adjusting to life's disappointments—if serious financial problems had not been a chronic issue in Faith's marriage. But Corra's own personal experience in the last ten years of her marriage, which were the first ten years of her writing career, led her to believe the prevailing gender ethos that women could not have both a successful marriage and a successful career.

By all accounts, Faith showed potential as a writer from an early age. Knowing that and knowing of her volatile temperament, Corra hoped again the odds that Faith would choose a writing career over marriage. On that subject Faith followed her mother's advice, but it was advice not intended for her. Namely, Faith followed her mother's published recommendations about marriage rather than her private pleas directly to Faith not to marry. Whether or not Corra actually discussed with Faith the contradictions between her published and private sentiments on the subject of marriage and motherhood is unclear from her papers. She did write Paul More in 1907 that she knew her private attitudes on the subject of marriage and children were "very inconsistent with the doctrines I preach about marriage, etc.— But who on earth ever made a doctrine for his own consumption. None, but a fool or a crank!"[109]

In her writing, Corra advised women to marry and have children. The title to an article in the *St. Louis Post-Dispatch* capture her public sentiments: "There are no woman problems that love and marriage cannot solve" (March 29, 1914). And she dismissed as selfish those who refused to do so. In an article published in 1911 she targeted educated women who chose not to marry and have children, calling them "the waste material of the race," "selfish," and "cowardly." Presaging ideas found in works such as Madison Grant's *The Passing of the Great Race* (1916), which would give eugenics an air of credibility through pseudoscientific claims, Harris admonished women who chose either not to marry or who married but then chose not to have children: "The children we *ought* to have for the next generation are not born at all because the women who are broad-minded, wisely sympathetic, splendidly capable of rearing them properly 'elect' either not to marry at all, or being married, not to have children. There is not a corporation in this country that cheats the nation so ruthlessly or out of so much important material. . . . One of the prayers of our times should be, 'Good Lord deliver us from the feeble and sterile chastity of highly educated females.'"[110]

Such sentiments however were definitely not what Corra conveyed to her daughter.[111] She wanted Faith to follow in her footsteps as a writer, but to do so without the attendant distractions of husband and family. Corra knew from personal experience how difficult it was to have both a family and a career. She knew what Georgia writer Frances Newman knew about marriage and hence why Newman avoided it: "It would seem like suicide to be submerged in a lasting loving affair . . . because I don't think it possible to tie your emotions up in someone and still be free to do your very best work."[112] She intended her own writing career and the contacts she made through it to serve as Faith's entrée into the literary world.[113] Against her mother's wishes, Faith married Harry Leech on December 24, 1910, her twenty-second birthday, at her mother's home in Nashville, just a few months after her father's death. Much to Corra's relief, the couple never had children.[114] Reminiscent of her own mother, who had seemed to know what was ahead for her daughter, Corra had a strong foreboding about Faith's choice of partner. Similarly, Corra's worst fears about Faith's marriage came to pass.[115]

Besides not wanting Faith to marry, Corra had particular reservations about Harry Leech. It was, in fact, a mutual antagonism. Corra doubted Harry's competence as a provider, and Harry had no use for willful women. Talmadge summed it up best: "Harry came from a good, but impoverished, Nashville family. He was handsome, educated, and personable, but, in Mrs. Harris's opinion, completely unfitted for the ruthless world of modern business where only strong people, like herself, could succeed. Besides, Harry had those very same weaknesses that had handicapped Lundy; he was highstrung, inordinately proud, and far from robust. He could never give Faith the security and comforts she deserved and must have."[116] Faith might easily have become the submissive wife he expected if he had been able to keep her mother out of their lives, but that proved to be impossible for a number of reasons, not the least of which was his difficulty finding and keeping suitable employment. Much to his consternation, breadwinning was more of a challenge than he had presumed. He worked variously in business, industry, and banking but seemed suited to none of them. Time and again for survival's sake he took jobs that had come through his mother-in-law's connections, but then lost them. Corra's increasing success compared with Harry's inability to make a comfortable or secure living resulted in perpetual tension. He resented her success; she resented his failure. At best they lived at polite odds; at worst, total estrangement. During the latter times Corra grieved most that Harry prevented her from expressing her natural generosity to her daughter. Among her greatest heartbreaks was being forbidden to exercise what she called her "inalienable rights as a mother," namely, to share her abundant means freely with her daughter.[117]

Corra was perpetually torn between two fundamental beliefs that seemed at odds. She firmly believed it was her "inalienable right" to share her prosperity with her daughter, but she also believed that Faith had to "keep faith" with her husband.[118] This was especially difficult when Corra would remind herself that Faith and Faith's security had been one of the primary motives behind her own ambition. She often sent Faith money or offered her money that she knew her daughter might not be able to accept. "But when I look back upon the years of indefatigable labor I have lived through in order that you might not suffer the terrors and anxieties which have ruined and darkened more than half of my life, I know you will understand and pardon me for offering you this small sum even if you cannot keep it and keep faith with your husband."[119] To take care of Faith, she wrote, "is now the only real interest I have in life which is my own and dear to me. I still have a few duties to perform. But within a few months, I shall refuse to bear a single responsibility except those incident to my own life, and the comfort of yours."[120]

If not always, at least sometimes Corra's assurances worked to bring about the result she wanted, namely, Faith's peace of mind. "Your love and the knowledge that you have a home and an income that makes you secure from the world are my great comforts," Faith wrote her. "I revel in them and hold them close to me in my times of trouble."[121] Ultimately, Corra's security was Faith's, and Faith was assured by her mother's financial security, even though "keeping faith with her husband" kept her from benefiting from it. Faith knew she would have to try to emulate her mother, not just professionally as a writer but as a person who had weathered certain personal storms and survived. Faith's domestic trials proved she would also have to develop her mother's emotional fortitude, which, considering that she inherited her father's temperament, would be no small accomplishment.

In early 1915, Faith and Harry moved to the Valley to help Corra manage the home and farm. Corra turned the place over to them so that Harry would have a secure job and so that Corra would be able to travel freely and write without worrying about the hired help at home—a constant refrain in her life. Plans were to build the couple a separate house on the property and to give them managerial control of the farm; until their house was completed, Faith and Harry would live in Corra's home. Corra traveled on assignment frequently in an effort to eliminate the problems inherent in having two families live under one roof. Farming proved, however, to be a lot more complicated than Harry expected and, much like his other work, something for which he was not temperamentally suited. Despite all their efforts, Faith and Harry were never able to operate within a budget, and as a result they had to remain in much closer contact with Corra than either of them planned. Moreover, it meant that Corra traveled more frequently and stayed away longer than she had intended.

The effects on Faith of the conflict between her husband and mother were profound, exactly what would be expected from a highly sensitive woman who took to heart her roles and responsibilities as wife and daughter. The two "pulled poor Faith to pieces between them," wrote Bettie Rains Upshaw.[122] The correspondence among the three in the spring and summer of 1916 reveals as much, but the letters between Faith and Corra throughout 1917 highlight the effects. For example, after telling her mother that she regretted being unable to visit the Valley, as they had planned, Faith wrote: "I have always told you that Harry made my trips out there difficult for me. He views you as his blackest enemy and he is inordinately suspicious of my relations to you—he is so afraid I may confide in you something about our life. . . . My life will always be divided into two parts—yours and Harry's—for nothing can affect [*sic*] a reconcilement."[123] At times Faith managed with artful diplomacy to keep a fragile detente, but at other times she came undone either psychologically or physically. Frequently, both conditions plagued her. The outcome depended upon the proximity of the couple to Corra and reflected anything from alienation among the three to quiet fights between Corra and Harry over who was most responsible for Faith's troubled state of mind and body. Corra and Harry managed for Faith's sake to coexist in states of relative tolerance until the summer of 1916.

Relations became worse when Corra was home, and they reached a nadir in the summer of 1916 when Faith suffered an acute bout with gynecological problems and in June had to be rushed to Nashville for surgery.[124] The situation became intolerable with Faith bedridden and unable to arbitrate between her husband and mother. What had been a cold war between Corra and Harry devolved into hot verbal exchanges, with each accusing the other of various nefarious motives.

By midsummer all pretense and hope for the three to live together as a family ended, and the couple moved out in early August 1916. In Corra's published account they left because they simply failed at farming. In fact, the tensions within the extended family had grown insufferable. In Talmadge's account of the estrangement, Corra comes off the heavy and Harry the victim of overbearing matriarchy. However, if what Harris writes in her journals is even half true, Harry was at the very least guilty of psychological abuse, having continually threatened both Corra and Faith with having Faith committed to an asylum.[125]

Once the couple moved out, Corra and Faith visited regularly, and in some ways they valued their relationship more because of the encumbrances Harry's disposition imposed. But the couple's financial insecurities and Harry's on-again, off-again refusals to allow Faith to receive financial help from her mother anguished Corra to no end.[126] The first few months on their own were especially difficult. Faith believed she and Harry would "always have to be struggling" financially.[127] Their economic future seemed so bleak at one point, she feared that if Harry faced reality as she saw it, "the horror of it would kill him."[128] Eventually, Faith began to think that if the couple had any chance of moving away from the edge financially, she alone had the key.[129] "Our great chance I know lies with me," she wrote Corra.[130]

Corra spent much of her time during this period getting support, both moral and financial, to her daughter without her son-in-law's knowledge.[131] It was not just money to keep body and soul together that concerned Corra—she wanted Faith to have domestic help to enable her to write.[132] Corra wrote Faith shortly after they moved out of the Valley that she wanted her to "take up some form of personal expression," to have "some life of your own which is neither mine nor Harry's life, but your own."[133] She had wanted her daughter's success to surpass her own, and in the early days of her own career she began to promote Faith to her editors and to encourage Faith's interest in a literary career. After reading correspondence between Faith and her mother that Corra sent him to demonstrate Faith's potential as a writer, Hamilton Holt wrote back, "She is a remarkable girl and when she gets your age may beat you."[134] His comments about Faith and similar observations by other editors gratified Corra and explain her determined efforts to encourage Faith in a writing career.

From the earliest days of her own career until Faith's death, Corra held on to "wishes and . . . plans for us both" to write.[135] It was an interest that remained secondary to Faith until the last two years of her life, when she realized what her mother had tried to tell her for years. It was rewarding if demanding work that could also be quite lucrative. Corra's efforts to keep Faith interested in writing finally paid off in 1917, when Faith's writing career began in earnest. The year 1919 looked especially promising. Faith had begun publishing regularly and had secured several writing assignments, including a novel. She had finally gained confidence in herself from earning her own income.[136] Corra, deeply gratified at Faith's newfound confidence and the "brilliant career" ahead of her, believed her daughter had the ability to surpass her own achievements.[137] Together they wrote and published *From Sun-up to Sun-down*, a serialized collection of fictional letters between a daughter and mother about the relative merits of "scientific" versus traditional farming.[138] Faith had come into her own as a writer, and Corra and Harry were back on speaking terms, when Faith died in May 1919 from a sudden onset of a former medical condition that she and her mother had sought to keep concealed.[139]

For Corra, Faith's unexpected death was more devastating than Lundy's had been. Although Faith had had health problems much of her life, she seemed to grow stronger and healthier physically as well as psychologically in 1919. Further, her success did not appear to threaten her marriage. On the contrary, the financial relief it afforded had facilitated goodwill in all directions, including between Harry and Corra, and life had finally started to normalize for them all. When Faith died, a sense of fatalism and disillusionment was renewed in Corra. Her immediate response seemed to be an uncanny detachment reflected in what observers believed an unnatural control of her emotions. Corra, to the surprise of many, showed a "frightening composure" at the funeral.[140] She explained her reaction in a letter to her editor and friend George Lorimer a couple of weeks after Faith's death: "I cannot weep, nor breakdown, nor give up. It would be such a relief if I could. I do not even suffer except in a dull way as one suffers pain under the influence of an opiate. At first this seemed indecent, horrible to me, that I could go on with my duties and responsibilities when there was no longer any reason for duty and responsibility. Then I experienced a curious impression, so strong it has been almost a conviction."[141] The "curious impression" she had was that Faith had made her way into heaven more quickly than the norm and "arranged it with Him at once that those whom she loved should not suffer. . . . I understood [then] why my mind seemed holden against the obligation of my bereavement. I was not bereaved. Faith still loved me somewhere and had cared for me. I came back to the house refreshed."[142] Although Corra did not retain that sense of "refreshment" or "hold the illusion" for any length of time, the conviction that Faith's spirit had provided for her and kept grief from overwhelming her sustained her through the earliest grieving stages.

Still, Corra struggled to understand what kind of God could allow her daughter to die. She had handled Lundy's death by blaming the administrators on the church board for provoking his last state of despair. Besides, Lundy had made it clear that he wanted to die. Knowing that and being able to focus her anger on human agents made grieving for him less tragic. Faith's death was not as easily explained. Unlike her father, Faith had "loved life," Corra wrote. "I have never known anyone who had such . . . delicate courage for living."[143] Trying to explain to herself how God could take Faith provoked questions that Corra was unable to answer and required her to grapple with her religious beliefs, to question God, and to wonder seriously if there was life after death. Was Faith living in the spirit somewhere, free, once and for all, from "all her anxieties," "fresh and shriven from every mortal tie"? These were questions she dared not ponder too long for fear of what she might discover. The best she managed under the circumstances was to console herself that Faith's death must have meant that she had "escaped something awful here by her passing." Because of her inability to face the magnitude of her loss and the questions it provoked, it did not take Corra long to "come to myself and begin again." She coped by doing what she had always done before: she buried herself in her work.

Tragic as it was, Faith's death was also liberating, if in ways Corra did not fully comprehend. Contemporary writer Ellen Glasgow captured a similar feeling. "A tragic irony of life," Glasgow wrote, "is that we so often achieve success or financial independence after the chief reason for which we sought it has passed away."[144] It was a bittersweet irony to Corra. All her adult life she had coveted happiness and personal freedom. After Faith's death, she realized, if nothing else, for once in her life, that she had nothing to lose.[145] While Faith lived, Corra shouldered both their burdens, financial and emotional, to spare Faith the grief. The letters between them are filled with agonizing concerns on Faith's part and irrepressible efforts on Corra's part to counter her fears. She "would tell any number of lies" to give Faith peace of mind, Corra wrote Lorimer.[146]

Although Corra was generally long-suffering with her daughter's despairing temperament, there was one concern over which she lost patience. "It is the only selfishness I know in you—this excess of anxiety about me," Corra wrote.[147] Wherever Corra was, if Faith did not hear from her frequently, she grew irrationally afraid that something had happened. "It amounts to slavery to feel that you will become 'frantic' if you fail to hear from me," Corra wrote.[148] Consequently, she felt "compelled to write at times when I have not the strength."[149] She repeatedly assured Faith that she was strong and healthy and, prophetically, that she was sure that she would outlive Faith.[150] As vulnerable as her daughter's emotional needs made Corra feel, she also assumed responsibility for Faith's financial and professional future, which put her at the mercy of editors. She felt obliged to remain on goodwill terms when she doubtless preferred to deal with them less cautiously. So for a time she cheated grief with the consolation, however hollow, that she had "escaped from the long bondage of love."[151] Finally, she gained release from the "necessity of love and sacrafice [*sic*] which compells [*sic*] submission to the inevitable."[152] Speculating on how long that fragile sense of invulnerability might have lasted is futile.

In May 1921, just two years after Faith's death, Corra's sister, Hope White Harris, died. Faith's death had caused Corra to reach a new level of resignation over life's fatal necessities, but it had not undermined her faith, she claimed. Hope's death, on the contrary, provoked a genuine, if short-lived, crisis of faith.[153] The two were not especially close, but Hope's death brought to the surface the grief that Corra had suppressed, forcing her to deal with some of the questions she had refused to face when Faith died.[154] Their relationship had been stressful at times when Corra felt Hope's medical problems were, at best, the result of tension caused by three undisciplined sons. However, she really suspected the worst, namely, that Hope was one of the hopelessly "neurasthenic" women about whom she often wrote.[155] She used the term as an epithet to dismiss people who she believed had crippled themselves psychologically to step out of life.

Corra changed her mind about Hope, though. In a letter to Faith in 1918 Corra wrote, "I should have been more patient with your Aunt Hope all these years when she whined so much, for she was evidently ill."[156] Once Corra discovered that Hope's medical problems were not "in her head" but rather in her heart, literally, she began to feel more sympathy, empathy, and affection for, if not intimacy with, Hope. Afterward, the sense of having nothing to lose made her relationship with Hope rewarding, if not as mutually gratifying as was hers with Faith. The ability to love someone with minimal strings attached was a new experience for Corra. However, this ended with Hope's death of apparent heart-related illness in May 1921.

The gravity of all her losses weighed Corra down. She claimed to see "reality" for the first time, and it seemed to confirm that God had simply been a "trick" she had played on herself to cope with life.[157] Faith's death had crushed whatever capacity for emotional expression she had left, but it had not entirely crushed her faith in the God who met her cry for help in 1898. Although she suffered a real crisis of faith with Hope's death, it was at least the last debilitating loss she suffered. Her mother died in 1888 and her father in 1930, and although she loved both parents and delivered a memorable eulogy at her father's funeral service, she did not suffer the same kind of deep grief at the loss of either as she did with that of her husband, daughter, and sister.

Corra recovered the faith she lost at Hope's death the way she resumed her inner balance throughout her mature years, namely, by losing herself in work. She found her internal center by displacing painful emotions with work. Throughout the 1920s she published prolifically, including three autobiographical works between 1923 and 1927. *My Book and Heart* (1923) and *As a Woman Thinks* (1925) purported to convey, respectively, the life of the heart and the life of the mind. *The Happy Pilgrimage* (1927) was to be a travelogue of her journey to the Far East in search of happiness. Illness cut short the trip and the book ended up being an account of the few months she stayed in California recovering from a heart condition.

Talmadge and Holt believed *My Book and Heart* was better than *As a Woman Thinks*. Talmadge dismissed the latter as the meandering digressions of one wrought down by fatigue. Harris thought differently, though, and so did many others.[158] "I know that *As a Woman Thinks* is the best thing I ever wrote," she told Lorimer, "and whether anybody else says so or not, I know it is a great book."[159] Writing the book proved emotionally beneficial; readers' response to the book was deeply gratifying to Corra. In it she wrote candidly about her regrets and disillusionments over having chosen the life of the mind—a choice that was necessary for her to write and publish—over the life of an ordinary woman, which allowed more time, energy, and natural emotion for human relationships. More than fatigue, as Talmadge concluded, the book reveals Harris coming to terms with her gender identity.

There were any number of reasons why Harris, a woman considered and consulted as an authority on gender roles, might have been confused over what it meant to be a woman. She grew up in a household where gender roles were somewhat reversed, married a man with as many traits considered feminine as masculine, and watched as her daughter did much the same. Moreover, American culture in general and the South's in particular challenged and punished strong-minded, bright women of her day, especially when they became public and independent.

However, Harris attributed her disillusionment, emptiness, and alienation neither to overwork, nor to the obvious losses of those she loved most, nor to family relationships, but rather to the fact that she had believed it necessary and so had forsaken womanhood for personhood. The price for professional success and personal liberty was more than she expected to pay, but in the end, writing *As a Woman Thinks* brought a degree of resolution. Giving voice to what had been inarticulate ponderings proved to be cathartic.

Her final book-length autobiographical work, *The Happy Pilgrimage* (1927), was a travelogue of sorts written over a period of months spent in California in 1925. *As a Woman Thinks* provoked a sympathetic response—her readers wanted her to find happiness and encouraged her not to give up. Encouraged, Corra left for California determined to discover and write about the happiness that had continually eluded her. Unfortunately, both the trip and the book were disappointments. She suffered a heart attack while in California and was bedridden much of the time. Moreover, her southern witticisms did not charm Californians in the mid-1920s as they had charmed New Yorkers in the 1910s. Californians were far less forgiving when she made factual errors or violated local taboos, such as making an issue out of the unsettling nature of earthquakes when public authorities went out of their way to downplay the phenomenon. Never one to ignore the elephant in the living room, Harris proved unwilling to back down when the president of the San Francisco Chamber of Commerce challenged her sensationalized account of an earthquake incident. But being right did not assuage the disappointment she felt when reviewers considered her reflections in the book regressive rather than quaint.[160]

Between the deaths of her daughter and sister and her own in 1935, Harris spent her time writing and entertaining family and associates in the Valley. Her personal life revolved around three nephews (Hope's sons) and, to a greater extent, Bettie and Trannie Rains, two neighborhood girls who came to live with Harris in the mid-1920s to work off their mother's fifty-dollar debt. In short time Harris found the two girls amiable companions and all but legally adopted them both, though she was fond of claiming they adopted her. Not surprisingly, the young women became surrogate daughters. After her sister's death, Harris needed merely to find the right ones "upon whom to spend my affections."[161] The three wrote numerous letters, most of them between Harris and Bettie, and many of them written in 1925 when Harris was in California working on *The Happy Pilgrimage.* The Rains sisters, nephew Al Harris, the staff of the *Atlanta Journal,* and many of the paper's associates were Corra's companions the last years of her life. She lived both for the serenity, solitude, and isolation of the Valley, on the one hand, and for entertaining guests with famed and memorable hospitality on the other. After Faith's death she wrote Lorimer that from then on she lived and wrote to make enough "money to spend on this land which is the only dear and living interest I have."[162]

Harris's literary career slowed down by 1930 when she had all but quit publishing nationally. One of her last involvements that made more than local news was her appointment by Holt in the spring of 1930 to a visiting professorship at Rollins College in Winter Park, Florida. In 1926 Holt left the *Independent* to become president at Rollins. Soon afterward he conferred an honorary degree on Harris (her third—Oglethorpe and the University of Georgia had done so previously), and in 1930 he created a visiting professorship to gain publicity for the school. Holt named her "Professor of Evil." It did gain publicity, but not the kind he wanted. That a woman from Harris's background presumed to instruct young people on a subject that had stumped philosophers for centuries seemed too naive for anyone in the press to take seriously. Critics from Orlando to London mocked the appointment.[163] Harris confided to educator and author William Lyon Phelps her "suspicion . . . that Dr. Holt regretted [creating] it and had much ado defending the 'Department of Perdition' in his college over the country."[164]

Although Harris spent the final years of her life nursing a heart condition, she wrote regularly the *Atlanta Journal's* "Candlelit" column from late 1931 until her death in 1935.[165] These brief columns capture well the ways Harris remained enigmatic and "seemingly contradictory" until the end of her life. Some of them reveal her at her best. They comprise a good deal of the concluding analysis of Harris in chapter 8 of this book. On religious issues her "Candles" show that she could be remarkably progressive. Her refusal early in life to give in to the constraints of southern evangelicalism and fundamentalism served her well in her last years. Between the influence of the conservative religious ethos of her upbringing and the regressive "humanism" of Paul More, her most influential mentor at a crucial stage of her intellectual development, it is little wonder that Harris lived a life of marked contradiction. The wonder is in the remarkable ways she let nothing, not even deeply held beliefs, keep her from being true to herself, no matter what the cost.

The Influence of Paul Elmer More

Editor, essayist, and literary critic Paul Elmer More (1864–1937) was a brilliant, polished, sophisticated, Harvard-educated scholar of Sanskrit and Greek. Harris's and More's paths crossed at a pivotal stage in the former's intellectual development, shortly after her literary career began. Although they corresponded throughout the decade, the primary years of their association were from 1901 to 1904. And though they met face-to-face on a few occasions, the venue for their relationship was almost exclusively correspondence. Harris and More coauthored Harris's first book-length work, *The Jessica Letters: An Editor's Romance* (1904), a book of epistles between two fictional lovers, Philip Towers (More), a New York editor, and Jessica Doane (Harris), a Georgia reviewer. Talmadge rightly concluded that Harris "revered" Paul More as a "literary oracle."[1] During their comparatively brief association More influenced Harris in ways as consequential and abiding as any other single source. As with practically everything else in Harris's life, her relationship with More reveals contradiction. While she acknowledged the "profound impression" some of his ideas made on her at the time she encountered them, she variously challenged, accepted, adapted, and eventually outgrew some of his regressive ideologies.[2]

During their years of association, Harris was very enamored of More. On the one hand, she admired his dispassion and self-possession as strength of character. At the same time, she lamented his emotional distance and asked repeatedly in letters for him to be more self-revealing. In real life as well as through the fictional character of Jessica Doane, she challenged his cold, dispassionate, and sterile philosophy. However, when tragedy struck her life repeatedly over the first two decades of the century, she turned to More's use of "indifference" as a personal coping strategy. Later in her life, however, she began to internalize what she learned from More to construct a perspective that helped steel her against personal tragedy. But it also robbed her of what she regarded as the birthright of women, namely, an emotional sensibility. More's prescriptive philosophy helped her reject her own emotions as an outlet for grief, a choice she regretted later in life.

Whether Harris felt more than respect and admiration for More is a matter of speculation.³ That he strongly influenced her thinking and writing is not. She regarded him with an unrestrained awe, as something of a modern visionary. He was her "literary standard bearer, rather far in advance" of his contemporaries.⁴ Harris looked to More, she told him, for the same reasons Lundy turned to God: "I always read whatever of yours I find, and for the same reason that Lundy prays and fasts,—to chasten my spirit, to keep me humble."⁵

She told him early in their association about the profound impact one of his ideas had on her. His assertion that "oppression is an illusion" and "liberty" a state of mind, not of material circumstances, literally changed her consciousness.⁶ She was so influenced by his opinion that a mere comment from him could turn her thinking and her own opinion completely around. A negative comment from him about a book she had previously admired "so turned me against that book that now I would not stay in the same room with it!"⁷

In More's writings Harris found what seemed a universal language and validation for traditional southern conservatism as well as the misogyny one finds in some of her works. His ideas about social responsibility, social reform, human nature, and what he believed were innate differences between women and men influenced Harris most. Clarification of More's influence on Harris requires a close examination of his reputation and ideas.

More's reputation as a scholar and philosopher came chiefly from his *Shelburne Essays* (1904–21) and *New Shelburne Essays* (1928–36), fourteen volumes on philosophy and literature. Although More never completed his graduate degree at Harvard, he taught Greek and Sanskrit there, at Bryn Mawr, and later at Princeton. He held several prominent editorial posts beginning at the turn of the century and was literary editor of the *Independent* from 1901 to 1903 when Harris became associated with him. From there he moved to the *New York Evening Post,* where he stayed until 1909. During his tenure at the *Post* he also served as literary editor of the *Post*'s weekly paper, the *Nation,* from 1906 to 1914. Although all three periodicals were known during More's day for being liberal, More himself was an avowed conservative. He and Irving Babbitt, his mentor at Harvard, led in the articulation of a philosophy and form of literary criticism they called "New Humanism" to distinguish it from humanitarianism, which they regarded with contempt. New Humanism was a reaction to romanticism in literature and to modernity's influence on religion and politics, specifically the changes science brought to religion and the influence socialist ideas had on Progressive Era politics.

Harris and More shared a similar legacy. Both were well known during their lifetimes and largely forgotten shortly after. Unlike Harris, however, More was neither an enigma nor difficult to categorize. There is nothing hidden in his works, no mystery to unravel. To him there were few riddles to life that could not be solved with some formula of logic and rationality. Whatever the questions, the answers were close enough to the surface. Though More was not a simpleton, his philosophy of life was quite simple. In his thinking, right and wrong, good and bad, black and white, were readily distinguishable; there were no shades of gray.

More's ideas evolved through several religious and philosophical phases, including Calvinism, Hinduism, Anglicanism, Buddhism, and Platonism, with elements of Calvinism and Platonism exercising the most lasting influence.[8] More believed foremost that dualism was the key to the mystery of "man." He had serious misgivings about women in general, or woman's nature, and Pauline misgivings about marriage—the ability to be committed to both a profession and a family—although he himself managed both. He had an abiding mistrust and insurmountable disdain for sentiment, emotion, and human nature. The nature of More's conservatism is captured in his celebration of the way the country's legal structure had come to value property rights over human rights. He proclaimed unashamedly that to "the civilized man the rights of property are more important than the right to life" and that "rightly understood the dollar is more than the man." More thought it progress that "law is concerned primarily with the rights of property" as opposed to human rights.[9] He emphasized above all else the need to constrain the lower impulses in humankind.[10] After pondering the "first and last things of human experience," he became convinced of "the inherent combativeness of human nature."[11] "We think we have grown and changed our nature," More wrote relatively late in life, "but in the end we fall back into the pit from which we were digged."[12]

More vehemently opposed social reform of any kind. A passage from a letter he wrote Harris in 1909 summarizes his thoughts on the subject: "As for those socialists, nihilists, and other ists, remember one thing: No reformer is ever to be trusted! My hand and seal to that. The amount of virtue possible to cram into any one man is limited. If he uses that virtue in regulating society and the lives of sinners generally, he is pretty sure to have little left for himself. As for me, not being a reformer, I am virtuous or nothing."[13] Such sentiment about personal virtue echoed the perspective of Harris's mother, who Harris claimed would die for a doctrine or a creed.

Opinions about More varied, but most of his contemporaries, even those who disagreed with him, took him seriously as a scholar who dealt with "the fundamental questions of what is the nature of man and how should he believe and act."[14] A number of celebrated men respected More's intellectual dedication. Biographer Stephen Tanner wrote, "T.S. Eliot considered More one of the two 'wisest men' he had known." Even caustic veteran editor and satirist H. L. Mencken, who had no regard for More's ideas, conceded that More was "the 'nearest approach to a genuine scholar' America had."[15] With his usual wit, Mencken told More that he would have been "a good fellow" if he had only "drunk more whiskey and begotten more bastards."[16] Journalist and foreign policy analyst Walter Lippmann characterized More as a "man who, in the guise of a critic, is authentically concerned with the first and last things of human experience."[17] Moreover, More came close to being the first American Nobel Laureate in 1930 when it went instead to Sinclair Lewis.[18]

On the other hand, More had a reputation for being a "cold and heart-less intellectual."[19] His reserve, aloofness, and disinterested nature was no secret to anyone, not "even those closest to him."[20] Biographer Arthur Dakin attributed More's disinterestedness to "the complexity of his nature."[21] But many others were less generous and described More as stiff and intractable rather than complex. Even though Mencken respected More's commitment to scholarship, he had no patience with his intellectual arrogance, intoler-ance, and elitism.[22] Some of his college classmates saw him as "critical, self-centered, unsociable, and aloof." One of them wrote that More "felt his su-periority . . . and was at no pains to hide it."[23] Whatever More accomplished, he was limited by his "inability to face up to the abhorrent or to identify himself vicariously with sensual, feckless, and untidy human nature."[24] His contempt for "untidy human nature," for the body through which it ex-pressed itself, and for the resulting mind/body dualism had a lasting impact on Harris's thinking.

The New Humanism movement articulated by More, Babbitt, and oth-ers suited conservative intellectuals who wanted to steer philosophically between organized religion and science.[25] They were careful everywhere to distinguish their brand of humanism from "its presumptive brother, hu-manitarianism."[26] More associated his "humanism" with the idealism of Plato, while he associated humanitarianism with socialism and materialism or naturalism, all of which he loathed.[27]

For More, dualism was the cornerstone of his philosophy and "the distinctive mark of humanity."[28] It was both man's cross to bear and his glory to find resolution of warring opposites in the soul. In More's thinking, the primary dualism was between reason and emotion. As More defined it, reason was humanity's one indispensable faculty.[29] He elevated human reason not only at the expense of human emotion but to emotion's full displacement. The capacity to reason, he believed, was the highest accomplishment of human evolution.[30] This bald displacement had a profound impact on the ideals and values Harris developed.

More's conceptualization of reason is clearly among that feminist philosopher Linda Alcoff calls "outdated." Yet revisiting the tenets More upheld, which were very much explicit in Harris's day, helps explain why Harris and other woman writers of her day thought that to be human meant to be masculine. Alcoff writes:

Feminists have argued that concepts of reason and knowledge, as well as those of man, history, and power, are reflections of gendered practices passing as universal ones. The problem is, not simply that men have been biased against women's capacity to be rational, but that . . . in modernity, reason has been defined in opposition to the feminine, such that it requires the exclusion, transcendence, and even the domination of the feminine, of women, and of women's traditional concerns, which have been characterized as the site of the irreducibly irrational. . . . This is how Kant is able to make rational his claim that the woman who reasons might as well have a beard. . . . Like any other concept, rationality is defined by reference to some contrast, and the association between rationality and masculinity dictated that contrasting site as the female.[31]

Distancing oneself from the feminine seemed essential to appearing to possess rationality, reasonability, and other traits associated with sound thinking. In As a Woman Thinks, Harris reveals the confusion that could result when women chose to cultivate masculine traits and deny feminine traits so they could write with a masculine voice.

More could never have fathomed the struggle Harris articulated in As a Woman Thinks, in which she wrestles with the contradictions between her purported gender ideals and her reality as a successful, independent woman. More could not have fathomed it because he believed women's souls were "singular," or simplistic and uncomplicated, compared with men's souls, which were dual and more complex. This becomes clear in excerpts from *The Jessica Letters*. It is this understanding of reason as implicitly sterile and explicitly masculine that one finds Harris refuting in both Philip Towers and Paul More, and it is this conception of reason that she believed robbed her of the ability to be at home in her body as a woman (a subject covered in chapter 5). Yet she turned to this understanding of reason as she sought coping strategies in the second half of her life.

More's solution to whatever dilemma humanity faced could be found in what he called humanism. For More a "true humanism" "mediated" the dualism in human nature. "And such a mediation is not a mechanical compromise or a flabby wavering between two moods," he explained to Robert Shafer, a friend and fellow proponent of the New Humanism, "but an intimate marriage between passivity and activity, contemplation and self-direction, emotion and will, of which is born a certain *tertium quid*."[32] More's use of the term *tertium quid* here and the double consciousness to which he refers in the passage below recall W.E.B. DuBois's use of the term and the concept in his essay on the freed slave's effort to reconcile racial and national identity in *Souls of Black Folk*. Yet the outcomes sought by DuBois and More could not be more disparate. DuBois promoted resistance to "fate," while More valued unquestioning acceptance.

More's *tertium quid* was the consciousness of the individual whose "lower nature" had been "charmed by the voice of his higher instincts."[33] More explained this condition and its relevance in a letter to his sister, Alice, a lifelong confidante. The passage illustrates something of More's philosophy of justice and how he simplified the "mysteries of human condition":

One key, one solution to the mysteries of human condition . . . to the old knots of fate, freedom, and foreknowledge, exists, the propounding, namely, of the double consciousness. A man must ride alternately on the horses of his private and his public nature, as the equestrians in the circus throw themselves nimbly from horse to horse, or plant one foot on the back of one, and the other on the back of the other. So when a man is the victim of his fate, his sciatica in his loins, and cramp in his mind; a club-foot and a club in his wit; a sour face and a selfish temper; a strut in his gait and a conceit in his affection; or is ground to powder by the vice of his race; he is to rally on his relation to the Universe, which his ruin benefits. Leaving the demon who suffers, he is to take sides with the Deity who secures universal benefit by his pain.[34]

This passage includes several key ideas. More believed that the human condition made all things equal. All men suffer; each was the "victim of his fate." Whether his fate happened to be the physical pain of "sciatic loins," emotional pain from a deformed body (club-foot) or mind (club wit), a limitation such as conceit or selfishness, or that he was merely "ground to powder by the vice of his race," no man could legitimately question his fate or claim to be baffled by "the mysteries of human condition." The problem was solved by recognizing the universal existence of the "double consciousness," which, because it was universal, was also democratic—no respecter of individual men, so to speak. Each man needed to believe that thereon was equality. No man's pain was more or less important than another's. Virtue resulted from the individual's attitude of acceptance toward his particular fate.

More believed the duality of human nature inhered in man's capacity for both a private self and a public self and that only men had such a capacity. Dualism also explained the irreconcilable differences between the sexes. Writing as Philip Towers, More explained that "in this duality lies all the reason of that enmity of the sexes, which draws us together yet still holds us asunder."[35] This also explained why men understood women better than women understood men: "It is so much easier for me to understand you than for you to understand me, because a woman's nature is single, whereas a man's is double."

Because man had both a public and a private experience, and a natural capacity for both within himself, he could understand woman's private nature, but because woman had only a private nature, she could never understand his "iron determination . . . in public affairs." The duality between a man's private and public self was but "one case in point of the eternal dualism in masculine nature which a woman can never comprehend. . . . For a woman is not so. There exists no such gap in her between her heart and brain, between her outer and inner life."[36] A similar sentiment informs Harris's autobiographies more than two decades later. Harris wrote in *As a Woman Thinks* that "once a woman's mind is divorced from her affections it is a trifle unbalanced and untrustworthy, no matter how brilliantly and broadly she uses it."[37]

For More, dualism explained why men were initiators and women responders in relationship. Woman is "less efficient in the world and is never a creator or impresser of new ideas," he explained. "She calls the man selfish and is bitter against him at times, but her accusation is wrong. It is not selfishness which leads a man if needs be to cut off his own personal desires while sacrificing another; it is the power in him which impels the world into new courses."[38] Such a belief could lead one to conclude, as Harris did, that man was simply the "one sex there is. . . . And you cannot get around that with all the thinking and doing that can be thought or done."[39] Man was to her the human norm. It explained to Harris why women would never have monuments built to them, why there were no women Isaiahs or psalmists, why women could never write great autobiographies, and why "there is no history of woman."[40]

The same ideas that encouraged Harris's misgivings about women governed More's misgivings about marriage. More wrote to his sister in 1900 about his feelings over his forthcoming marriage: "I cannot but feel a little anxious about my approaching marriage. I have no doubt I shall be happy, and it is probably the best thing for me from every point of view; but on the other hand I have done so little and want to do so much, that I dread any curtailment of my liberty and choice in working. At any moment I may feel a terrible impulse to throw up everything and follow some new impulse."[41] Nor did marriage to a woman who was apparently in every way capable of living up to his expectations about women change his mind about the institution. With all the compelling evidence to the contrary in his own life, More held to his belief that married men were less productive than single men.

In 1921 More wrote that it was women who had ruined the quality of education at Oxford—both from the enrollment of women and from the increasing numbers of married professors. In accounting for why Oxford had been on the decline since the mid-nineteenth century, he wrote: "At least one can safely say that a unique interest was lost to learning with the admission of women into Oxford's cloistered society and the banishment of God." Moreover, it was not just "the presence of the undergraduate in petticoats that marked the revolution; wives, too, were multiplying, and with them came a great alteration in the habits of the faculty. In the generation preceding, none of the tutors were married and very few of the professors."[42]

Whatever his misgivings about women, More apparently made an exceptionally wise choice for his wife. Nettie More was known to be the heart and soul of the family, the "active and stabilizing factor," the one known within and without for her "charitable disposition." Dakin wrote about the complementary domestic relationship between Paul and Nettie More and the benefits to the former from the typical sexual division of labor:

Fortunately for Paul, the details of daily existence, so boring to him, fascinated his wife [though Dakin offers no evidence to support the latter observation]. . . . She devoted herself as intensely to housekeeping as he did to intellectual work. This, from a writer's point of view, being an ideal division of labor, he left everything, except the ordering of the coal, which he claimed was a man's job, to her, aided by such occasional cleaning women and maids as they could afford. When he closed the library door, she saw to it that no uninvited caller or other annoyance obliged him to open it.[43]

Whatever anxieties More suffered before the wedding over his decision to marry, Dakin suggests that he soon realized the folly of his anguish.

Nettie was not always able to run interference, though, and when circumstances prevented her intervention, the experience could be especially frustrating for More. He took consolation, however, when one particularly trying occasion actually led him to a breakthrough on the subject of human nature—one of his favorites. Obliged by family responsibility, in 1907 he found himself confined at a Lake Seneca farmhouse with Nettie, their daughter, and several members of his wife's extended family, some of whom vexed More plenty even from a distance. Living confined with them drove him first to distraction but then to a revelation that affirmed him once and for all in his disregard for human nature. More wrote a letter to Prosser Hall Frye, a friend and instructor at the University of Nebraska, in which he remarked that after "a month in 'that home of bawdy, bedlam-and-babies'" he no longer doubted what he had always believed about human nature, namely, that it tended toward evil. His suspicions had been confirmed, and he had thus gained inspiration to write the essay on Pascal that he had been struggling with for some time.[44]

You will be surprised to hear that the people of the house here have in a way, and certainly without their own volition, helped me in this task. You see Pascal's faith was based on a contempt for human nature unrestored by Grace. Ordinarily the conventions of life so overlay the real instincts and acts of men that we see mankind in a kind of solid respectable gray. Now here I have been brought in contact with real unadulterated undisciplined human nature, and it has the effect of opening one's eyes to what we all at bottom are—a poor, restless, animal, evil thing. And as a moral I have before me the two opposite results of indulgence—a stupefied paralytic [his wife's aunt] in whom the springs of action have been dried up, and an imbecile [his wife's mother] who has lost all power of inhibition so that there is no buffer of convention between fluttering impulse and action.[45]

More preferred his life in "respectable gray," and Nettie generally provided the conditions that made it possible. But when he discovered reality in face-to-face contact with a "stupefied paralytic" and "an imbecile," he realized, in essence, that human nature was an "evil thing."

This view of human nature caused More to fear the world and to suspect all within it. "The world at large," he wrote his sister in 1898, "seems to be only a great instrument ready to the hand of the jealous Nemesis."[46] By 1909 his cosmic outlook had grown even bleaker. "My own life . . . is a crushing grind," he wrote his sister that fall. "I feel that cynicism and indifference creep every day closer to my heart; I read books by habit, and write for God knows what reason."[47] Still, even if his professional environment did not bring the satisfaction he sought, he was more comfortable behind the closed doors of his study, where he could remain lost in the abstract, keep his hands clean, and continually "see mankind in a kind of solid respectable gray" rather than in his personal world, where there were diapers and wheelchairs and where he saw his fellow humans for what he believed they really were "at bottom": "poor, restless, animal[s], evil thing[s]." In either case, his thinking made it difficult for him "to establish any sufficient bond between my intellectual life and my personal relationships."[48] Life for More was a series of unresolved bifurcations.

More knew that people considered him a "cold and heartless" intellectual. In a letter to his sister in 1906 he implored her to preserve her capacity for human sympathy. Even then he recognized the cost of living without it. He confided:

If I wrote what was really in my heart, I should merely blacken paper with a long commentary on the emptiness of life—of my own life in particular. Here I have been toiling and renouncing and wrestling with heartache since I was a boy for fame, and now, when enough praise falls to me to show what fame would be, I find it adds not one jot to the meaning of life or to the pleasure in my work. This is a mystery the world has been trying to solve for a good many years, and apparently the solution is not to come from me. And withal I have a number of things which you have not. I do not wonder that you feel the bitterness of it. *I beg of you, however, to keep one thing which I have lost—that is the power of sympathy* [emphasis added]. . . . And above all don't grieve over having spoiled me! I have not yet found that anyone has been spoiled in this world by affection, have you? As for Darrah [his daughter] I feel sometimes that my own absorption produces a chilly atmosphere about her, not altogether wholesome.[49]

The doleful sentiment was hardly a passing one. Four years later, he wrote Alice: "The dreadful truth is that the struggle for life has a sad disheartening effect on most of us. I feel it only too strongly in myself—feel a kind of hardening of the fibres, a disinclination to give myself out in sympathy, a shutting in within an ever narrowing circle."[50]

By the time of More's letter to his sister, Harris and More were no longer corresponding. If Harris could have read the letter, she would not have been surprised at his disillusionment, as she had chided him frequently—as both Corra Harris and Jessica Doane—for his inability to feel human sympathy or empathy. Had she been able to see, however, the toll his path would take on him, she might have been less inclined to adapt his ideas to her own series of tragic circumstances. Just over a month after More's letter to his sister, Lundy Harris took his own life. Around that time, the effect of More's influence on Harris is seen in a letter Corra wrote to her daughter, Faith: "I am glad to see that you are learning 'indifference.' You will find that a hard plant to cultivate in your nature. But cultivate it. Study the philosophy of life—what it shall profit you to earn. I found the less agonizingly I cared, the less I suffered."[51] Harris reveals that she had learned well by then to integrate More's philosophy of indifference into her own life.

Indifference was not all Harris adopted from More's moral philosophy. More's influence on Harris was profound and lasting because of where she was in her own intellectual and moral growth at the time they met. When Harris met More in 1901 she was thirty-two years old and in transition, in an intense phase of "becoming." Becoming *what* she was not sure, but she was moving toward something different from what she had been. In April 1903 she wrote More about how the experiences of 1898 and 1899 had profoundly marked her and changed her life: "In the old days when I was just a little feminine creation in my home in Oxford, I was not happy, but I was very simple. Then the shock came [her family's destitution] and I was thrust into the strange world of a new life [a writing career]. . . . The world I knew went out in one lightening [*sic*] fizzle, and although I escaped on the 'ladder' . . . I can't come down because I cannot trust the ground again. And I can't go up because I am not finished.—So I just sit up here and talk and talk of you all to pass the time and to grow wise."[52] With this metaphorical depiction Harris reveals her affinity with her time and place. Her description of being trapped on a ladder escaping from one phase of life to another recalls Daniel Singal's passage about the thinking southerner at the turn of the century being "trapped in an intellectual no-man's land between the thought of two centuries."[53] Harris was among the number of women forced by financial circumstance to become a writer. A large percentage of her income over the first decade of the century came from reviewing books for the *Independent,* a job for which she felt ill suited but took on nonetheless. As book review editor, More became her primary contact at the periodical and eventually an unquestioned mentor.

The Jessica Letters took their inspiration from correspondence between Harris and More in the early 1900s. About the book's origin, Dakin wrote: "When she had sent More scores of reviews and every few days for a year had deluged him with correspondence whose exhausting length, pronunciatory spelling, and unrestrained temperamentality accompanied an amusing, intelligent, and intense interest in fiction, he proposed they write a novel, the first at which she tried her hand." Dakin called the novel "sweet, flimsy, and ephemeral as a valentine." More's biographer and friend Robert Shafer wrote that More "had not the natural aptitude for the undertaking that Mrs. Harris so evidently had." Harris's "creation of Jessica" is "inimitable. By comparison . . . Philip Towers is almost tame." Talmadge suggests rightly that "Mrs. Harris's letters to More during the writing of the book are more entertaining than those she contributed" to the book itself.[54]

The surviving letters between Harris and More from 1901 to 1909 include half a dozen from him and more than six dozen from her.[55] Her letters are generally long, chatty, intimate, self-reflective, and self-revealing (she called them "affectionate, impudent, guileful, truthful").[56] His, by comparison, are brief and focused, yet cordial and kind, if not as self-revealing as she would have liked. In them, as in *The Jessica Letters,* Harris praises More (Philip Towers) for his brilliance as a literary editor but also chastises him for his cold aloofness as a person. In all, though, even when she bemoans his emotional distance and regrets the coldness of his classically trained mind, she defers to him as the superior and more advanced of the two.

The Jessica Letters were supposed to be a dialogue reflecting different regional perspectives on politics and society. More as Philip, being from the North, was supposed to reflect liberalism; Harris as Jessica, from the South, was supposed to reflect tradition; their dialogue and ultimately their marriage were supposed to harmonize and reconcile the two ways of thinking.

What the correspondence actually became, however, was a forum for two shades of similar social conservatism, as years later the assumed antagonism between the Agrarians and New Humanists concealed as much concord as discord between the two. With the possible exception of one or two ideas More had on religion, there was nothing progressive or liberal about him. "Paradoxically, the characters do not express the prevalent economic and social views of their sections," wrote Talmadge. "Phillip's attacks on social humanitarianism would have found no favor with Northern intellectuals, and Jessica's defense of this trend would not have been echoed in the South. In reality More and Mrs. Harris saw eye to eye on such questions." Talmadge is correct that they "saw eye to eye on such questions," but a careful reading would have revealed no "defense of this trend" of social humanitarianism on Harris's part. Her "attacks" were against Philip's incapacity to feel, not against his "social humanitarianism," because he had none.[57]

An encouraging letter from More could carry Harris a long way. One in particular "gave wings to my fainting spirit," she wrote him. Harris was discouraged by the condescending manner of one of Lundy's high-minded colleagues. Corra's naturally feisty temperament never sat well with the clerical authorities surrounding Lundy, but once she identified herself as a writer her demeanor tested them beyond endurance. They had no regard for her increasing success as a literary critic, but by the time she established a name for herself with the *Independent* they held barely veiled contempt for her growing self-confidence.

On one occasion, More's letter praising a review by Harris encouraged her to challenge an unkind criticism from Dr. Sasnett, a colleague of Lundy's who was always accusing her of "impudent, blankety blank ignorance." And she defended herself against another colleague who told her she did not write reviews but rather "'little essays' and called them reviews, but that as a matter of fact I only used the titles of books as an excuse to air my own reflections in general."[58] Thanks to the letter from More, though, which arrived the same day as Dr. Sasnett's unwelcome visit, she spent a "*heavenly day* . . . celebrating another lawless literary victory at the expense of his [Sasnett's] opinion."[59] Whatever Lundy's colleagues' opinions and reputations, those of the literary editor of New York's *Independent*—a periodical southerners disliked but begrudgingly respected—could and did put them in their places and silenced their condescension toward Harris.[60]

Unfortunately for Harris, such letters from More were few and far between. She grieved once the correspondence slowed after *The Jessica Letters* was published (in book form in 1904, the year after More left the *Indepen-*

dent) and all but ended by 1909. When he moved from the *Independent* to the *Post*, the change was painful enough for Harris, but she continued to write him occasionally and he continued to help her find editors to publish her work. When he took over as literary editor at the *Nation*, however, she felt she had lost touch with him for good. She could no more "'sass' an editor of the *Nation* than I would the author of the Book of Job." She had "missed you sadly" enough already, she wrote in 1906.[61] She knew that once he moved to the *Nation*, a periodical for which her writing would not be appropriate, their association would eventually end.

Harris kept up with More's work for several years after their professional relationship ended. Even though their formal association ended in 1904, in 1909 Harris wrote to thank More for sending her the latest copy of the *Shelburne Essays* and told him that she had received directly from the publisher and read copies of all but one of the previous issues. She also lamented the fact that the two of them were no longer closely associated, a circumstance that she was sure had retarded her literary development. "I have lost infinitely," she mourned in 1909, "qualities that I might have developed if I had stayed under your influence."[62]

Whether or not Harris consciously linked some of the changes that occurred in her thinking and ways she began to espouse the very ideas that she had once condemned in him in personal correspondence and the published *Jessica Letters* is not clear. What is clear is the way the stark contrast between their perspectives in the early years collapsed into striking similarity once Harris articulated her thinking in print. More influenced Harris's thinking on human nature and on gender identity, both of which shaped her politics. Much of the outcome of that influence is seen in chapters 4, 5, and 6.

Although Harris idolized More much as Jessica Doane loved Philip Towers, the feelings were blind in neither case. Speaking as both Jessica and Corra, she was astutely insightful in her harsh criticism of his bankrupt emotions, of his living in abstraction, of living in his head as if the body were superfluous. Such was pathetic enough if he could live alone in his head without affecting all those around him, but that was impossible. It had serious effects on anyone with whom he shared a relationship. In a separate letter Harris called More a "stiff faced man" who "should burn for being so cold."[63] "I know the cold scholarly atmosphere of your mind as well as you do yourself," she once told him in her all-too-familiar tone.[64]

More was, in fact, *all* mind, the consummate "disembodied self," as otherworldly in his intellect as religious people were in their spirits. "You seem to me," she wrote in 1902, "to be, not a person so much as a mind of varying moods when it comes to personal contact of any sort. I have never got acquainted with you. The fact is you are not *there,* your personality seems to me to have been sublimated into some sort of intangible intelligence. If when I meet you, you prove to be a real human being, I should not believe the evidence of my own eyes."[65] In sharp contrast to More, who abhorred the body and longed to live in the mind, to escape the human nature he feared and loathed, Harris was very much at home in her body and in the world. In 1902, in a telling letter to More, she wrote: "I have got a natural antipathy for the disembodied myself. And if its [*sic*] just the same to the ruling saints in heaven, I think I will have my same body rejuvenated and fixed over to wear while I am there. I am such a savage by nature that I should feel unnaturally apparent without it to hide in."[66]

Harris accused More of being "a wanderer out of time into space and mysteries. . . . You don't need people. You could go on freezing forever and never know any better."[67] Loneliness was a feeling that haunted Harris, but at least it was a normal human response. "But *you* don't know anything about it!" she wrote. "You were born lonesome and you like it."[68] In January 1905, after he wrote her that the "bowels of human feeling" had "dried up within" him, she informed him that although he had many traits to recommend him, including "an impersonal faculty for justice and mercy," he was clueless when it came to human feelings:

> Man, you do not know any thing about "bowels of feeling." That is an inordinate figure of speech with you. You can interpret the spirit of man, but his heart action is a blank mystery to you. There are certain places in human nature that have been domesticated . . . but I believe you crawled out of your cradle beyond them. There are *homeless* tracks in human nature that lead "to fair lands forlorn" with which you are well acquainted. Their topography belongs to the spirit altitudes of man, and few have the speech to define them, but you can. You can give a voice to this region, cold, thin, remote and to most people unintelligible. . . . I mention all this lest you should imagine you had really lost something in realizing the fact that the "bowels of feeling have dried up in you." Don't worry about it. You never had any.[69]

On the surface Harris clearly admired More's ability to interpret "the spirit altitudes of man," but she intimates that something valuable was missing from a capacity so refined. However cultured or civilized the "spirit altitudes" were, they were also "cold, thin, remote and to most people unintelligible." In contrasting herself with More, Harris portrayed herself as being more at home with the "heart action" and "bowels of feeling." Not long afterward, however, she began to struggle with the tension between naturalness and refinement as she understood them. In her own "savage" or unrefined state she appreciated the value of naturalness, but she also knew that refinement defined the powerful and self-possessed like More, and self-possession became her chief aspiration.

However awed Harris was by More, his intellectual origins were not a mystery to her. It was his classical education. Harris had decidedly mixed emotions about the classically trained mind, well aware of how exacting such an education could be. Hence she knew she had achieved no small victory when More wrote approving words about something she had written: "I always think that a word of praise wrung from a man with the Greek 'accent' of mind and spirit is a great concession to a barbarian like me."[70]

But the classically trained mind could be blinded by its own light, she told him. His certainly was, as he revealed after a trip to speak at Bryn Mawr where he discovered that women there did not like him. "Not because I was unamiable, but because I was indifferent," he believed.[71] Harris set him straight. He was not "indifferent" to women. No man in his right mind, or no man who was not "stupid or very old," could be indifferent to women. No, his attitude toward women was much more pernicious. "Mr. More, you exorcise women, you cast them out of your mind like you would seven devils." The ability to "exorcise women" was uncommon; in fact, the only men she knew who were capable of such an exploit were those like More, trained in "ancient classics whether Greek or Sanscrit [*sic*]." She had known many of them, among whom her husband was only the most intimate. But they all had the ability to "cast out from his consciousness every living vital thing."

Whatever irresolution Harris had in her love/hate relationship with classical education, her deepest conviction appears in the following excerpt from a letter to More: "That is why if Lundy dies and I am asked to marry again, I shall ask the rash man if he knows any of the ancient languages. If he does, I will not marry him though he owned a whole big forest and a castle besides! I know some of the pangs of being exorcised, cast out, looked at as if my features [illegible] some kind of hieroglyphics! Never call a classical minded man's attitude to women mere 'indifference.' It is something far more offensive."[72] Indifferent men at least coexisted with women, but men like More (with inference perhaps to Lundy) "cast them out."

Although More's ideas influenced Harris before the end of the decade in which they met, when she first encountered those ideas as Jessica Doane she laughed at their presumption. Jessica had plenty to say about men "impelling the world into new courses," but first she addressed the effects made on individual male/female relationships. This dual nature was a flimsy ruse, the trick of a "magician." "Two things I never suspected: that love is the kind of romantic exegesis you represent it to be, or that every lover, psychically, is a sort of twin phenomenon—that he is *two* men instead of one! And after he is married," she wrote facetiously, "I suppose he will be a domestic *trinity,* but with his godhead concerned with the affairs of the world at large."[73]

Such was the source of man's virtue, his *tertium quid,* Philip explained. Moreover, virtue was not the same for man as for woman. A man's virtues "are aggressive and turned outward toward conquest. . . . But a woman's virtues are bound up with every impulse of her personal being; they work out in her a loveliness and unity of character which make the man appear beside her coarse and unmoral." Virtue was "not a man's character, but a faculty of his character." It was something "removed from himself, something which he analyses and governs and manipulates." In the woman, however, virtue was "an integral part of her character," and hence was simply expected of her. Harris would express the same sentiment many times over the years.[74]

The unspoken implications in Philip's interpretation of male and female nature were not lost on Jessica. Men could take credit for their virtue as something they developed. Women, on the other hand, could claim no part in the development of their virtue because they had not actually developed it—it was a gift of nature. It sounded like a trick to Jessica. The "way you have multiplied yourself and doubled forces upon me," she wrote, "may be good masculine tactics, but I am sure it is an unparliamentary advantage you have taken." Jessica was not quite sure who was to blame for it: "I do not know whether I cherish them [my convictions] against you or against the God who made me simple and you double."[75]

Whoever was to blame, the whole thing was unfair and, in Philip's case, hypocritical. "But granting all you say to be true," Jessica wrote, "that every man has a personal life and at the same time a universal life energy as well, that there is in him a little domestic fortress of love, and a battle power of life apart,—admitting all this, how do you reconcile justice with the fact that you frankly offer only half of your duality for all of Jessica?"[76] She found it difficult to believe that someone who spoke so often and authoritatively of justice could be so blind to this unjust reasoning against women.

Women gave their all in relationships; men gave only half, and with Philip it was not even the better half. It was the half left over, not that from his "higher self," which he gave to the world and to his work. Moreover, the half he brought to relationship was not offered to Jessica to keep but merely for her to nurture and inspire so that he might be empowered to do the work of the world. This was how women contributed to the public realm—through the men they served to empower. Jessica never got a satisfactory answer from Philip on the apparent injustice of this arrangement, so she gave up questioning, buried her misgivings, and married him in the end. Women, after all, could not "live without a lover."[77]

Before she gave in to marriage, however, Jessica predicted that Philip's obsession with the life of the mind would divide them irreconcilably. He so represented the mind/body split, she wrote, that "With you life is but a breath without form, a whisper out of your long eternity. And I confess that to me the impression of a man not being at home in his own body is nothing short of terrifying."[78] She could respect his intellect, but she was "too much alive to be offered up" for a man who was nothing more than a mind.[79] Jessica compared Philip as she saw him to "Nature." At first that might have seemed like a compliment, considering the appreciation they both claimed for nature. But Jessica meant it as no compliment. Humankind might be a part of "Nature," but it was also distinct.

> For in the forest, ever present, is the intimation of Nature's indifference to pain. There is no charity in the commonwealth of trees. They live, decay, and die, and there is no sign of compassion anywhere. It is terrible, but there is a Spartan beauty in the fact.
>
> But suddenly, as we sat there in the sweet green twilight, the thought pierced me like a pang that . . . you are more nearly related to the life of the forest than I am. I merely love it, but you are like it in the cold, ruthless, upward aspiration of your soul. I long for a word with the trees, but you are so near and kin that your silence is speech. And then I asked myself: "What is the good, where is the wisdom in loving a tree man, who may shelter you, but never can be like you in life or love?" Always his arms are stretched upward to the heavens in a prayer to be nearer to the light.[80]

That "light," in Jessica's mind, was cold, clinical, and impersonal. There might be a "Spartan beauty" in nature's impersonality, and even in the "cold, ruthless, upward aspiration of [the] soul" stretching heavenward toward the light, but because it lacked feeling, it was not human: it lacked the capacity to empathize or sympathize with anything outside itself.

Before Jessica made final proclamations of love, she had to penetrate Philip's natural reserve, a forbidding task. And it was his reserve toward

her, not toward humanity, that was her concern. Ostensibly, she was supposed to be chiding him for his harsh judgments against humanitarians and
humanitarianism, but in actuality it was not sympathy for the humanitarian
cause that provoked her responses. Her grievance was that the same dispassion and indifference Philip felt toward humanity at large ultimately governed his private relationships as well. While Philip maintained that what
Jessica interpreted as indifference was actually his *"sereine contemplation de
l'univers,"* which was essential to the "peace and better growth" necessary for
him to do his work, Jessica focused on the result: his complete self-absorption.

Jessica saw early that Philip was ultimately incapable of grasping anyone's
needs but his own. This was never more evident than when he wrote in his
diary months after their engagement ended (at her father's insistence) that
he suddenly wondered if she might be as aggrieved and distressed as he:
"My own misery has lain so heavily upon me that it has not occurred to me
to imagine what you too must have suffered. Indeed, the wonder of your
love has been to me so incomprehensibly sweet that the notion of any actual
suffering on your part has never really entered my thought. My own need
I understood," he confessed, but it was months before the thought of hers
ever occurred to him. "Can it be that our separation has caused the same
weary emptiness in your days that has made the word peace a mockery to
me? Can it even be that while I have sought refuge and a kind of forgetfulness in the domination of my work, you have been left prey to unrelieved
despondency?"[81]

Jessica knew that Philip's self-absorption was not malicious; it was a trait
common to those who lived the life of the mind. Her chief complaint was
that for Philip the preoccupation tended to be total. More importantly, the
part that he jealously withheld from her was the part of him she coveted
most:

Your faculty for projecting yourself in spirit further than I can follow,
excites in me a terror of loneliness that sharpens into resentment. I am
widowed by the loss of the higher half of your entity. Can you not see,
Philip, it is not your views I combat, your theory about humanitarianism and all that? They are but the geometrical figures of thought in
your mind; and I have no wish to disturb your "philosophic proposi-
tion." The point is, I love that in you more than I love the lover. And
the passion with which you cling to it as something apart from our

relationship offends me, excites forebodings. Tell me, are "philosophic propositions" alien to love? And after all do you think you are the only one who may claim them?[82]

Why could not Philip share his "higher half" with Jessica? She feared that he never would, and pondered her fate if he never learned to do so.

Her fate would likely be the same as that of Jack, the orphan child Philip rescued from the New York City ghetto. "So you are keeping Jack mured up with you and your *magnum opus*," she wrote. "No wonder he 'crouches in sphinxlike silence on the curbstone.' He prefers it to your company. You once told me that you found humanitarians difficult to live with: I wonder what Jack thinks of mystical philosophers in the domestic relation. It almost brings tears to my eyes. And some day in a similar situation I may be driven to seek the cold curbstone for companionship."[83] The story of Jessica and Philip ends with their betrothal. All things considered, had a sequel been written, readers likely would have found Jessica "seeking the cold curbstone for companionship." But the writer Corra Harris would have related to the situation differently.

By the end of the decade in which *The Jessica Letters* was published, Harris had developed a different voice. She had become something of a "mystical philosopher" in her own right. Both because of and in spite of More, she had glimpsed into those "portals" reserved for men's "higher entity," and she had crafted a new identity for herself based on what she found there. She learned to value and write in the masculine, to eschew the feminine, to cultivate indifference and dispassion. They helped her come to the abject conclusion that if tragedy was one's fate, then "the less agonizingly I cared, the less I suffered."[84]

Harris remained at war with herself over the incongruity between what she had valued and cherished before she met More and what she learned from him that displaced those early values. Of all that his philosophy taught her, his belief in the single, private nature of woman versus the dual, public/private nature of man had a far greater impact on her career than she anticipated at the time. Having that implicit belief so explicitly articulated by More and having his direct order never to trust a reformer and never to become a reformer if she wanted to keep her "virtue" affected her political views, including her stand on women in politics and particularly on woman suffrage, as the following chapter explores.

4

"A Woman Takes a Look at Politics"

More than a decade after women gained the vote, Corra Harris wrote: "It may be right but I cannot believe it is becoming for a woman to be interested in politics."[1] Therein lay much of the source of her ambivalence on woman suffrage: the belief that women could not be who and what they were supposed to be and political at the same time. Her sentiments echo those of Sara Haardt, who wrote satirically that it was an "utter impossibility" for women to think and "look pretty" at the same time. In 1925, Haardt, Montgomery belle and later wife of H. L. Mencken, published "The Southern Lady Says Grace," a satire about the tenacity of the myth of the southern lady. In spite of the advances in women's rights and the popular flapper image at the time, in 1925 the southern lady "is still, and rather proudly, a slave of the conventions." She "shrinks from the shrillness, the vulgarity, above all, the pettiness of 'taking her own stand.'" Most significantly, this lady prefers to "follow the old order," because it "saves her from thinking, and she has witnessed the utter impossibility of thinking intently and looking pretty at the same time."[2] Though a satire, Haardt's observations regarding the hold of convention on southern women rang true, even for those who saw through it. Exploiting the myth could be the most expedient way of living with it. Some middle-class black women employed the myth for the cause of racial justice.[3] White women might do the same for any number of causes.

After much posturing on the subject, Harris eventually supported woman suffrage. Her lukewarm attitude came in part from a general aversion to women's involvement in the public sphere. Unlike many southern women who challenged the constraints of southern ladyhood through various "respectable" reform efforts, such as Lost Cause memorializing, education reform, temperance, and eventually woman suffrage, Harris avoided and ridiculed all such efforts, if not the causes.[4] "Let somebody else do it!" was her simple reaction to whatever activism was needed.[5] "I could never lead a movement or get stirred up about public affairs," she wrote. "Let the public manage its own affairs."[6] "I have felt obliged for conscience' sake to believe in equal rights for women," she wrote in 1925, "but the best success

I ever had along this line has been to go out and win by my own words and wits the rights I preferred and that would be the most becoming to me in the end."[7] She claimed toward the end of her life to have remained "atavistic in my political proclivities," nostalgic for a time in the past before women "lost our grip on the situation and became public-spirited citizens at large."[8] "My idea is that the good little life, with no publicity screen in the background, leads with less confusion and certainly less embarrassment to peace and happiness."[9]

Harris avoided writing about politics for many reasons. Although she held strong political opinions, she claimed to regard herself as a "simpleton in the art and practice of politics."[10] Every time she wrote openly on the subject, it seemed to backfire. She provoked public rows with Jack London and Upton Sinclair, for instance, and they both cost her considerable embarrassment. It was difficult enough living the contradictions for which she was well known. But she wanted to avoid political controversy. Hence she frequently wrote about the need to "retire from politics." She could not write as freely about the pointedly political as she did about the heart and mind, romantic love, domestic relations, or even religion, which, given the unorthodox nature of her own beliefs, was surprisingly less consequential in provoking backlash than her political candor.

Harris's definition of politics limited it exclusively to government, which to her in any case ought to be extremely limited. Not until a couple of years into the depression, which was late in her life, did she invite the opportunity to write about politics, and then only locally.[11] Favorable response, she claimed, to "A Woman Takes a Look at Politics," published in 1931 in the *Saturday Evening Post*, motivated her to write more on the subject. The article reflected her strong conviction in limited government.

Harris vociferously opposed women's involvement in the public sphere for numerous reasons, but for her the image of the southern lady governed what was and was not "respectable." Marjorie Wheeler writes about the pains southern suffrage leaders took to "present themselves and their cause as nonthreatening and in accord with traditional Southern values. Proud to be Southern Ladies, these women took care to look and act the part."[12] Having helped start the Equal Suffrage League of Virginia, Ellen Glasgow was less equivocal than Harris on the subject of suffrage, but her views of activism were similar to Harris's. Glasgow explains in her autobiography why she was "lukewarm" on woman suffrage even though she supported the cause. Her words demonstrate how deeply ingrained anti-activist thinking was in the minds of southern women, even those not blindly obsessed with "looking pretty." She writes in *Woman Within*: "Like Voltaire, 'I am an ardent friend to truth, but in no sense a friend to martyrdom.' More-over . . . I have never believed that either woman's acknowledged intuition or woman's unacknowledged intelligence would change so much as an atom in man's practical politics. If women wanted a vote, I agreed they had a right to vote . . . and I was willing to do anything, except burn with a heroic blaze, for the watchword of liberty."[13]

Although Harris preferred private over public life, her national repu-tation brought her into the discourse on social problems from the begin-ning of her career at the turn of the century until her death in 1935. Of all life's mysteries with which she grappled, none troubled her more than the liabilities of gender identity. Yet she wanted to keep her legacy free from (what she considered) besmirchment by the political nature of gender is-sues. Long before "the personal is political" became a slogan defining the movement, Harris bemoaned that the personal had become political. "The greatest change I have seen during my lifetime," she wrote, "is that there is now no distinction between the problems men formerly worked out for themselves and public problems; but every issue that arises now in the lives of the American people, whether private, social or industrial, is immediately resolved into a political issue."[14] Where she lived, she was happy to report, "the issues we make are personal, not political."[15]

Aside from cultural discouragement, her own private nature by tem-perament, and the need for privacy to write, Harris may have developed an aversion to politics from experiences during the first decade of her career. Unhappy incidents with two particularly forthright socialists left a mark on her in the early years of her career. Charlotte Perkins Gilman had been Harris's nemesis since they debated the nature of home in the *Independent* in 1906, but Gilman caused Harris far less grief than either Jack London or Upton Sinclair. Her debate with Gilman actually enhanced her reputation and brought out a number of supporters. Gilman was, after all, challenging the conventional notion of the home as transhistorical. Harris argued under the banner of home, hearth, and family.[16]

Public sentiment in the Progressive Era was generally more tolerant of socialist ideas interpreted by men critiquing the class structure than those interpreted by women such as Gilman questioning the fundament of male-female relations and women's economic independence. When the subject was home, the debaters women, and the issue tradition versus anything be-sides tradition, the woman representing the traditional home, as was Harris, generally came out the winner. The same was not the case in her rows with

London and Sinclair. She paid a price for airing her differences with them. Her squabble with London eventually caused her to resign her membership in the Author's League of America, and her altercation with Sinclair temporarily put a brake on her publication with the *Independent*.[17]

Harris considered both London and Sinclair morally suspect. London's "cosmic consciousness" and "splendid sense of humanity" were not "altogether desirable morally in their effect upon others," she wrote in 1906 in "The Walking Delegate Novelist," an article largely committed to exposing the evils of "socialistic" writers. Moreover, that "consciousness" and "sense" were contagious. London's uncanny ability to capture and re-create the consciousness of the "enemic classes" and thereby to "preach the gospel of the poor" was so persuasive that he had the average man on the street, who formerly "was content to be a respectable member of society," wishing that he could "know how it feels to be a tramp also." In the review Harris condemned not only London and Sinclair but also Edith Wharton, Frank Norris, and William Dean Howells for inciting "lasting hatred between the masses and the classes." They all had "the literary neurosis of a sort of moral despair."[18]

Harris and London crossed swords through the mail after publication of "The Walking Delegate Novelist."[19] The exchange is comical. Harris sent London an "apology form" to sign and return to her for an "obscene" insult she felt he had directed toward her in an article on the "House Beautiful." London refused to sign the form, which he found humorous and "deliciously ridiculous." In a mildly mocking retort, he wrote:

> While we're on this subject of obscenity, in the very letter accompanying the apology form, you yourself confess to a consciousness of the obscenity of your reference to what I said in the last paragraph on the House Beautiful. You yourself say: "I have ached, but with shame and regret, every time I thought of it since." Why shame? . . . Imagine my surprise and consternation when in this letter of yours I now have before me I learn that you have misconstrued my meaning and given me to understand that it is not becoming on my part to intimate 'that sort of thing' to a woman of your age. Heavens on earth! I never thought of such a thing until I read it here in your letter.

London suggested that she not take things so seriously: "You say you have to keep on respectable terms with me. Why sweat about respectability? It is so bourgeois." In any case, "as regards disrespect," he pointed out to her, "in this very letter you've called me a fool twenty times." "And now, a final paragraph," London writes. "Do you know the whole cause of conflict between you and me? I'll tell you in two words. It is the inevitable conflict that arises between the simple mind and the complex mind. You are all complexity, I am all simplicity."[20] Harris and London did not actually meet until they both attended the Author's League banquet in 1914. Knowing that Harris would be at the banquet, London wrote the month before to ask if he could "call on" her sometime before the event but after he was finished with his business, to which he attended "like so much medicine. When the dosing has been accomplished I shall become human and social and come to take you by the hand and arrange truce or loose the dogs of war according to your heart's desire."[21]

Whether because of Harris's unwillingness or his failure to follow through, London did not "call on" Harris beforehand but met her for the first time at the banquet. It is difficult to say what event at the 1914 banquet was the leading cause of Harris's resignation, whether it was the altercation there with London or the fact that she was "extremely unhappy over having dined with a negro" that evening. London was "probably far from being as decent a man as DuBois," she wrote a friend, but character had nothing to do with propriety, which London and DuBois both transgressed—London by behaving like a "ruffian," DuBois by dining with whites.[22]

Harris was surprised to discover that London was not, after all, the "magnificent brute of a fellow with noticable [*sic*] fists" that she had always "supposed" he was but was rather a "fake ruffian." She found his behavior that evening scandalous, and the fact that she catered to rather than ignored him became a source of humiliation and regret for her, so much so that she decided afterward "never to go again among so many strangers, not even in Paradise." Shortly after they had all finished listening to "William Jennings Bryant [*sic*] . . . make one of the poorest Sunday School speeches" she ever heard, Harris wrote, London "caught sight of the name tag on my button." It was not an accident. She was embarrassed to admit to Ms. Nealle, editorial associate at the *Saturday Evening Post*, that she had actually "meant that he should." But she had no idea what would follow. He "stood up and announced Corra Harris so loud that Charlie Towns the poet heard him." Towns then responded, "'Corra Harris! Madam I love you! I always have.' I did not think that was so bad," Harris confessed, "though I was embarrased [*sic*]." But "everybody seemed to be loving somebody." "I just bowed to him and said I was much obliged."[23]

Unfortunately for Harris, London would not let it go at that. He went over and "sat down by me," and with his "loud talk" and audacious behavior he managed in the brief encounter to offend practically every sensibility Harris had. To try and calm him down she "compromised by writing my reply to something he said on a little pad he had. He retorted, begging the question, but telling me quite gratuitously that he was 'born in the stocks' and that he did not believe in God." It was the height of impropriety for a reputedly pious southern woman to converse openly with a professed atheist, but she had lost her window of opportunity by that time and could not figure out how "to get rid of him" graciously.

Besides, something in her kept her from either excusing herself or bidding him leave. She told Ms. Nealle she knew "that he is a man of genius. That he is doing better, not worse with himself. It seems to me honorable always to be for such a man, not against him." Clearly, she had mixed feelings. As much as she despised him, he touched some heartstring. "I know that such a man must be at bottom sensitive," she observed, but then curiously wrote, "he has good reason to despise himself, so I didn't want him to think I did not like him." As unruly as he was, for whatever reason, "I couldn't bear to snub him."[24]

Finally, London did go away, and parted with a gesture that left Harris the golden opportunity to put him in his place, which she was confident she had. "At last he did go, tearing the leaves out of his little pad and presenting them to me. I think he thought he was presenting me with a valuable souvenir. The next moment he knew he was not. I tore them up and laid them in my coffee cup saucer." Then she began to ponder what had made her feel so "miserable" and "embarrassed": was it more his obnoxious behavior or the fact that she had indulged him? Likely it was because she simply had not been able to expose him in all his "conceit," and she felt "miserable" for having tried. "I hope God counted it to me for a grace that I endured it and was as nice to him as I knew how to be," she wrote. "I told him he made a fuss like a lion and that he had the heart of a lamb. I did not really believe that, but I did not think I ought to tell him he made a fuss more like an ass. An ass never likes to be recognized by his voice if he is a man." But London was no man. He was a "fake ruffian," merely a pretender of a man, and no such effeminate infidel should have been able to get the best of her. But the fact that he had and that the Author's League officials had seated her at the table with "a negro" was more than she could take. She resigned within a matter of days.[25]

Harris's dispute with Upton Sinclair caused her even more public humiliation. Her disregard for Sinclair was no secret. The *Independent* had published many of her tirades, which had proved to be good for business. While some of the editors there wondered how far they should let her go, editor Hamilton Holt told her that he would not limit her "freedom of speech on account of a 'few old socialists'" and "to keep it up," which she did.[26]

In 1907 Harris reluctantly accepted an invitation to stay at Sinclair's Helicon Hall, a commune for the dispossessed—or, as she called it in a letter to Paul More, "some wild-cat club on Fifth Avenue." Holt, Harris complained to More, had suggested that a stay there might have "a good and broadening effect . . . upon my soul" and give her "southern prejudices" a needed "shock."[27] It had the opposite effect, however, and roused further contempt on her part for socialists and their cause. Harris's stay there ("for which I paid regular hotel rates!") convinced her only that socialists were guilty of "bribery" and "double motives."[28]

Sinclair's effort to "appease" her had the opposite effect. Harris wrote that the place "sheltered more ungrateful guests and ignoble spies than any other home in New Jersey." "The host could," Talmadge wrote, "but did not, point out that she had qualified for both categories."[29] In a review of Sinclair's *Advance of Civilization* at the end of 1908, Harris reported "gossip" that the author had deceitfully "played butler behind a rich man's chair in order to eavesdrop from him material for his last novel."[30] That was more than Sinclair could take. He wrote a scathing protest in the *Independent*. Harris wrote Paul More that Sinclair "said he would like for me to be sentenced to a year of poverty and misery in a garret."[31]

The incident with Sinclair caused a ruckus, wrote Faith from college: "What on *earth* have you been doing lately to Upton Sinclair, Mama, that he should be so bursting with rage? . . . He is mad with a vengeance."[32] The altercation temporarily halted Harris's publication with the *Independent*. The response of the editorial staff actually made Harris angrier than did Sinclair's rebuttal. Editors William Ward and Edwin Slosson refused to publish Harris's "temperate" response to Sinclair's "half a page of invective at my expense."[33] Their reason for not doing so was what stirred her most. "Slosson and Ward said it would be a reflection upon my hosts among the socialists I met in New York two years ago," she wrote More. She was particularly incensed that she had not been "allowed since then to express a single opinion of socialism without having my obligations as a guest cast up as a buffer."[34]

Harris never softened her antagonism toward socialism, which explains in part the dispassionate way she viewed the poor. Her writings on poverty and the poor are as contradictory as any. At times her attitude mirrored those of her region, namely, a belief that "poor whites" were governed by what Duke University professor Edgar Thompson called "improvidence, moral degeneracy, lack of ambition, and indifference to profitable labor."[35] Regional attitudes toward poverty and the poor, Lundy's misled generosity, and More's dispassionate "humanism" made it difficult for Harris not to think of poverty as a personal problem, as the fault of imprudent individuals.

About the problem of the poor, Harris believed the best any individual could do was to be a good example. She wrote the following observations in 1914 after several visits to New York City: "You can only supply the right condition for him to uplift himself by behaving your own self. . . . A lot of people would die of starvation here if this rule should be followed. But a lot of grass dies also. It is not so great a misfortune to die sometimes as it is to live. Besides whether one is sure of life or not, the next is assured."[36] The thing that most impressed her about philanthropic people such as those in New York City was "the utter futility of them and all their goodness."[37] They could all work themselves "to a frazzle in 'settlements,' in 'diet kitchens,' on 'welfare committees,' in labor unions, and even in church bazaars. But you cannot really accomplish any good. It is like trying to sweep the Atlantic ocean back with a broom."[38]

Harris's writings on poverty did not change substantially over time. Wayne Flynt observed that people's sympathies for the poor were typically greater during the depression: "When a quarter of the American labor force was out of work in 1932, few citizens tried to explain the national disaster in terms of indolence."[39] Harris did. Generally, until the 1930s her writings on the poor were variations on a theme of romanticizing the rural poor and demonizing the urban poor; after the depression, her views hardened and she more often portrayed all poor as lazy but clever people who were encouraged to exploit the rich by the charity trickling down through the New Deal.

Harris know from personal experience that there was something "reducing to the soul" about poverty. "No one was ever more reduced in poverty than I have been," she wrote.[40] And her letters to her daughter reveal an acute awareness of the relationship between the personal liberty she treasured and the economic means necessary to have and keep it. But because she thought of herself as a self-made woman, and because she had beaten tough odds to achieve financial success, she believed a level playing field existed economically for everyone. Her attitudes toward the poor and her aversion to charitable efforts to alleviate conditions were influenced by her husband's indiscriminate contributions to the "unworthy" poor and validated by More's misanthropic philosophy. Both made it easy to interpret her own life story as evidence that hard work and virtuous living led to success.

When Harris began to publish, her reflections on poverty linked it with southern identity, romanticizing it as a part of the nobility of the native southerner devastated by the war but still proud in character. During the 1910s her promotion of poverty as a way of life was an effort to privilege rural over urban living. She wrote often after or during trips to New York City paid for by the *Independent* and designed to facilitate her comparison of the two regions. They became a comparison of the worst of New York City with the best of her pastoral Valley.[41] Harris's conservative agrarian thinking again mirrored that of her home state, which was 68 percent rural in 1910.[42]

Harris's romanticization of the rural poor and demonization of the urban poor may have resulted from the prevailing town-country divide at the time. Although there was considerable distance in her thinking between the southern poor anywhere—be it Atlanta, capital of the New South, or her Valley neighbors—and those in New York City, the northern poor about whom she believed she knew the most from personal experience, the precedent of juxtaposing town and country was well established in the thinking of Georgians in both locales. Numan Bartley wrote that "By the early twentieth century the chasm between town and country was a fundamental fact of Georgia society."[43] His characterization of rural Georgia life as "simpler" and "in many ways more satisfying" (so long as the weather and crops cooperated) than life in the towns and cities underscores the basis of Harris's portrayal of an ideal, serene, and peaceful life in the Valley versus one of chaos, crime, and pollution found in the cities.

In her works observing conditions in New York City through the 1910s, Harris wrote that the moral degeneracy of the urban poor and the misguided efforts of socialists were the chief causes of urban poverty, and by inference of the nation's economic ills. And there was really only one solution, however unrealistic it might seem.[44] "Deport about three million nine hundred thousand of these people to the country."[45] In any case, Harris believed no city should exceed a population of one hundred thousand.

At bottom, a firm belief in meritocracy governed Harris's thinking. Her own success in life against the odds convinced her that success was within the reach of anyone willing to work hard enough. She also believed that if the South could recover from the total devastation brought by the Civil War and Reconstruction and become a "new, safer, saner civilization" because southerners "behaved ourselves," any people in any region of the country could do the same.[46]

Some of the ways Harris battled with herself in her thinking can be found within a "Candle" article she wrote on "Success." "The very ten commandments of success are only two . . . to fear not, and to be willing to go through every hardship in order to come up under your own power. This is success. The measure of it is negligible, depends upon your opportunities and a little, not much, on your natural ability."[47] In one sentence she claims that courage and hard work are the top two commandments, but immediately afterward she says that the measure of success depends upon one's opportunities, likely sensing no incongruity in the concepts.

Two "Candlelit" columns published just a few months apart in 1934 demonstrate something of the division in her mind on the subject of poverty. In December, just two months before she died, she wrote "To Restore Poverty's Good Name," in which she praises the virtues produced by poverty. She claims to want to "write a textbook on how to be poor and happy." "Poverty properly practiced is the finest of all arts in living. The life it produces is truthful and convincing." "As mammon is the root of all evil, so is poverty, vigorous, clean and able-bodied the inspiration of energy and courage, the very life of virtue, dignity and modesty."[48]

In August of that year she had written a scathing denouncement of charity, but the poor she referred to there in no way resemble the "vigorous, clean and able-bodied" she would write about four months later. "I see good people who have earned peace and the right to be comfortable but cannot be because there are so many weak and selfish people clinging to them, obstructing them, appealing to them one way or another, deliberate invalids of courage and honor. I have seen this everywhere during the whole of my life. The weak, the greedy and the irresponsible, resting and fattening on what the strong and industrious have earned, but cannot enjoy because they must support and protect shrewder dependents."[49] A character in one of Harris's autobiographical novels, *My Son* (1921), represents one of the "shrewder dependents" she wrote about in 1934. "Sister Sally Tears" is a widow who tricks the county, the church, and others in the community not only to support her but also to support her "disgracefully extravagant" charities to others. She is "a perverse old woman" who adopts "an orphan, and not a serviceable orphan at that, but a crippled boy who was about to be sent to the poorhouse."[50] This makes her an "autocrat" who forces onto the community not only her own upkeep but that of an apparently useless child.

Whether romanticizing or demonizing the poor during the depression, Harris saw a different face of the poor from that seen by Georgia writer Erskine Caldwell, who "could not become accustomed to the sight of children's stomachs bloated from hunger and seeing the ill and aged too weak to walk in the fields to search for something to eat."[51] Harris's thinking resonated more closely with that of journalist Ed Howe, whom she quoted: "It is the poor and the shiftless who keep the world in trouble, not the rich."[52]

By the time of the depression, Harris's ideas linking urban poverty with the immorality of the poor were solidly entrenched. Harris had long since divided the poor into two opposing categories: worthy and unworthy. The worthy poor deserved liberal moral support but cautious material support. Neighboring children suffering during the depression were among the worthy for whom she purchased oatmeal and raisins in the winter of 1933.[53] But she was hypercautious about charity of any kind, especially in government programs, and was "opposed to government and all its works so far as the same affect our fortunes."[54] She even had serious doubts about private charity.[55] She had misgivings even about Christian charity. On the subject of poverty she revealed her preference for the Old over the New Testament. Experience taught her that "giving a man your coat also because he took your cloak . . . leaves you naked, cold, and bruised in the face, and the other fellow strutting around bragging at your expense."[56] And in 1934 she accused people of mistaking sentimentality for Christianity.[57]

Harris heard from critics disturbed by her interpretations of the causes of poverty, her romanticization of rural poverty, and her dispassionate attitude toward the urban poor. After reading an article in *Ladies Home Journal* in 1925, J. E. Blair from Alabama wrote questioning not merely her politics but her Christianity.[58] "Charity begins at home," he stated, "but it should not stay there." "I wish you would NOT discourage" attempts by women to alleviate the conditions of poverty, he wrote, especially when they involve helping children. Blair "noticed a hard-boiled in a way, non-Christian vein, in all your writings." He further doubted if she had "ever cried over Christ's words if ye love only them that love you, etc."[59]

In a four page, single-spaced, typewritten reply to an article in the *Saturday Evening Post*, a C. G. Fry from California chided Harris for being "so intolerant, illogical, and childish." After four pages, he realized he had probably wasted his time, since "Any person who could write so illogically and vindictively as you have done is not likely to listen to patient argument."[60] A reader from Georgia asked her in 1934 to stop using her "genius" to "glorify poverty."[61] Another wrote to persuade her she was wrong about the "form and extent of the wave of 'moral leprosy' afflicting the poorer classes of Georgia." He asked her to consider the implications of her words when she could better use her "pen [as] a potential source from which the most good might come."[62]

One reader from Illinois suggested that "success has made you forget something," namely, what it was like when she herself was a poor circuit rider's wife.[63] In a letter to Warren Candler in 1899, after observing poor people on the streets of Atlanta, Harris wrote, "Oh, if people could realize how identical Christ is with the poor and misfortunate the cruel comfortless, suspicious stare would go out of the face of the croud [*sic*] and we would recognize each other as children."[64] Such ability to connect with others was lost over the next few years. She recovered an empathic sense later in life, but her conviction that poverty was chiefly a matter of personal responsibility changed little.

Harris's conservative ideas about the poor and about the causes of and solutions to poverty derive in part from her generally negative view of human nature, which was at least validated by More's philosophy. It was most often critical and unforgiving, as revealed pointedly in her debates with other writers in 1930 when she accepted what became the position of visiting "Professor of Evil" at Rollins College. Most often she expressed fear of and aversion to human nature. At other times she could be thoughtful and forgiving. In 1905 she expressed a positive outlook: "Goodness," she wrote, "is so inherent in human nature that it is found nowhere else," and in 1914 she referred to it as the "sane prose of life."[65] Some of her best insights on the subject came in thinking about how it affected literature. In an article in which she criticized southern writers for their blind allegiance to the past, she identified what was missing from southern literature: the "dynamic life-element in human nature which raises it up or casts it down according to some eternal law, and not by some arbitrary, romantic departure from it."[66] Here the origin of human behavior is more a sense of Providence than fate, suggesting more possibility for the positive than fear of the negative.

But for many years a fear of the negative rather than a hope in the positive governed her thinking. Harris wrote repeatedly that because human nature was essentially unalterable, efforts to change were practically futile. In 1914 she wrote: "You cannot change the real nature of men and women . . . it is the same old everlasting element today it was in the beginning."[67] "Vices" are "the only things that never change in men and women."[68] In 1924 she wrote that although humans might be "born innocent," they have a "very dangerous" nature.[69] Humans are the most "tragic figure in all creation."[70] They are tragic because, knowing good from evil, they are generally powerless to choose the former over the latter.

At Rollins College in 1930, Holt, then president, held a forum to discuss the nature of evil in human existence and appointed Harris to guestlecture on the subject. Poet and dramatist Percy MacKaye challenged her grim view of human nature: "I am astonished at your belief . . . that there is nothing good in us," MacKaye said. Harris answered that modern young people who had all the benefits of modern society were yet "without moral power." When MacKaye countered, "That takes patient development," she responded, "How long are you going to live? A thousand years?"[71] No amount of patience, Harris believed, could outlast the strength of human nature. "Every man is forever guilty of himself, what he is by nature."[72] The human, she had written earlier, was after all "a criminal either really or potentially."[73]

Harris's belief that humans are private by nature supported her aversion toward women's involvement in the public sphere. For Harris, a political identity or a political role in the classic sense went against the even more intensely private essence of woman and undermined her ability to be effective indirectly, behind the scenes, where Harris and many others believed women were more successful. In 1909 she wrote: "Women are all tribal in their instincts. Their diplomacy has to do with one man, not with a thousand, and this is one pathetic boundary of their political faculty. They cannot think beyond the tent shadow of something primitive in them. There is something catholic about political thinking of which they are still incapable."[74] Harris believed that all humans were private by nature but that women were much more so than men: "Nature intended them [women] for private life," she told a reporter who interviewed her about the social changes since World War I. It was regrettable that the "war made a lot of women with neighborhood minds world conscious." Taking them out of the home "brought only an increase of personal expenses and more competition against" the women themselves. It might be true that "the service of women in public affairs . . . commands immense respect," but they would be much better off to return to their homes, to their "career behind the scenes, where most power is exerted with less noise."[75] The "foundations of society rest in no small measure upon the success of this vocation wherein women are called," that is, the "supreme ability" of one woman's love and virtue to reform one man.[76]

Harris believed women's reform efforts damaged the economy and contributed to juvenile delinquency. "Mark my words," she warned, "the rich, restless, tender-hearted, public-spirited women are doing as much as the most adverse conditions in the labor market to increase pauperism in the country."[77] And she was convinced that there was a direct "connection between the development of women's interest in the welfare of the whole world and the astounding increase in the youthful criminal class."[78] But it was not the effect women's involvement in the public had on society that Harris was most passionate about. It was what it did to them personally. It ruined them for private life.

For Harris, what happened to women after they became "public-spirited" was worse than any good they could accomplish in the balance. Once women gained a "sense of their duty to the world," then "a pain[ed] and changed expression" came over them. "They no longer merely twinkle; they achieve and shine." An awakened social consciousness caused women to "wear the sharpened, hurried, worried look of workers and burden bearers at large, not the sweet dim, withered look women wear like decoration, performing their own duties and prayers."[79] This awakened consciousness was "bad for them [the women themselves], profaning to some essential decency and delicacy of womanhood."[80] The more militant a woman was, especially if the cause was her own rights, the more unattractive and unnatural Harris believed her to be.

Furthermore, it was not just agitation or activism that bothered Harris. Women's clubs and organizations "used up more wasted feminine energy than any other power company known to civilization."[81] In Harris's mind, most social problems resulted from women having traded the private for the public sphere. She believed that the "woman of yesterday" who worked behind the scenes influencing opinion rather than expressing her own or becoming directly involved was much more successful working alone to accomplish goals, whatever the cause, than any organized group of "new" women in the current generation. Such a woman "practiced her virtues delicately . . . in secret . . . and in the grace of silence."[82] Harris had an aversion to collective organization of any kind.

Historian Darlene Rebecca Roth found that Harris's antipathy toward public involvement and her preference for a privatized life were by no means unique to her. Roth finds a rejection of public interest in most southern women's literature of the period. In her study of women's organizations in Atlanta from 1890 to 1940, Roth found prevailing in the literature a strongly individualistic nature as well as a rejection by most southern women authors of the time of any form of women's "collectivity." Harris, Roth writes, merely represents the "clearest expression of this rejection." After quoting a long passage from *As a Woman Thinks* in which Harris derides women's organizations as parasites of individuals' achievements, Roth concludes that Harris's sentiments represent a "previously unrecognized" tradition, namely, the artist opposing not just society but an "explicitly female society—one created by women, for women, to which she does *not . . .* belong." The point is important, Roth writes, "as it appears that the female literary tradition (at least in some of its forms) has evolved in conflict with other female traditions within the American culture. That is to say, not only has it evolved separately (alienated, perhaps) from the female collective experience, it supposes itself to be in actual conflict with that collectivity."[83]

Much of Harris's published work, though not her lived experience, supports Roth's conclusion that some writers consciously opposed collective involvement. The conclusion does not account, however, for Harris's strong sentiments not merely against women's organizations but against women as women. One reason why Harris was opposed to women's organizations, and to being involved in them, was her general belief that women had a natural antipathy to each other. Women simply could not get along with women and quite naturally "despised and envied" each other.[84] Characteristically, she defied such a belief through some of her friendships with women over the course of her life, especially the last decade. She believed that there was a more natural kinship between men and women, and a natural antipathy among women that made the "sisterhood of women inconceivable." The reason was simple: women "have no mutual consciousness upon which to base such an ideal. . . . They will never co-operate with one another, because, in the very nature of things, their chief hope and happiness depend upon their co-operating with men." "It is not that they are vicious," she wrote, "but naturally treacherous to one another."[85]

To Harris, women had no choice but to cooperate with men, which made cooperation with other women impossible and made competition among women inevitable. Such sentiments contrast sharply with Ellen Glasgow's comment in 1913 on the "vast strides" women had made toward political rights chiefly because they had learned to cooperate with each other. "The point of value," Glasgow wrote, "is that we have realized our plight and have set ourselves to abolish it, and that we have stumbled on the important truth that co-operation is strength. That will lead us out of the wilderness."[86] During the years of suffrage activism, Harris could not grasp cooperation as a strength. She felt that cooperation among women was unnatural and hence exhausted energies that could be used more productively elsewhere.

Harris expressed a common belief about women that no doubt factored into her thinking about woman suffrage, namely, that women were much better at influencing indirectly, behind the scenes. She believed this throughout her life. Writing in 1900 about the southern woman, she stated that the "keynote" of this woman's "character" is that "she is not a force in the life about her, she is only an influence."[87] Writing more than two decades later, she stated the same thing about women everywhere.[88] It was a prevailing view, as Glasgow illustrates. "What I secretly felt," Glasgow wrote in her autobiography, "though I did not offer this as a reason for lukewarmness [over suffrage activism], was that, so long as the serpent continues to crawl on the ground, the primary influence of women will remain indirect."[89] In a memorial service for Harris in June 1936, the year after her death, Hamilton Holt praised her for recognizing the abiding "truth" "that everybody knows, namely the man functions directly, woman indirectly."[90] This tired argument about women being their best at indirect influence was what finally provoked southern suffragists into action. Marjorie Wheeler writes that the southern women who became leaders of the suffrage movement in the South "grew more and more cynical about the celebrated chivalry of Southern men, and denounced the Southern woman's enforced reliance on 'indirect influence' as degrading as well as inefficient."[91]

Harris's ambivalence toward woman suffrage captures well the cognitive dissonance so characteristic of her thinking. Harris waffled over the issue until at least 1915.[92] She had a difficult time taking a stand on the issue, though when forced to choose she supported it resignedly. "I believe in it," she wrote shortly before the amendment passed, "but with that practical resignation one acquires believing in the remission of sins, as a sort of sublimated condition that must come. . . . I am not a fighting suffragist, nor a termagant suffragist, nor a gall-embittered one, but I am a suffragist."[93] Later she described herself as a "sufferance [sic] by conviction, not by temperament or disposition. I am one regretfully, because I ought to be one."[94]

By 1914, the year she claimed in retrospect that she "began to emerge in consciousness," Harris had begun to call herself a suffragist, but she refused to "ally . . . with any suffrage body."[95] She published Co-Citizens in 1915, a novel written ostensibly, one journalist wrote, to "silence the report that she is an anti-suffragist."[96] However offensive she found suffrage activism and activists, she found their opponents even more so. About anti-suffragists Harris wrote in 1919: "I thanked my heavenly bodies for the instinct, whatever kind of instinct it was, that led me to avoid that group."[97] But neither cause would claim Harris's unreserved support. Even though she despised "cat-spitting antis," she considered herself a "sluggard . . . about correcting the abuses from which women suffer. I have never been able to cast myself or my pen whole-heartedly," she wrote in 1925, for any "campaign to clean up the men and bring them to repentance for their trespasses against us."[98]

Anytime Harris was forced to take a stand on the issue of suffrage, she followed her endorsement by distancing herself from suffrage activists, especially the "virago branch," or those she saw as "offensively militant."[99] "My interest is like that of Zaccheus up the tree," she told a reporter. By comparison with suffrage activists, Harris was careful to portray herself as "gentle, mild, peaceful, not excited over it."[100] Once suffrage had passed, she was proud that she had not been "one of those who pranced and champed the bits to bring this great responsibility upon our shoulders."[101] Nor to Harris was there a distinction in behavior between suffrage activists in the South and elsewhere. She was no more inclined to ally herself with the Equal Suffrage Party of Georgia than with a sister organization in one of the more radical states, such as New York, where she believed there were the most "vicious-minded ballot-banging suffragists" anywhere.[102]

Harris's reservations did not end once the amendment passed. She was convinced in 1925 that after a few years of "associating too intimately with men in the political [and] professional" arena, women would "suffer a revulsion of sensibility . . . take to their heels," and return to their "tasks at home." She admitted that her "opinion may spring like hypocrisy from cowardice, because I have not the courage to risk the losses these women sustain."[103] For Harris, however much women gained with political rights, they lost more in private life. Her ideas on the subject contrast with those of Glasgow, who also believed women had "lost something precious" over the years but considered the loss to be more than offset by what women had "gained . . . by the passing of the old order."[104]

The two women saw the responsibility of voting differently. In Harris's thinking, the ballot was being forced on women.[105] Glasgow believed southern women were "less appalled at the gravity of being allowed to vote, and of helping govern, than the women of any other portion of the country," primarily because of the responsibility they had assumed during the Civil War in men's absence.[106] In contrast, Harris wrote in 1928 that "To be a successful woman calls for meekness . . . and I had no conscientious scruples about practicing this kind of womanly wisdom until Suffrage was thrust upon me."[107] Gaining suffrage had made women "more alert mentally [but] less satisfied" otherwise, Harris believed.[108] She wished that "the mind of our times would settle down, and that we might be given, as we used to be, to revivals, picnics, and romance."[109] Harris personally found the "obliga-tion" of voting onerous. "I still despise to vote," she wrote in 1929, "but do it indignantly for conscience's sake."[110] She accepted her responsibility to vote "much as one recites a prayer without believing the Lord hears his petition," but she had serious doubts about what the outcome of full citizenship would be.[111]

Virtually all of Harris's statements on suffrage are ambiguous, half-hearted, and buttressed from all sides with rhetoric that echoed far more the socially conservative ideology of anti-suffragists than of suffragists.[112] She claimed, as did most anti-suffragists, that being involved in politics would desex women and make them unfit for their primary role in life, which was to be a wife.[113] Like most anti-suffragists, Harris believed politics was a messy business and saw voting as a burden more than a right. She was extremely conservative on the issue of divorce, claiming that a woman was entitled to leave and divorce her husband only when he physically abused their children, though the same did not apply to a husband's abuse of his wife. Harris "doubted if she [a woman] has the right to save her own life by getting a divorce."[114] A reader pleaded with her to let up on divorced women: "It is a very black world for divorced folks, Corra Harris. Please will you not build up instead of tearing down? We need your help and your mothering instead of invective."[115] Harris also shared with anti-suffragists a belief in the antipathy of women for each other.[116]

With all her outspoken reservations about the political capacities of women, it is impossible to say conclusively why Harris chose, when forced to take a stand on suffrage, to support it, or to call herself a suffragist, even if a "regretful" one. But the evolution of her position is worth tracing. At no point did she claim to support suffrage because of a belief in women's moral superiority, as did many suffragists in the National American Woman Suffrage Association. "It is ridiculous to claim that, granted the ballot, they would purify politics," she wrote candidly.[117] In 1903 Harris had been quite willing to review any books or write on practically any subject editors of the *Independent* asked, but she adamantly refused to write or review anything on "sufferance."[118] Apparently, by 1908 she was unable to avoid the subject any longer, but when she wrote about it then she clearly sounded more like an anti-suffragist than a suffragist.[119] "I have never worried over the serfdom of my sex," she wrote. "I prefer to remain the victim of man's love and injus-tice rather than compete with him politically, face his temptations and risk the chance of being elected to some indelicate office like that of sheriff."[120]

Harris's concern over her public image related to suffrage activism becomes clear the next year. In a 1909 article lamenting the inevitable "price of suffrage for American women," Harris predicts that southern women will be the first to gain the ballot, partly because they know how to ask for it. Southern women "probably understand better than any others the gentle art of winning their franchise rights," hence from them "there is no 'agitation,' and there never will be." For her the reason is evident: there is no agitation for the vote or any other cause among southern women, because there is "less opposition between the sexes" in the South.[121] There "men and women are still very much in love with one another." Therefore, women "will simply begin to vote when they all make up their minds to it. And the men will count the women's ballots in with their own, without any misgivings about their women becoming less attractive or faithful because they have taken a notion to vote for themselves. This may seem absurdly optimistic to those who do not know that it is first and second nature of every Southern man to humor his womenkind in every possible way. And I stick to my prediction that he will be the first man in this country to concede to her the rights of citizenship."[122] Indeed it is "absurdly optimistic" to think that southern men will be the first to vote for woman suffrage, since only three southern states voted with the rest to ratify the amendment. Her own beloved Georgia, moreover, was the first to reject the amendment; it did not ratify it until 1970.

Significantly, however, Harris was not alone in optimistic sentiments about southern men coming to see eye to eye with women on suffrage. In a 1913 *New York Times* interview, Glasgow expressed sentiments very similar to Harris's. She also "deplored" the "tendency" to "foster sex antagonism." It was simply not necessary. "I am convinced," she stated, "that when women have once made it plain to men that they all want the ballot and that suffrage is not merely the hysterical and agitated ambition of a handful of overwrought women the men will promptly let them vote."[123] That two women who understood the constraints of southern ladyhood believed that southern men merely needed to be asked politely by southern women for suffrage to grant it says a great deal about the hold of romance on the region.

Given the fact that Harris had published dubious statements about women in political life, it is difficult to take seriously her quandary regarding why suffrage activists were not seeking her out. In an interview in 1911 she felt a "keen disappointment" that she had never been "invited to a meeting to see the suffragists actively at work" during her trips to New York City.[124] At least by then, though, she was claiming an "interest" in woman suffrage. A year or so later she told a women's club in the Northeast that the "leading women's club in Nashville" had expressed open "antagonism" against her for her "lukewarm" position on suffrage published in the article "The Price of Suffrage for American Women." She admitted her article was "guarded because I have never been able to commit myself to the idea," though she conceded that by this time there was really no way to avoid the issue. The "new mind" and a "new order of things" had already come to the South. Interestingly, she reported that women were going to have to gain suffrage without "assistance from men," because men were afraid of the "new woman," who "appeals more to their anxiety than she does to their admiration."[125]

The novel *Co-Citizens* captures Harris's ambivalence. The pretext of *Co-Citizens* was to promote woman suffrage. It was apparently endorsed by Harris's fellow Georgian Rebecca Latimer Felton, famed first U.S. woman senator and ardent suffragist, upon whose life Harris based the protagonist in the novel.[126] The novel was also endorsed by a number of state suffrage associations.[127] And although Florence Kelly, writing for the *Bookman*, classified the book as "lighthearted" satire that "bubbles with humour from beginning to end," a reviewer for the *Nation* interpreted the novel differently.[128]

The *Nation* reader was not fooled. "Surely an enemy hath done this," the reviewer wrote. "We trust we shall not be doing the author an injustice in describing her book as a peculiarly subtle and underhand attack upon the feminist cause. . . . It is more effective," the reviewer continued, "because Mrs. Harris presents so successful a simulation of sympathy with that cause." After summarizing the plot, which involved women of the fictional town of Jordantown in a local suffrage organization, the reviewer writes: "So far this is very good, and the feminist may well tingle with gleeful expectation. But then comes the author's betrayal. Having set them [the women] well on the road to obtaining their rights, she delivers them—respect for Mrs. Harris's ability compels us to assume deliberately—into the hands of the mocker and the ungodly." Rather than showing sympathy with the cause, the book was to the *Nation* reviewer quite obviously a "shameless betrayal."[129] This was demonstrated perhaps subtly to a point, and then more boldly in the character of Selah Adams, the young heroine suffragist who manages to turn a town of passive women into ardent suffragists. In the end, however, she declares unabashedly to her fiancé, "I'll make a confession to you, now it's over and we have won; it's been horrid, from first to last. When we are married I want to sit at home and darn your socks—you do wear holes in them, don't you?"[130]

The ironic and paradoxical nature of *Co-Citizens* is seen further in an exchange of correspondence between Harris and editor Arthur Vance of the *Pictorial Review.* She proposed a follow-up serial to the novel, and Vance wrote back that although the story idea sounded good, "you want to remember that we are in favor of woman's rights and the new woman, so we don't want to go back on our propaganda."[131] Vance's letter suggests he was not altogether sure Harris felt the same. He later wrote to her that they expected "the club women throughout the country, and the woman's suffrage associations to take up 'The Co-Citizens' and make a lot of noise about it."[132] Unfortunately, the novel was not popular enough for anyone "to make a lot of noise."[133] But it well demonstrates Harris's mixed feelings about suffrage.

Rebecca Latimer Felton (1835–1930) and Mildred Lewis Rutherford (1851–1928), two Georgia contemporaries, provide a context for Harris's suffrage position and show how a life of contradiction characterized southern women who stepped outside their homes. Southern white women in general had made an art form of using femininity to gain what the majority of their male counterparts regarded as unfeminine goals.[134] Suffragists and anti-suffragists alike used the tactic. Felton and Rutherford demonstrate similar contradictions between rhetoric, stated goals, and experience. Rutherford, an avid anti-suffragist and one of Georgia's most prominent public figures, extolled the virtues of the southern lady, all of which were to be practiced in the private sphere. As state historian for the Georgia United Daughters of the Confederacy and historian-general of the Confederate Memorial Association, Rutherford traveled and spoke widely, often outside the South. In doing so she "constructed a strong public role for herself [yet] was still considered a southern lady."[135] In this respect, Rutherford and Harris represent any number of women whose rhetoric expressed one ideal yet whose experience reflected another.

Nor were suffragists such as Felton without contradictions between their rhetoric and their tactics. Besides being a widely known suffrage activist, Felton was a highly visible Women's Christian Temperance Union leader; an education, prison, and labor reformer; and (briefly) the first woman U.S. senator. Hers is also an "ambivalent and contradictory story" that reveals goals and ends inconsistent with the means used to attain them.[136] Felton, like many other southern white women who wanted their domestic roles valued and saw gaining political rights as a means to that end, used rhetoric laden with domestic images about the virtue of women and motherhood to argue for suffrage. Gender became the "key to their agenda." But the price Felton and other southern women paid for the "protection" they demanded from white men was akin to what women in wage labor paid for the protective legislation passed earlier in the century.[137] For women in the New South, using femininity as a means of breaking "into the public arena not only failed to undercut white male domination, it in fact served to reinforce it."[138]

Just as Felton's appointment to the Senate seat left vacant by Tom Watson's death was nothing more than a "half gesture," suffrage for southern white women turned out to be a half victory when protection became a means of penalizing and restricting their freedoms. Felton's rhetoric demanding white men's protection undermined the autonomy and independence she hoped white women would gain through gender reforms; similarly, Harris's rhetoric glorifying Victorian gender roles within marriage defy, and in complex ways undermine, the life of relative autonomy and economic independence she gained and kept by remaining a widow the last twenty-five years of her life. This, moreover, was only the most obvious of contradictions in Harris's life.

Harris is comparable with Felton and Rutherford in other ways as well.[139] Each came from a plantation background, and all three were from north Georgia. Harris and Felton lived a few miles apart in Bartow County (northwest of Atlanta) and became associates if not close friends after they met in 1915.[140] Rutherford lived in Athens (Clarke County, east of Atlanta). The three women shared national reputations: Harris as a widely published novelist and essayist; Felton for her activism in causes such as temperance, education, and prison reform; and Rutherford for her writing and national speaking engagements as spokeswoman for the United Daughters of the Confederacy. Felton, Rutherford, and Harris also shared a similar understanding of the definition of the southern lady. Each expanded the boundaries of how that image applied to her personally as well as to southern women in general. Finally, although they existed at different levels on a continuum of paternalistic race ideology, they shared a public commitment to white supremacy.[141]

Beyond a few generalizations, however, Harris differs in fundamental ways from these two native Georgians. Though they were not close friends, Harris knew Felton well as a familiar and celebrated personality in her home county.[142] Harris may have appreciated Felton's political success, but she did not regard Felton as someone to emulate. She may easily have said about Felton what she said about Carrie Chapman Catt, whom she considered an activist to be "respected" but not taken as a model. Harris's "first impression [of Catt] was that I could never love such a woman, even in case I should feel obliged to honor and respect her." And although Catt's two husbands apparently did, Harris believed no man could "give his whole heart to such a woman."[143]

By modeling a central fictional character on Felton and by speaking in Felton's behalf on occasion, Harris paid homage to one of Georgia's most highly visible and prominent citizens.[144] She did not do so, however, as someone who was like-minded. The two women shared similar southern racial views, and if both regarded the home as a sacred place, they differed markedly in their ideas about women's role in social activism. If Harris tolerated social activism at all it was as a necessary evil, but she did not admire those who chose to become activists, especially women. However much she appreciated Felton's success in the public world, Harris did not regard Felton as someone to emulate. Nor could the protagonist of *Co-Citizens*, Susan Walton, be interpreted, by Harris's standards, as a proper role model. Walton was a successful political agitator, but she was also an agitating wife who controlled and cajoled her husband in his political career in ways Harris clearly held in low regard.[145]

Harris acknowledged Felton's political savvy, writing that Felton "was a fearful antagonist . . . an advanced woman before the rest of them girded up their loins for the fray . . . [she] made herself at home in any political party, and [came] precious near ruling the politicians of this State more than once like a schoolma'am who knew what they had been doing and would tell it for the dropping of a hat." But in a debate over education policy in Georgia between Felton and Warren Candler, Harris set the record straight. "The impression at the time was that she [Felton] had got the better of Candler," but that was not how Harris interpreted the row. In that debate it was Candler's chivalry that Harris admired, not Felton's political assertiveness. "What really happened was that he fled like a gentleman before her until she worked off her energy for the university, dropped it feminine fashion, and took up something else."[146] Harris respected Felton's success but not her tactics.

Harris claimed to support suffrage actively, but much of her rhetoric on the subject of woman's proper role in the home and on politics as a sordid business that would unavoidably desex women sounds much more like that of Rutherford, an outspoken anti-suffragist. Like Rutherford, Harris may have agreed that the hearts of southern women would never willingly be "reconstructed," but unlike Rutherford, a loyal proponent of the Lost Cause, Harris made a mockery of building monuments to the Confederate dead.[147] Most significantly, whatever Harris shared with Felton and Rutherford through their identities as southern women and native Georgians, in

her visceral opposition to activism and social reform of any kind she differed from each of them at least as much as they differed from each other in
their clearly opposing political positions. If Felton in her lifetime of political
commitment was an "archetypal woman reformer," Harris in her aversion to
politics could have been her archetypal opposite.[148]

Harris had an image of a role model for women interested in reform:
Ida Tarbell, a woman with a national reputation developed by her exposé
of John Rockefeller in *The History of Standard Oil Company* (1904). Harris
praised Tarbell for exemplifying the proper political tactics for women. Her
respect and appreciation for Tarbell are especially telling when compared
with her tongue-in-cheek portrayal of Susan Walton, the suffragist modeled
after Felton in *Co-Citizens*. Harris clearly admired those women who could
be both feminine and politically effective, which is how she saw Tarbell.
Harris may have been drawn to Tarbell because they shared similar convictions about suffrage, even if their stated positions finally differed, with
Harris claiming to support the amendment and Tarbell opposing it. Both
were deeply ambivalent, however, about affiliation with either suffragists or
anti-suffragists. "For my part," Tarbell wrote, "while I am not willing to work
for the ballot, I am not willing to work against it."[149] Harris's actions if not
her words echoed the same sentiment.

Harris advised suffragists to study Tarbell. Instead of resorting to "abusive
methods in . . . suffrage pleading" that promoted antagonism, they might
resort to "printer's ink" (as if they had not already) as Tarbell had.[150] It is
unclear from her published remarks on Tarbell if Harris knew she was anti-
suffragist in sentiment if not in open affiliation.[151] What is clear is Harris's
admiration for a woman who managed to keep the appearance of femininity while being active in political affairs. It was to her nothing short of a
"miracle." Harris wanted to make it clear that the press had misrepresented
Tarbell in portraying her "with a severe, almost masculine countenance. As
a matter of fact," Harris wrote, "she is distinctly feminine in appearance." It
was difficult to believe that the "gentle and engaging expression" on Tarbell's
face actually managed to "conceal a mind which has so tenacious a grip
upon affairs usually left for men to discuss."[152] Whatever Tarbell's position
on suffrage, Harris admired her tactics in investigating without fanfare and
revealing through the printed medium what she uncovered about Standard
Oil. Tarbell's tactics were so clever that if only a "few thousand well-in-
formed women with a place to publish what they discover" would follow
her lead, "suffrage [would] be actually offered as a bribe of silence."[153]

Harris's perception that activism, especially for their own rights, desexed women and made them unlovable influenced her convictions about suffrage. To Harris, as long as romantic love and women's rights could not co-exist—and in her mind, they never really could—she would claim to choose the security of love over the novelty of rights. It was among the reasons why Harris would admit late in life that no matter what she learned about justice for women, in her heart she had never been "born again politically."[154] But whatever her stated ideals about women, political rights, or the public sphere, her decision to remain a widow for the last twenty-five years of her life speaks to what were likely deeper convictions. Of all women, she would write, only widows are truly free. Her ideas on widowhood, addressed in chapter 6, reconcile some of the contradictions between her apparent beliefs about the inherent limitations of women and her claim to and experience of her own personal freedom. But first we will examine Harris's thoughts on what she called the "ancient fate of women," some of the most troubling ideas with which she struggled in her effort to reconcile contradictions between belief and experience.

5

The Woman of Yesterday
versus the New Woman

About no subject was Corra Harris more conflicted than gender identity—understandably so, given the contradictions between what she valued, what she believed, and what she experienced as a successful woman writer in the New South. She made a living seemingly promoting values that her life defied, and the effort to reconcile those contradictions caused her considerable turmoil. But if she never outgrew her misgivings over woman's nature or her convictions over women's role in the public sphere, she did come to see that whatever biology was, gender was a social construct. In addition to the effects of Paul More's misogyny on Harris's thinking about gender, this chapter examines the other influences in Harris' struggle to reconcile belief, values, and experience.

Woman, Harris wrote, was "created in the first place as a necessity for man, and has never been able to change her position in the scheme of things."[1] As an afterthought, women were "not quite normal as men are. We still have a futile instinct to escape from what we are. Thousands and thousands of years have not made us contented and at home in ourselves." When all was said and done, the situation of woman seemed dismal: "If we obtain the balance of power we seek, live the lives men live and do the things they do, we shall still be women, subject as usual to fits of nerves and tears on account of the long strain of not being quite normal and at home in ourselves."[2] Harris claimed her birth as a female was an "accident" she was never able to "overcome."[3] Perhaps in part that was due to an acute awareness she and her sister both experienced; as children they had been a "grief and a mortification" to their parents, who "preferred sons."[4] Even though in Harris's day the woman suffrage movement was challenging the myth of female inferiority, that myth had not yet been displaced in mainstream thinking.[5] And it took a toll even on women who knew better.[6] In many very astute ways, Corra Harris knew better.

Writing just before she died, Harris reflected on something that had always bewildered her: what she perceived as the prevailing attitudes toward women's emotions. On the one hand, women were expected to have volatile emotions; on the other, they suffered for any unladylike demonstration of them. "A strong emotional actress is one who wins applause and fame by having hysterics on the stage," she observed in 1934. "But in real life, the same capacity in a woman to dramatize her anger . . . is regarded as the antics of a termagant, or a neurasthenic.—Intolerable, no applause. And in extreme cases, where she might win a star on her dressing room door behind the stage, the family sends for the doctor!"[7] Harris determined early on never to give way to typical female hysterics. She might get angry—she would be the first to admit having a short temper—but she would not resort to what she considered a feminine display of anger.

Before Harris was a seasoned writer and trained in literary criticism, she privileged traits that would be considered feminine, such as emotion, sentiment, passion, and compassion, or some of the same sort of emotionality she attributed to southerners that made them such romantics.[8] Similarly, in the early years, even though she did not consider herself the "representative Southern woman" (because she saw "too keenly"), she did not try to distance herself from her femininity as she would once she began publishing the sort of fiction that made her nationally popular.[9] Her self-characterizations in letters to More compared with those in her autobiographies two decades later are striking in their differences. In the former she is self-consciously feminine; in her autobiographies she describes herself as "femininely stupid."[10] Throughout most of her maturity she described herself in very masculine terms and prided herself on having achieved a masculine voice in her writing.[11]

Early in the century Harris referred to herself as "feminine . . . as the God made me."[12] In her autobiographies, however, she portrays herself as just the opposite. She believed, writing in retrospect, that she "may have been a kind of idiot, femininely speaking . . . almost totally devoid of that engaging self-consciousness which makes women noticeable and attractive to men. . . . I do not recall ever being coquettish or feeling attractive; merely honest, kind, devoted, and at times freakishly witty or gravely intelligent."[13] Furthermore, she expressed a poignant anxiety about having chosen after a point to live "with all my feminine vanities prayerfully suppressed," which for her meant keeping her emotions perpetually in check.[14] She wrote *Atlanta Journal* managing editor John Paschall in the mid-1930s, "I have had such a poor chance in my life to be feminine at all that it is a great privilege to me to do something a man wouldn't do. I say, 'Ah, ha! Corra, you see you really are a woman after all.'"[15]

Any attempt to understand Harris must look beyond More's influence and examine why she chose to suppress her natural emotional responses. Part of the answer is found in her characterizations of model women, who bear the typical traits of the southern lady that prevailed in her day. In her fiction, Harris experimented with characters who defied prescriptions of the model lady, but it is clear in both her fiction and her nonfiction that she was both haunted and repelled by that norm. "For a woman to be a perfect lady, she should have a sterilized mind," Harris wrote mockingly in 1932. "She must use the weakest and most innocent words."[16] "Women are like words," she wrote. "It depends upon how they are used whether they look bright and make a pleasing sound," which is what a "perfect lady" did. This lady, to be wise, had to "practice . . . silences." And with typical wit, since she openly admitted her own nicotine addiction, Harris insisted that "no perfect lady" would smoke cigarettes.[17] Obviously, no person with Harris's mind, ambition, talent, and love of both language and cigarettes could live such an existence, no matter the cost.[18]

Besides having a personal disposition that warred against the social pressure to be a lady, Harris knew that the same emotional capacity that made the "more womanly women . . . the dearer kind to men" also made them acutely vulnerable to pain and grief and, importantly, the volatility of human relationships. She displaced her "feminine vanities" with "indifference," a trait she learned well from More. Indifference meant to her the skillful art of self-control or the ability not to feel emotions in the midst of situations that would normally provoke strong and painful emotions.[19] Passages from two letters to Faith illustrate the point.

> Pinkie, darling, peace and happiness . . . both depend upon . . . your adjustment to the inevitable. Practice that and shrewdness, but not malice. Take care of the honor of your soul. . . . Be patient but do not be a patient fool. There is a tremendous difference. And avoid bitterness. It produces a[n] acid of the mind far more fatal to peace and enjoyment than anything else. . . . I am glad to see that you are learning "indifference." You will find that a hard plant to cultivate in your nature. But cultivate it. Study the philosophy of life—what it shall profit you to earn. I found the less agonizingly I cared, the less I suffered.[20]

Above all, she cautions her daughter to "avoid the pulsing spirit of martyrdom, which is the lifetime temptation of all decent married women."[21]

The "philosophy of life" that would "profit" most was that of indifference. The advice to Faith was, with "shrewdness," to "cultivate 'indifference'" as the surest means of "adjusting to the inevitable"—a persistent theme throughout Harris's life. Cultivating indifference as a means of dealing with the tension between volition and fate was the most effective and reliable survival technique Harris had learned in life. As she wrote, the "less . . . I cared, the less I suffered." Indifference implied strength of character, a kind of self-possession. In retrospect, it was the thing about Harris's father that had "augmented his importance" in the eyes of Harris and her sister when they were children.[22] Indifference toward men was an asset that the "public-minded" woman stole for herself; it was the trait that "excited the marauding masculine instinct of each lover in turn to win her."[23]

In addition to instructing her daughter how to gain some control over her life by gaining control over her emotions, Harris suggested practical ways to deal with what she could not control: "You must try to get this in your mind, my dear. Peace of mind and spirit are . . . *entirely* dependent upon *inside* conditions, your health, and your mental ability to order your life, harmonize it[,] adjust it to whatever is inevitable for the *moment*, remembering that there is *nothing* more transient than the inevitable. . . . Submission and cunning are the great elements of peace making in life. Submission to what is and a fixed invincible purpose to make the future nearer to your liking."[24] One "ordered" one's life by developing the "mental ability" to submit. However, when coupled with "cunning," submission could be as much an active as a passive decision. One could willfully "order" and "harmonize" one's adjustment through a sort of cunning that cheated fate of its power.

During Faith's life, Harris wrote confidently about the ability to remain indifferent, but later in her own life she wondered if the suppression had not been unnatural and hence psychologically unhealthy. "I desire to show my tears like an honest woman," she wrote in 1923. "Not that there is anything the matter; I simply wish to exercise the emotional birthright of my sex. But I have never had the chance to do so."[25] Actually, during her marriage to Lundy Harris she had learned to control external displays of emotion before she had found ways to suppress them internally. Considering the realities she faced dealing with his temperamental excesses, tears were a waste of energy. She "had got out of the habit of crying" in those years, she told More, and afterward she "could not even when I wished."[26] By the time she was forty, she wrote in a letter to editor and confidante George Horace Lorimer, "I can no more weep than a man can."[27]

This non-emotional reserve had given Harris some "private peace" and a "quiet heart," but she wondered if it was actually "peace" and "quiet" or merely numbness and emptiness.[28] She wrote tentatively in her first autobiography and more resolutely in her second that suppression of her feminine side was the reason why she felt so unfulfilled and unhappy in her later middle age. "I am merely intimating that it is dry stuff being a woman when some dull wisdom in you keeps you from acting altogether like one," she wrote in *As a Woman Thinks.*[29] "If it was all to do over again," she wrote in *My Book and Heart,* "I should be careful not to develop a strong character."[30]

She would concentrate less on having a "strong character" and more on giving in to the instincts that endeared women more to men. "Sometimes it has occurred to me," she wrote, "that I might have done well to stick closer to my pudding making talent" rather than developing a literary talent. "The feeling I have now is that I missed part of my conduct as a woman at a time when it might have contributed some to that happiness which I have also missed."[31] Then, at least, no one would have resented her. Harris felt that both men and women resented her because she had developed her mind at the expense of traditional domestic skills. "I have observed that a woman may boast of the cake she bakes and no one resents her pride. . . . But give yourself some airs about a book you have written and see what happens! . . . Why do men praise a woman for her cookies . . . and shun her if she writes a poem? Maybe the divine fire that produces verse does something to her personally, liquidates her dearer-to-man charms. . . . I am not complaining. What I mean is that there may be something everlasting and providential in these instincts."[32]

Harris never fully reconciled her conflicted thinking over what was or was not instinctive for women. During the last years of her life her irresolution gave way in her writings to more reflections on the spiritual side of life. Composing her autobiographies in the mid-1920s may have helped her come to terms with conflicted thinking on gender roles. Whatever their tone, however irresolute, she was able in them to wrestle with ideas and issues related to gender roles—not in the abstract as they applied to others, not in fiction as she imagined they might apply in an ideal, but as they related to her personally—and this forced her to articulate and ponder her own irresolution.

Harris found writing about herself in a sustained, systematic way to be especially cathartic. She told a reporter in 1929, on her sixtieth birthday, "I have ceased to strive and am really cashing in with a happy heart."[33] The last five years of her life were not so uncomplicated as that statement implied. She had, after all, to tackle that centuries-old problem of evil in her appointment to the visiting professorship at Rollins College before she could settle down and reflect on the public dilemmas brought to bear from the depression and the personal dilemmas brought about through the process of aging.

Moreover, she struggled naturally with anniversaries of losses, and birthdays of those she had lost, especially Faith. A letter a few months before her death reveals that Harris was thinking about her suppressed emotions even then. Just before Christmas 1934 she wrote John Paschall, "Every year . . . I begin to take sick in my heart of hearts as Christmas Eve (Faith's birthday) approaches. . . . There are three favors I shall ask God on sight, and one of them will be to turn the heart of me inside out so that I shall seem more like what I really am. And I shall ask to go around behind a corner somewhere and cry like a woman until I have shed forty years of tears without getting a heart block or a sick headache."[34]

In addition to More's misogyny and gender-role expectations on southern women, academic and medical authorities promoted the sort of sex essentialism that troubled Harris. *Sex in Civilization*, a reader published in 1929, is an example. Dr. Joseph Jastrow, professor of psychology at Johns Hopkins and contributor to the volume, wrote: "There are no human beings, only men and women."[35] Sex, to Jastrow, was not limited to the body; the mind was clearly sexed. "A masculine body implies a masculine mind, and a feminine body carries even more significant implications." The reason was simple but profound: motherhood. "The potential mother in every woman penetrates deep into her nature, radiates intimately to the finer modes of expression, more than any other feminine trait." Woman was the "conservative element, the race guardian."[36] Such was a most potent argument for confining women to the domestic sphere.

Charlotte Gilman, a contemporary of Harris's and Jastrow's, wrote volumes on the social consequences of privileging the masculine, which invariably made the feminine the "other."[37] In the human race, Gilman wrote, man is "held the human type; woman a sort of accompaniment and subordinate assistant, merely essential to the making of people."[38] She understood well why women would want to write in a masculine voice: "Acting on this assumption [that man is the norm], all human standards have been based on male characteristics, and when we wish to praise the work of a woman, we say she has 'a masculine mind.'"[39] Society would have been better served, Gilman wrote, if it had "avoided that general prejudice born of the exclusive rule of man, which called all the conduct natural to him 'human nature' and all that was natural to her 'feminine.' His conduct he assumed to be typical of the race, and hers he deprecated as weak and unworthy."[40]

Considering the prevailing standards, it is understandable that Harris attributed her literary success at least in part to her ability to transcend a feminine voice in writing. The *Independent's* literary editor, Edwin Slosson, confirmed her ability to do so. "Did I tell you that the editor of *Current Literature* wrote in to inquire whether it [a review of *Marriage á la Mode*] was written by a man or a woman?" Slosson wrote. In keeping with Harris's wry wit, Slosson responded to the inquiry simply that "it was," leaving the inquirer to continue wondering.[41] Harris no doubt valued highly a commendation from novelist Will Harben. "The last sentence of your review is fine enough to be graven on the walk of the very Temple of Heaven," Harben wrote. It was so inspiring that "I am making arrangements to have it put on my tombstone as a justification for my having lived and as a lasting bit of philosophy too masculine for Mark Twain or Abraham Lincoln."[42]

Harris's favorite nephew, Al Harris, wrote her often with comments on her work. They no doubt had discussed the subject of voice in literature, and the effect of the gendered voice. Once when Al felt particularly moved by a piece of Harris's writing, he attributed the piece's success to Harris's ability to achieve "sexlessness" in her writing. More would have been proud of Al's conclusions. In response to one of Corra's articles published in *Pictorial Review* in 1922, Al wrote: "The great trouble with women writers"—his aunt excluded, of course—"is they are moved to words by the impulses of their sex rather than by cold, solemn facts. . . . That woman Clark who writes editorials for the *Pictorial* impresses me in this way. Her thoughts are splendid, but they need B.V.D.'s. There is a modesty to expression, an occasional note that bespeaks a friendly word for the great shortcomings of mankind, and this is the salt of literature. We refuse to view naked truths, there is something repulsive about them."[43] But Al believed his aunt had an uncanny ability to reveal "naked truths" as they were. "What I started out to say," he went on, "is that more and more I am discovering the power of sexlessness in your copy. Sex is more than a physical thing, it is spiritual and mental, and the only thing that overshadows sex, is the common heart. You appeal to this heart."[44] Through his use of the phrase "common heart" to illustrate the universal, and "they need B.V.D.'s" to discredit (if politely) the woman writer's voice, Al Harris demonstrates how conflated were masculinity and notions of the universal. More might have used a different discourse, but the conclusions would have been the same, namely, that only a masculine voice can speak the language of the universal heart or mind.

Expressing a view that medical science would have confirmed in her day, Harris wrote that the "purely feminine soul . . . is so intimately connected with her nervous system that only her Heavenly Father can locate it from day to day."[45] She believed this was a mystery best left unexplored and unexplained. A woman's soul, or nature, or perhaps it was something without a name, but "whatever" the "thing" was, it was the "secret psychic stuff which determines our place in the order of things [and] accounts for the fact that we have so few monuments raised to us."[46] It accounted for the fact that "All women are a foreign language. . . . Most [of them] pathetic, pidlin' souls."[47]

On occasion, Harris could reveal uncanny and remarkable insight when questioned specifically about the domestic nature of woman. Women were *not* naturally domestic, she claimed. Not when one admitted candidly how isolating and confining home could be, as Harris did on this and a few other rare occasions. Women "do not belong in their homes any more than birds belong in the cages where they have been imprisoned," she wrote. "They are there for the same reason—caught and put in and trained to service some thousands of years ago by men who chose them singly for this purpose. . . . Women have been trained merely to do what is to be done whichever way they are told to do it. . . . We are merely the trained automatons of an order of things we did not invent."[48] Ask "any modern American woman you will find" and she will tell you that "she does not really like housekeeping. She is restless, dissatisfied, and feels that she was cut out for something else."[49] Practically anything else, Harris might have added, believing that housework was unarguably some of the most burdensome, thankless, least-gratifying work a person could do, and certainly not the way for a creative person to spend her time.

If nature had not designed women for the domestic sphere, how did Harris explain their presence there? Harris explained that it was by design, but not God's, at least not nature's God. It was man's making. Cleverly and "shrewdly," men had crafted a feminine ideal that included temperament, disposition, and virtues. This ideal, this woman-in-the-abstract, was not really a person at all but only a "character," a creation of man's own mind. The beginning of Harris's unpublished essay "The Migration of Women" is noteworthy for its insight into the socially constructed origins of gender roles.

Until the present time, women have figured chiefly in religion, poetry and romance. They have been that part of the imagination of men which creates creeds, poetry, windmills and fiction. They have no reputation for any other form of existence. They are purely imaginary beings living in physical bodies. The quality of their intelligence, their emotions, even the fashion of their clothes have been made to confirm this figment of themselves. Their character is a legend invented by men. It is not a real character and could never fit real human beings. Yet they have accepted it and believed in it even more than the men do who mystified them with it. From Juno and Helen to Sarah and Mary, they have been merely the feminine, instead of the divine part of the creeds of men. They are not the authors of a single standard governing their own lives. They have never been priests. They have only obeyed priests. If it had been left to them to discover Almighty God, we should all have remained in ignorance of Him. They lack the tablelands of the Moses soul. This was why in the olden days the angels appeared first to men. No mere woman could have withstood their shining faces, nor believed them divine messengers. Women are the inventors of fairies, not angels. They were so made that they could only take the word of men for these things. But accepting that, they have been the portion of the race set aside more particularly by their helplessness to pray and believe in prayer and to practice the piety which was chosen for them.[50]

Significantly, women had not been the architects of their own design, "the authors of a single standard governing their own lives." God and man had conspired together to bring about woman. But while God might have been responsible for the fact that women had "been the portion of the race set aside more particularly by their helplessness to pray and believe in prayer and to practice the piety which was chosen for them," it was man who "even set the Lord himself up to be feared and served more particularly by women with their heads modestly covered, while they continue to hobnob opportunity with the easier devil. It has all been very shrewdly managed."[51] Women might have been "set aside" and "chosen" for their submissive roles by God, but it was not nature's God: it was the God of man's own making.

She continues, explaining astutely that so had the feminine character of woman been contrived by man. She was a figment of man's "imagination." This woman was a "purely imaginary being living in a physical body." Her character was a "legend invented by men." Furthermore, it was a character suited only for the imaginary world and in no way "fit real human beings." The motivation was obvious. "Whenever he considers woman, he is himself the standard, and he considers her only in relation to himself, what he needs, what he will have of her, more particularly what she cannot give and what he does not want of her, and nothing else."[52] Men had "defined all the virtues for their own convenience."[53] Women did not "own their own virtues, [because] they ha[d] never chosen them."[54] To own a virtue, one had consciously to choose it, or choose to claim it. The feminine "virtues" ascribed to women as women—modesty, chastity, deferential emotions—were "invented by men." This woman was "modest and chaste"; she "was sensitive, easily moved to tears or to laughter and was not expected to be healthy"; she "was bound to her pedestal by strangely enslaving virtues"—but these were fabricated virtues.[55] This creature was a phenomenon, "probably the most convenient ideal men ever actually produced in this world, one that never failed them in fidelity."[56] All this contrivance was clear. Men had determined what women were and what they were not, and by claiming it was woman's nature had justifiably left them at home where they conveniently belonged—a home that was a dirty place where some of life's most irksome tasks had to be done daily and when necessary, around the clock.

Harris demonstrates the importance of historical knowledge and the cost to individuals of views of history from which women were left out. Anne Scott identifies as "fiction [the belief] that women could not be significant historical actors" and "that society is made entirely by men."[57] When women do not know their own history, they have no model in mind of how women had not only been present at the making of history but were integrally involved in that making.[58] Harris reveals how vulnerable women, or any group omitted from the record, are when the only history they know is one from which they are written out, when they believe from what appears to be evidence that only men made history.[59]

Given this historical ignorance, Harris reasons that if domestic work was really as bad as women claimed, they should have done something to relieve the onus. If women were not "capable of exercising the genius of civilization," then they deserved the consequences. The evidence that they were lacking in such a way was overwhelming; the facts as she knew them were hard to refute. Women had been around, after all, as long as men had, yet clearly "every [technological] device known in the modern establishment for comfort or convenience was invented by a man."[60] One could find "few traces of the feminine imagination in . . . great accomplishments. . . . [Women] are . . . at best the patient conservators of what men make, win, and produce."[61] Apparently, women had simply drawn the short straw in the struggle for existence; they were responders, not initiators. Woman was "originally designed by her Maker to be the complimentary mirror in which Adam might gaze to spoof himself to greater endeavors."[62] Harris was convinced that not just man but "all history and the whole of Nature conspire to keep us in our former place."[63] Those were pretty dreadful odds.

Not surprisingly, "man," if not individual men, more often fared better in Harris's characterization than "woman." "At a safe distance, I have spent much time observing men and the world they are making," she wrote. However flawed it was, "I still prefer it to any world women can make."[64] Women were able to "endure" hardships of life, but only men were able to "overcome" them. "If we ever do become real people," she wrote of women, "we will never produce a psalmist or an Isaiah."[65] Harris's failed effort to produce evidence to the contrary underscores the power of history to make or break seekers of liberty. "It is not the nature of woman to achieve more than the minor notes in living."[66] Such was the record in the histories she read. This was why she "instinctively look[ed] up to men" and why she believed in women's permanently inferior status. "No man ever wished himself a woman, but ask any one of us and if she is in a truthful mood she will admit that she wishes she were a man. I have no doubt Eve regretted she was not Adam."[67]

Harris wrote a great deal of prescriptive literature for wives. Nearly all of it contradicts what she wrote in her latter years about the subject in private letters to a few select friends. For example, she wrote John Paschall about how a mutual female friend was catching on to a truth Harris had learned much earlier: "Privately my thought was that women who strive to make men happy always lose the power to do so. They only succeed in spoiling them [and] . . . making them dependent upon the ministrations of women, very irritating."[68]

In her prescriptive pieces, fiction and nonfiction, however, Harris wrote differently, portraying modern wives as culpable for domestic problems, especially those that resulted from adultery. Although it was "man's nature to wander from one woman to another [and] woman's nature to be faithful to her mate," she wrote, when husbands did "wander" it was nonetheless the wife's "fault."[69] Philandering husbands were the victims of "errant femininity."[70] Either a man was unfaithful because his wife provoked him to stray by her unfeminine behavior, or she invited him to stray by investing herself outside the home in clubs, social reform, or both. Harris spent her sharpest invective on women social reformers, but unkempt homebodies could be equally culpable. If a husband sat across the table at breakfast, "read the paper and had nothing to say to" his wife, she had either offended him with her "venomous tongue" or had "sinned against her marriage" with a slovenly appearance. The woman has asked for betrayal when she "does her hair up in kid curlers, creams her face and appears shamelessly disfigured before the man who chose her because he thought her pretty." A wife has also provoked her husband when she "always has a headache or a pain in her side or a sad tale to relate about her household difficulties."[71]

Harris also blamed relaxation of the double standard in sexual conduct for husbands' roving ways. That too was woman's fault for coveting man's "moral license." Cultural feminists of Harris's day also opposed the double standard in morals, but their solution was to raise the bar for men, not lower it for women. Although she admitted the unfairness of the double standard, Harris believed it a waste of time to impose a higher standard on men, and she was most critical of women who appropriated for themselves the same sexual license as men. If it was man's nature to be promiscuous, holding him to a higher standard would be an exercise in futility, but lowering the standard to give women a similar liberty, she argued, would make men worse. Still, in her judgment, it would be the fault of women. Men would be worse because they would have a greater variety of women from which to choose illicit partners. When "advanced women" adopted the morals of formerly "bad women," marriage did not stand a chance. "Every indictment that women bring against men as husbands is really an accusation of their own sex," Harris explained. "What I mean is that . . . we have an ever-widening group who claim . . . the right to conduct themselves with the same license in morals [as men]. And there are enough of these 'advanced' women prancing in every walk of life to be largely responsible for the ludicrous deflections of middle-aged husbands, so indignantly accused in divorce courts and dramatized in decadent fiction. They are the victims of errant femininity."[72] Middle-aged husbands were "the victims of errant femininity" the way preachers were victims of the "morbid feminine saint [who] is the most unscrupulous moral phenomenon in the spiritual world."[73] Harris was much more sympathetic with modern man than modern woman. The modern man was "at bottom a generous creature, only a trifle set in his ways."[74]

According to Harris, a woman of marriageable age who was single by choice was deluded at best but was in any case a social aberration. Any woman who claimed to want to remain single was either "unsexed," "proudly concealing her lack of lovers . . . or her nature has been singularly perverted from the eternally feminine desire for love—for all normal women wish to be loved even more than they are ever capable of loving in return."[75] Marriage was a woman's only natural state, and if a woman was daring enough to contemplate happiness, her relationship to a man through marriage was the only avenue there. "No thinking can get you beyond the everlasting truth," she wrote, "that man is the misfortune to which every woman must submit in order to obtain a modicum of happiness and to be normally unhappy. . . . Every other happiness and unhappiness for her is unnatural, harassing, never satisfying."[76] A woman who found herself unhappy in marriage had the consolation that it was at least "normal" unhappiness and that those around her regarded her as normal. But there was something pathological, even "perverted," about the single woman, whether she was happy or unhappy.

In 1922 Harris replied to a reader who had asked for personal details about her life, "I still like to live; I love above everything the earth, the grass, and the trees. I am afraid of the world, but I like men and women, especially women."[77] The sentiment about liking women was rare and offset by contrary observations. Most of Harris's writings about women were negative, even misogynistic, until the last decade of her life, when her invective tone softened even if her fundamental beliefs did not. At base in her thinking were several fundamental premises about the nature of woman, most of which were antipathetic. From works that span her publishing years one gathers Harris's ideas about woman's nature: the "normal" woman is the victim of her usually hysterical emotions; she prefers the love of one man to freedom; she is incomplete without a man; she is normal only in marriage; women who never marry are pathological; women who choose not to have children are selfish; the normal woman is naturally faithful to one man; women have an insatiable need to "fix" things; a woman is responsible for her husband's morals; women are naturally sacrificial; and the normal woman is naturally jealous of other women.[78] All in all, woman "by nature and condition was singularly subject to unhappiness."[79]

Harris believed there was a natural antipathy of women for each other; as a result, to her the "sisterhood of women was inconceivable."[80] Women naturally "envied and despised" each other.[81] She was by no means alone in her thinking. The editors of *Everybody's Magazine* wrote that there existed in the female sex "an instinctive suspicion and dislike" for each other. "In the hope of learning the reason for this attitude," the editors of the magazine asked journalist Dorothy Dix in 1904 to write an article on "woman's inhumanity to woman." "Just why women, who are gentle and considerate, tender and forgiving, in their dealings with men, should exhibit to their own sex a callousness that is almost brutal, even when they are not actively cruel, is one of the anomalies of life that no one can explain," Dix wrote. "Her heart is a storehouse full of tenderness and forgiveness and the milk of human kindness, but man has a monopoly on the latch-key that unlocks it. Whether or not this is because women have to use so much altruism in getting along with men that they exhaust their supply and have none left for the service of other women, can never be definitely ascertained; but certain it is that when it comes to dealing with her own sex the average woman is a female Ishmael, whose hand is against every other woman."[82] Actually, the attitude was not really a mystery to Dix, who observed at the end of the article that the mutual hostility among women was not innate but the result of woman's continued, forced dependence on man. "This theory is borne out by the fact that wherever women are most independent and freest, there does the spirit of sisterhood prevail."[83]

Dix lamented the absence of a sisterhood; Harris did not. Although Harris did not share Dix's sense of loss, she agreed with Dix that women spent their energies getting along with men. Women were antagonistic, according to Harris, because "They have no mutual consciousness upon which to base such an ideal. . . . They will never co-operate with one another, because, in the very nature of things, their chief hope and happiness depend upon their co-operating with men."[84] Men, conversely, never "felt the antagonism of sex, because they had more than sex as the basis of consciousness."[85] Women were defined by their sex, men by their humanity; as a result, men were left with more grounds for cooperation and less for paranoia and jealousy.

To Harris, jealousy was woman's most crippling weakness.[86] All women, to Harris, were innately jealous, and the unmarried woman especially so. The single woman was "restless, dangerous and incapable of a loyal, generous friendship for another woman, because she will not endure competition when it comes to the art of feminine blandishments."[87] Nor did education tame a woman's innate jealousy. When it came to sharing, whether it was attention or accolades, "the intellectual woman . . . apparently contradicts the theory as to the lack of relationship among women, but she is, in fact, the most conspicuous example we have of mental affinity to men on the one hand and of tempermental antipathy to women on the other."[88]

Well-educated and successful women intimidated Harris, though. Although her "awe of them [was] always assumed," she wrote More in 1901, she was mostly repulsed by an educated woman.[89] She believed education depleted women of their otherwise natural charm. A well-educated woman,

especially "the Ph.D.," was "the most formidable, the hardest, most unnatural form that intelligence can take in this world."[90] Educated women were
"the waste material of the race."[91] "One of the prayers of our times should
be," she wrote in 1911, "Good Lord deliver us from the feeble and sterile
chastity of highly educated females."[92]

Harris felt much anxiety when she had to speak to an audience of women.
She had fears about public speaking in general, believing that her ability to
speak had been undermined by channeling her creative energies into writing, something she discovered early. "Since I have learned to write," she
wrote More in 1903, "I do not talk as much nor as well as I did."[93] "Invitations
to speak upon public occasions are among my most grievous embarrass-
ments," she confided in *As a Woman Thinks*.[94] Harris discovered, however,
that most of her fears of public speaking came from her fear of speaking
to women. After a successful speech in Atlanta at a banking convention
where over two hundred men were present but only two or three women,
she wrote Faith, "there is no doubt about it, men are so much more generous
and cordial to a woman than women are. This was my first men's audience
and I felt the difference. There is a certain element of competitiveness or
antagonism in women to another woman. If I could speak always to men, I
could *speak!*"[95] With similar sentiments she wrote an editor in Philadelphia
that she would like very much "to make an address to a great body of men,
just men you understand, because if there should be a single woman present she would tie my tongue. I am mortally afraid of women, and there lives
not a man in creation whom I fear." She wrote that she had "just declined to
address the Convention of Business and Professional Women which meets
this month in Chattanooga, because I would not dare to appear before an
audience of highly efficient, mechanical feminine intelligences."[96]

At least some of her refusals to speak to women came out of resentment
toward the women who invited her to speak. In 1917 she asked Faith to
"apologize" to the women of the Atlanta Federation of Women's Clubs, who
had asked her to speak a number of times. "Since the women of Atlanta do
not endorse my work, nor buy my books it would be the highth [*sic*] of presumption to appear before them with a lecture," she wrote. "The excuse that
they read my stuff in the *Post* does not hold. The *Post* is widely read outside
Georgia, and the book sells widely everywhere else except in Georgia."[97]

It is sometimes difficult to tell if Harris believed half of what she wrote
about women, or if she was writing mostly what she knew would sell. But
when she was called to account for some of her provocative statements, her
reflections could be telling. In a letter to More in 1901, before she was widely

known, Harris responded to an apparent caution from him against being so boorish in her statements in print about southern women's need to be ruled with an iron fist:

You advise me to be careful about cultivating the Southern point of view about women,—and for instance some body is annoyed because I said that it requires a proportion of Oriental brutality to govern women. I am very sorry I said that then. The truth is so often incredible even to those who practice it. But *is* that a particular Southern observation? I should have supposed that even the polar bears in the far North knew that about women by this time. You have to frown and show your teeth when you advise a woman, or she will not think you are divinely appointed to look after her wellfare [*sic*], and she will do the job herself.[98]

At face value the sentiment seems reprehensible, but whether it was conscious wit or unconscious insight, she was here holding up a mirror to More (as she did many times): "The truth is often incredible even to those who practice it." If Harris believed that women required "Oriental brutality," a constant show of force, to govern them, she also believed that women could be measured by the "amount of power and energy . . . men use in order to crush them and hold them back."[99] It took "Oriental brutality" to govern women, the passage suggests, because women were capable of governing themselves. Whatever else was going on in Harris's mind at the time, she suggested insightfully that More found this frank awareness embarrassing because it hit so close to home.

More's caution reveals at least as much about the culture's inability to deal with Harris's particular brand of candor as it reveals about a lack of propriety. But propriety frequently tripped Harris up, as she confessed to More in a 1904 letter: "I never do know exactly what is conventionally scandalous and what is not."[100] In 1922 she wrote, "I have very little to do with people because I seem to do and say things that they do not like or do not understand."[101]

Harris's belief that anatomy was destiny colored her ideas about aging. One newspaper reporter who interviewed her on the celebration of her sixtieth birthday described her as "a woman who likes growing old," one who has a "complacent contempt of Archaiphobia . . . a word to denote the fear of old age."[102] Nor was she above describing herself as aged, as she did to an editor she was trying to persuade to accept her proposal for a story. She was simply, she wrote, "an old woman, with a fat face, a sardonic eye, a tender heart, a mischievous and valliant [*sic*] mind with two fighting horns in front and a forked tail of humor behind and a highly developed spiritual nature, commonly known as imagination."[103] But these sentiments belie stronger feelings of contempt for aging found elsewhere in her writing.[104] Until she became one herself, she could be especially harsh when portraying older women.[105]

In *My Book and Heart* she wrote, "age does make astonishing changes in the human countenance," and more so for women. In fact, "nature seems to lose interest in you, once you have fulfilled her purpose," which for woman was reproduction. Women beyond the childbearing years were to be pitied. The forces of nature mocked and played tricks on the aged. "I have noticed this about the wind," she wrote, "when it catches the skirt of a middle-aged woman, it flaunts the thing roughly, as if nothing mattered; but it whisks the skirt of a girl softly, meaningly, as a handkerchief is prettily used in a flirtation, or like a neat little cloud that belongs to her."[106] When nature had no more use for a woman, "the wind," or life, flaunted or exposed her. For a woman without a purpose, "nothing," not even such exposure, "mattered." Life had "meaning" for, and "belong[ed]" to, the young woman, for whom there was yet a natural, biological purpose.

Harris's feelings on aging are poignantly captured in a birthday note she wrote to her daughter on the occasion of her twenty-first birthday, which Faith had to spend away from home at college. Corra is sorry Faith will have to "come of age" alone, without the "props of father's and mother's presence," but considering that they sent her away to college to grow up and "learn how to live," being alone on her twenty-first birthday actually might be the "proper way to do it." "And here is my wish for you," Corra writes just before her own fortieth birthday, "my only child, my dearest possession in the world, my peace and my crown—That you may learn to make life your own, not to be driven and frightened by it. That you may achieve peace and happiness out of the strength and calm of your own spirit. That you may have health and hope and energy and much to do in the world, and that you may do it well with all your might and mind. That you may be a good woman, live well and die before you are old."[107] If she recalled this birthday wish later it was likely with acute grief, since Faith died not long after her thirty-first birthday. Significantly, in addition to what it reveals about her thoughts on age, it is conspicuously silent on the subjects of marriage and motherhood.

If Harris expressed fears over aging, disregard for the experience of women beyond middle age, and scorn for the concept of sisterhood, elsewhere she wrote about the capacity of women in their senior years to outgrow natural and characteristic jealousy and rivalry. At age thirty-five she published "A Woman's Relation to the Two Sexes," in which she discusses why women cannot think in terms of solidarity until they reach a certain age. After explaining all the reasons why there never would or could be a sisterhood among women, Harris ends the article on a different note:

> After middle age . . . the average woman begins to care more for women than she does for men. Her allegiance undergoes a psychic change, her eyes are opened, her judgment cleared, and she learns to appreciate her own sex fully. The characteristics that seemed to her hateful frailties long ago are defended now as their poetic distinctions. . . . And for them all [men and women] she has a chastened affinity. Men have passed out of her calculations. They are the things with whom she failed or succeeded, from lover and husband down to her youngest son. And however much she remains dependent upon them, she is no longer related to them in the same near way. She has survived them and returned to her own.[108]

Harris at least envisioned a time, if she did not seem to look forward to it, when men would become "things" in a normal woman's consciousness, and other women would be those with whom she felt most "related" and toward whom she felt least antagonistic.[109]

Whatever confusion Harris experienced about gender identity, she came after a time to see that what seemed to be a given of nature was not such at all. Men had it and were not willing to give it up. She differed in many ways from feminists who had the same insight. For one thing, she was not willing to challenge the reality directly. Life was too short, and it seemed best to recognize it and find the most plausible way to live with it. She did so personally by remaining a widow for the last twenty-five years of her adult life. But she imagined other ways to do so, ways that show up in select women characters in her fiction, some of whom are subjects of the following chapter.

6

Widows as the Only "Free Moral Agents"

In the prime of her writing career Harris venerated domestic tradition in the popular press and blamed and condemned women for straying from its security, yet in some of her fiction there is marked uncertainty and equivocation about traditional roles. Several of the female characters with whom she as author clearly identified do not celebrate traditional domestic roles, but defy and resist them in subtle ways. Some of the characters reveal confusion more than anything else about gender identity; others reveal clear feminist insight. Six characters from three novels and a short story demonstrate the insight: Jessica Doane in *The Jessica Letters* (1904), Mary Thompson and Sal Prout in *A Circuit Rider's Wife* (1910), Sylvia Story in *The Recording Angel* (1912), and Miriam Ambrose and Millicent, the narrator, in "The Widow Ambrose" (1920).

Jessica Doane illustrates how Harris's complex ideas on gender roles were developing before Harris established a reputation as a novelist, and how she had come to question traditional gender roles even as she began making her living advocating them. Although the character Jessica Doane waxes eloquently about the strength of romantic love to redeem woman from herself, about the way a woman's worship of her lover transforms her into the ethereal Goddess of romantic tradition, behind that rhetoric is an astute awareness that conventional young women were not supposed to possess. Jessica is a southern lady, but one far wiser and more self-aware as an affianced youth than the "sad-eyed Madonnas" Harris had used to represent southern women in essays published shortly before *The Jessica Letters*.[1]

Unlike the model southern lady, Jessica is by nature a rebel, and this is an instinct she does not want to give up.[2] Giving in to love, she explains to her suitor, Philip Towers, is the ultimate sacrifice for her because it means death, "annihilation of self," loss of "character and personality," total "absorption" into the self of the lover. Moreover, she knows that she will never be able willingly to commit this act of spiritual suicide; it will take the force of circumstance to bring it about. For her the circumstance, not surprisingly, is love.

However, it is not love of her betrothed as a lover but rather as a "portal" to an intellectual and spiritual reality to which only men have access.[3] She wants more than anything else in life to reach the same intellectually and philosophically satisfying heights he has. In her mind he has been able to solve the mysteries of life through mastering philosophy. For her that represents freedom, the kind a woman could only hope to achieve, if at all, through intimate association with a man. Some of the passages from Jessica's pen mimic more the mystical language of the Song of Solomon than that of the kind of domestic fiction for which it was dismissed by critics. They also reveal Harris's mystical tendencies and her gradual moving away from institutional Christianity more than they reveal a budding novelist who would make her living selling fiction laced with Victorian domestic ideals. Harris was in her mid-thirties when she penned the letters of Jessica Doane. By then she understood that, unlike many women of her time and place, the concept of personal freedom, but she had not been able to reach it for herself and that motivated her for the rest of her life.

In her early forties Harris created the most beloved of all her fictional characters, Mary Thompson, who expresses a greater feminist consciousness than any of Harris's other characters. *A Circuit Rider's Wife* begins with the marriage of itinerant Methodist minister William Thompson to Mary Thompson and ends shortly after William's death thirty years later. The novel, set in Hart County, Georgia, at the turn of the century, is ostensibly about the hardships William and Mary face on the circuit and about William's struggle to reconcile his traditional faith with liberal theology. As popular reviewers wrote, it is supposedly about the triumph of marital love and religious faith. An underlying purpose of the book, captured in more critical reviews, was to expose the autocratic nature of the Methodist Church hierarchy as revealed in their calculated unwillingness to support the denomination's circuit riders. Reputedly autobiographical, the book is based marginally on the short period in Lundy and Corra's early marriage when Lundy started his career as a circuit rider. It is actually the spiritual autobiography of Corra Harris, revealing her spiritual and psychological struggles during the first decade of her writing career, roughly from 1898 until 1909, when she wrote the book.

Mary Thompson and a lesser character in the novel, Sal Prout, reveal Harris's growing doubts about the church's ability to meet the spiritual needs of the modern world. Harris was applauded for the candor and courage the novel expressed in exposing the Methodist Church hierarchy's abuse of power.[4] She conceals in domestic rhetoric the way Mary and Sal shore up William, who is, much like Lundy Harris, too otherworldly for his own good.

Mary never doubts God's goodness, she says, but she does doubt that God can work all things out for good, "especially in any kind of a church."[5] Furthermore, the really wise ones (spiritually speaking) in this novel happen to be these two women, both of whom wind up, if unwittingly, confounding William, the hero, who goes to his grave as he lived most of his life, discomfited and troubled. If Harris keeps Mary and Sal deferential in tone at all times, she allows them to emerge as autonomous thinkers who manage to see the "truth" more clearly and more astutely than the minister to whom they both give rhetorical obeisance.

Although Mary is aware of the church's inability to meet its members' spiritual needs, both she and Harris have less regard for traditionalism's nemesis, the "higher criticism," than they do for the legalistic excesses of William's brand of faith. Mary is not above calling William to account when he "backslides" and gets in "a blue funk spiritually" by flirting with the "mischief" of "rationalism" that, she says, "curtail the Divinity of Jesus Christ and make your Heavenly Father just a natural force in the Universe."[6] Even if Harris had disdain for the doctrinal legalism of rural Methodist faith at the time she wrote *A Circuit Rider's Wife*, she had even less tolerance for the doctrinal latitude that she saw making its way into urban areas all over the country.

Eventually, Harris adopted a naturalistic discourse about God and a universalistic discourse to explain salvation and an afterlife, but for Mary Thompson the "truth" is somewhere between the constraints of evangelical zeal and the license she saw in liberal theology (chapter 8 explores Harris's religious identity further). And the God she serves clearly favors the spirit over the letter of the law, which is something she is infinitely better at divining than her husband. William, with all his genuine devotion to his calling, is blinded by the letter of the law. He, like his God, is limited by a piety that makes no allowances for human nature. "William's greatest limitation as a minister was his firm conviction that the world was a drawback to Heaven," Mary says.[7]

The God whom Mary worships understands human nature and does not regard as sinful her desire for "real laughter and lightness and play of life." William needs those things, too, she knows, "but the difference was he never knew it. When he felt world-hungry he thought it was a sign of spiritual anemia and prayed for a closer walk with God," Mary says, "as if God was not also the God of the world even more than he is the caste Deity of any church or creed."[8] William cannot see the forest for the trees, or the spirit for the letter of the law. Although he can extend the spirit of the law to a woman on the verge of suicide from fear of the weight of her sins, he cannot get past the letter of the law to help out "apostates" who are "looking for God and praying for the witness of His Spirit," Mary says, those who believe they have "sinned away [their] day of grace."[9] Before apostates he stood "powerless."

One of the biggest "skeletons in William's doctrinal closet" is Sal Prout, a woman whose name reveals her position as a social outcast: "The omission of the last syllable of her given name implied social ostracism and personal contempt." Prout is, Mary says, "a soul without a country," a woman for whom the "truth" is that people can connect with God as well outside as inside a church—and in her case, much more effectively outside.[10] Sal lives her faith by taking care of the "wicked" and basically anyone who needs help. For those in her village, Mary says, "all you had to do to get her was to need her."[11]

Prout is ostracized by the members of the church because they fear the message she is sending to the unchurched, which is that love and goodness are not limited to those within. Her good deeds have "done more harm than a dozen wildcat stills," one of the local preachers tells the Thompsons.[12] It is William's duty as the new circuit pastor of her village to bring her into the church. However, as she is forever busy helping others—everything from "pulling fodder to nursing a teething baby"—William and Mary can never catch her at home.[13] She winds up calling to help the Thompsons, however, after William has been "down with sciatica" for a month.

While taking care of William she talks about the difference between her faith and William's and between his and her "vision" of God. William's God is exclusive, helping out only the good, only the churched; Sal's is inclusive, providing for both the sinner and the saint, the unchurched and the churched. She tells William that he believes in a limited God, one who plays favorites, who is "mean and partial . . . a Paradise capitalist and aristocrat."[14] Her God, however, does not turn his back on or hold unduly accountable people like her who have had, she says, "no chance to be good." On the contrary, her God is "One that makes flowers like them bloom for sech as me . . . that lets His rain fall in my garden same as He does in your'n; that never takes His spite out on me for bein' what I was, but jest made it hard for me and waited patient for me."[15] William's "aggrieved" retort that Sal did not "put it fair" convinces neither himself nor Sal. He recovers from the rheumatism from which he was suffering, but he never recovers from the spiritual "trance" he had fallen into, and not long afterward, Mary confides, he "turned over on his spiritual ashheap and died."[16]

If Mary and Sal illustrate in a subtle way a higher spiritual wisdom on the part of two women over the male minister, Mary's "experience" of finding herself—her own "I am" shortly after William's death—cogently reveals Harris's awareness of women's position in traditional marriage and how the absence of autonomy affects women. The "experience" is exclusively her own, Mary says immodestly: "unglorified by William, so strange that I cannot explain it unless there is what may be called a reversion to type in spirit like this: that a person may be absolutely dominated for years by certain influences and not only feel no antagonism to them, but actually yield with devotion and inconceivable sacrifices, yet, when the influence is removed . . . the person finds himself of his original mind and spirit, emancipated, gone back to himself, what he really was in the beginning before the domination began."[17] The language she uses to describe her experience of being "emancipated" from "domination" needs little explication. The "experience" is, in essence, a rebirth. After William dies, she grieves intensely and falls into a "trance of sorrow."[18] But, "Then suddenly the veil lifted. . . . At once my own mind came back to me, not the humble, church-censored mind I had during his life, but my very own, and it was like another conversion. . . . For so many years I had not belonged to myself. . . . Suddenly it came to me that I was a free moral agent for the first time in my life—widows are the only women who are."[19]

Even if Mary had loved her husband and grieved deeply after he died, she nonetheless realizes what that love had cost her. Both here and in *The Recording Angel,* Harris describes romantic love between men and women as an illusion.[20] "Love is not love in either men or women," she writes. "It is the instinct to subjugate, an instinct of which Nature makes excellent use for purposes of keeping the earth properly populated."[21] Women "devour" men before marriage as husbands devour wives afterward.[22] Moreover, wives love husbands because they have no other choice.[23]

Importantly, none of Mary's revelations about her newly discovered and cherished moral agency are reversed in the end. She does indeed return from a visit to her sister in New York City feeling chastened for her "world-hungry" desires, but her change of heart comes not from what she finds in the world outside the church in New York but rather from the emptiness she perceives on the inside of the church, and more to the point, on the inside of the people in the church, even her own sister.[24] The simple folk back home who have enough faults to keep them ever in need of the altar at least have souls that need saving. "If they ever had souls," however, the people in the churches in New York have "had them removed, probably by a kind of reasoning surgery quite as effective as the literal surgery with which so many of them have their poor appendixes removed."[25]

The change of heart that sends Mary back home to a simpler place has nothing to do with her second thoughts about once again becoming her own "moral agent." It has everything to do with the liberal theology, which is influenced by liberal politics—that is, "socialistic scantlings . . . and barbwire theories of the brotherhood of man"—in the churches in New York and elsewhere.[26] They are the same theories that Harris will adapt to her own universalist beliefs during the last years of her life. The people who believe liberal theology, to Mary (and to Harris), are the most deluded of all.[27] For her, the issue is simple. Rationalism governs the new interpretation of scripture, which she believes is sterile and allows no room for human individuality. Furthermore, the ostensibly progressive theology is not progress, but arrogance. But she believes that rationalism, by questioning Christ's divinity, also displaces the love of Christ. She sees the theology and its proponents as devoid of love and the capacity to love. Although Mary will return home totally unconverted by liberal religion and politics, she has no intention of renouncing her "conversion" to the autonomous self she discovered after William's death.

In *The Recording Angel,* Sylvia Story reveals Harris's unwillingness to believe all she wrote about the domestic ideal. The story, told by an omniscient narrator, begins at the turn of the century with prodigal son Jim Bone returning home to the sleepy little town of Ruckersville, Georgia. Bone had fled as a youth twenty years earlier after knifing his best friend in a fight over a card game. Although he plans merely to pass through, on the first day of his return Bone falls in love with the beautiful Sylvia Story. Determined to win over his new love, Bone forgets about his travels and decides to devote a fortune recently earned in speculating to making Ruckersville livable— which means, by his lights, modernizing the town and shaking its residents out of their lethargic allegiance to Lost Cause ideology.[28] Bone buys up the land for sale in Ruckersville (which includes most of the town) and begins a series of aggressive building projects, including a theater. Bone partners with Amy White, an elderly woman blinded by cataracts who serves as the novel's title character and primary heroine, in the theater project. Bone decides that the first play in the new theater will be adapted from a series of biographical vignettes of a typical day in the life of the town's residents written over the years by Amy. In the novel's concluding chapters, Bone wins Sylvia's heart, Amy gets her sight back, and industrialized Ruckersville grows into a model New South town.

Amy White might possess many of the feminine traits traditional society expected of white women, but she would not have been the envy of most women readers.[29] Twenty-five-year-old Sylvia Story more likely would have. Because of her mother's early profession as a courtesan, Sylvia has been "designed by inheritance for the brothel," the narrator states, and hence is hardly high-minded Ruckersville mothers' choice for their sons, but Sylvia nonetheless is the one who manages to steal the heart and become the first true love of the novel's hero.[30] In many ways she is the envy of some if not most of Harris's women readers, as she appears to have been in curious ways for Harris. Sylvia is beautiful and self-assured, the desire of every single man (and some not-so-single) in Ruckersville.[31]

Clearly, Bone's ability to "tame" Sylvia with a kiss, which she bears "as a tamed filly bears the shock of a saddle flung across her back," might be interpreted as fairly traditional romance, but little else about Sylvia will fit her into a domestic identity.[32] For example, she is nothing like another character in the book, Mildred Percy, a middle-aged "gentle beauty." As a single woman, Ms. Percy is growing distressingly into old age when she is rescued just in time by Jim Bone's artful persuasion of Tony, one of the available bachelors, to make her his wife.

Unlike Mildred or a number of other single women in town who could easily have "shriveled into reputable old maids" had Bone not shown up, Sylvia would more naturally have become a "female bachelor."[33] The difference between a "female bachelor" and an old maid is significant. Female bachelors are agents in life; they can reconcile life to themselves. On the contrary, life forces old maids into stoic resignation. Harris's descriptions of Sylvia are telling. If she represents a particular type or a "peculiar kind" of woman, Sylvia is decidedly distinct from all other women in Ruckersville.[34] She is beautiful, but something about her beauty sets her apart from the "gentle beauty" of Mildred. Sylvia has a "muscular grace" of sorts.[35] In more than one place Harris portrays her as an archetypal woman who transcends history and culture. She is "mysterious . . . with that strange authority of the Delilahs, Jezebels, and Cleopatras."[36] She knows nothing of coquetry and is above playing hard to get. Rather, she is a "singular human pyramid full of the silent secrets of former creations."[37] She is the type of woman who has no maternal instinct, one whom children "instinctively" avoid, but whom a man will "wear himself to the bone in order to discover." [38]

Sylvia's self-assurance comes with a price, of course. She might never suffer the fate of a fool in the game of love, but neither can she feel love's ecstacy. She can "calculate emotion" but cannot feel emotion herself.[39] She is a "cool mathematician" whose physical beauty suggests that "she had been chiselled instead of being born of flesh and blood."[40] Inside she has "no tenderness," merely "intelligence and passion."[41] "Such women do not love but they desire more than others in the world to be loved."[42] Sylvia could "no more open it [her heart] to the tender fires of love than a ruby can bleed. She is a thing to possess, to keep, to hold, to have and to love, but that is her desire and her limit. She is so made that she cannot love in return."[43] But that is her obvious attraction.

In Harris's thinking, women and men have fundamentally different experiences of romantic love. Men crave more to love than to be loved; women crave more to be loved than to love.[44] "A man infinitely more enjoys loving a woman than he enjoys having her love him," the narrator writes, reflecting on Jim's feelings for Sylvia. Because of that, a woman should do whatever is necessary "to keep her lover in love with her." She should "cultivate more her own lovableness, and place . . . as little emphasis as possible upon her devotion to him."[45] Sylvia is a natural at that sort of thing, and for that reason "she is the . . . untrodden frontier toward which all lovers strive in vain."[46] Her frontier is coveted because, although she is incapable of experiencing the felt joy of love, neither can she feel the pain. With love there is always pain, an experience Harris knew intimately. Sylvia avoids pain by cultivating the trait of indifference, one that Harris also cultivated to cope with grief and sadness.[47]

Finally, two women from the short story "The Widow Ambrose" illustrate subtle forms of defiance as well as the way Harris drew back from accepting the feminist insights her own life brought her. Set in the small southern town of Rochford around 1920, "The Widow Ambrose" chronicles the friendship between Millicent, the town librarian who narrates the story, and the title character, Miriam Ambrose. Millicent makes a series of visits to Miriam's farm, purchased after Mr. Ambrose's death, in hopes that Miriam will donate her books to the library. As the two women become friends, Millicent notes that although Miriam is a competent farm manager, she struggles to command the respect of her hired hands. Later, after returning

from a tour of postwar Europe, Millicent discovers that her friend, now betrothed to her former husband's law partner, has adopted a more feminine
persona and that her ability to manage her farm employees has improved
as a result. At the story's close, Millicent reflects on her friend's transformed
behavior; this meditation leads her to consider her own gender identity and
her loneliness as a single woman.

Harris clearly admires the character Miriam Ambrose, a forty-nine-year-
old widow of a small-town lawyer who left her with a "modest competency."[48]
But she just as clearly admires Millicent, the narrator, a thirty-eight-year-old
independent, never-married woman. Much of Mrs. Ambrose's life parallels
Harris's. In many ways Mrs. Ambrose's story is more autobiographical than
that of Mary Thompson in *A Circuit Rider's Wife*. She cares little for going
out in public, but rather "conducted" "her social life . . . in her own house
at Sassafras Plantation, where she had the advantage." Harris and Mrs. Ambrose have many of the same traits, physical and otherwise. They both move
from town to a farm at their husband's death, and neither is typically feminine in dress, speech, or manner. Mrs. Ambrose bears masculine traits similar to ones Harris used to describe herself. She is rather "tall" and "portly,"
"a fine fighting man of a woman, with a gleam in her eye."[49]

The bane of Mrs. Ambrose's widowed life, as it was for much of Harris's,
is the hired help on her farm. Millicent describes Mrs. Ambrose as being
"subject at all times to altercations with her hired men or with her tenant."
Harris's unforgiving sentiments toward "labor" are reflected in Mrs. Ambrose, who discusses the "question of labor with the wit of one who is eye to
eye with a dangerous force." And, like Harris, Mrs. Ambrose "thought her
difficulties came in a great measure from being a woman. The most ignorant
man resented taking orders from a woman." Like Harris, Mrs. Ambrose believes not even suffrage would help. She doubts "if having the ballot would
afford me any additional advantage in managing labor on this place." In fact,
having the ballot, Mrs. Ambrose believes, would make women less feminine
and hence would handicap her in her relationship with the hired help. "We
must do what we can do as women, employing the usual arts and policies of
the strictly feminine in our relations to men."

Mrs. Ambrose knows she has the solution, but since it contradicts her
self-image, it takes time and thought before she can "find out how to apply
the theory" to practice. Once time has passed, however, and Fortson, her
tenant, begins "practicing [the] newfangled doctrines" of labor, that "dangerous force" that "had its head in the air," Mrs. Ambrose swallows her pride

and turns to what she had known all along would work. She—a strong-minded, self-confident, independent woman who had dressed for comfort in some of the "homeliest and most durable garments"—dons the dress and manner of a delicate, dainty, and somewhat helpless woman and takes on her tenant.[50]

When asked by Millicent what had brought about the change, Mrs. Ambrose responds that she had finally, after "studying . . . these men who work for me . . . [put] two and two together." She found out for herself "where they were least guarded against me. It is what everyone does in the competition of working or selling the other fellow."[51] She does not care at all for the frills she wears. She dresses "attractively for purely business purposes," she tells Millicent. Mrs. Ambrose's motives are not only mercenary; they reflect a feminist awareness of the affected nature of femininity. "If you are a woman," she continues, "you must answer first to what men think women are, which is not what they are at all, nine times out of ten, but what their clothes represent them to be. And the lighter, more frivolous these are the less they resent you, the less you must overcome in order to carry your point, whatever kind of a point it is. They will not allow *you* to do it, but they will allow your frocks and parasol to do it for you." She has put Fortson "off his guard" and has him eating out of her hand. Nor does it bother her that he has begun to take credit for implementing all her ideas. As long as he is getting the work done, she can tolerate the "theft." "Now he begs my brains, uses them, and does without knowing it what I want him to do. It is an excellent arrangement," she adds proudly.[52]

Soon, as fate according to Harris would have it, the new Mrs. Ambrose takes a lover and becomes betrothed. She "had not only dressed for purely 'business purposes,' conquered the will of her tenant and hired men with her organdies and silken girdles. She had achieved a lover—at the age of forty-nine!"[53] Harris's message in the story becomes mixed with this change in the heroine.

Mrs. Ambrose moves from the self-confident, hardworking, sure-of-herself woman one meets in the beginning to one who is as self-conscious and diffident as her dress and manner are feminine and dainty. "The snap seemed to have gone out of her," the narrator writes. "She was placid and uninteresting." Some of her friends have surmised that there is a man in the picture because she shows all the "signs" of being a "gratified woman." "She showed other evidences" as well, Millicent tells us, like "a somnambulant wit, peculiar to people who have lost the edge of their desires."[54] The "signs" seem to be in conflict. Whereas before Mrs. Ambrose had dominated all the conversations between herself and the narrator, after her "metempsychosis," the narrator writes, "I only remember that, if anything, I had the conversational advantage because she forced it on me with undue silences."[55] Was the change in Mrs. Ambrose qualitatively positive or negative?

In spite of the apparent devolution of Mrs. Ambrose, the narrator becomes envious as well as curious. "The cat in me wondered," says Millicent about Mrs. Ambrose's clandestine affair. "When you are thirty-eight and have never had a lover it is very difficult to purr at the sight of a woman eleven years your senior who has got one. . . . She was smiling, not the smile of a productive and satisfied farmer, but one of radiant, strictly feminine happiness. . . . I arose languidly to meet her and she embraced me, a thing she had never done before."[56] Millicent seems to envy the woman lost in love, preferring the "radiant and strictly feminine happiness" of Mrs. Ambrose transformed by love to that of the "productive and satisfied farmer" without a lover. "For the briefest moment," Millicent confesses, "I had a vision of myself in a pansy-figured organdie of robin's egg blue with a ribbon tied around my waist and a rose-colored parasol over my head sitting in a meadow somewhere. How would I look; above all, how would I feel?" Would she feel at home with herself? Would she be comfortable with the alien identity? Probably not. She regains her senses, as she relates, and perceives that Mrs. Ambrose "was a shattered woman, that she had lost her grip. . . . For the only time in my life, I felt superior to her. I was still sane, and I belonged to nobody but myself."[57]

Which does Harris want the reader to value more: the "radiant, strictly feminine happiness" of the heroine, or the "sanity" of the narrator who "belonged to nobody but myself"? It is not entirely clear, though with certain imagery she seems to try to persuade the reader to sympathize with Mrs. Ambrose. Certainly none of the alternative images of Millicent are appealing: "I sat down, feeling more like a priest about to receive a confession and less like a cat ready to scratch somebody," as she had felt when she first recognized the change.[58]

Through the character of Mrs. Ambrose, Harris exposes the powerfully alienating effects of a certain forced femininity by pointing out how Mrs. Ambrose, by internalizing the superficial behavior and mannerisms required of the feminine ideal, literally became that ideal.[59] Mrs. Ambrose became what she was not, a dependent and "irresponsible" woman, willing to relinquish all the traits that the narrator had admired about her in the beginning. Why? Mrs. Ambrose explains her personal surrender: "I have proved my point, that a woman can farm and make it pay, that she can control labor and make labor earn its wage. What else can I do that would not be a vain repetition? I am tired of the repetition, even of good harvests. . . . I am worn out watching the weather and trying to outdo it and outwit it. I want to be just a woman again and fold my hands and not be obliged to do and do and think and think. It really is very hard on a woman."[60]

Millicent understands this very well. She herself is worn out: "How many times had I longed, not for a husband, maybe, but for the feminine state of irresponsibility which they provide." The end of the story leaves the reader with the image of a forlorn narrator. After being invited to be the widow's bridesmaid, Millicent departs knowing that after the wedding she will never go back. She leaves "feeling very lonely, merely one of the bystanders, watching life and love pass by, fading and growing dimmer in the minds of men and women, while yet I lived and went on working just to live."[61]

For a woman, having the freedom necessary to belong to oneself and no other means shouldering alone the burden of supporting herself in a competitive world where even honest men sell their souls for some kind of security. "In this desperately competitive world an honest man may change his character overnight," Harris wrote elsewhere, advising widows not to tempt their financial agents, even those proven honest, by trusting them with their inheritances.[62] If an honest man could not be expected to keep his soul untarnished, how could a woman with fewer means financially and psychologically be expected to take care of herself?

The characters of Millicent and Mrs. Ambrose before and after the metamorphosed state of love-struck mindlessness may reflect Harris's conflicts over the value of traditional gender roles, but they may just as well reflect a need to sell the story. Why not end the story with Mrs. Ambrose's clever and successful experiment in gender role-playing? Mrs. Ambrose had exposed the myth of feminine fragility as a hypocrisy that smart women used and not-so-smart women got trapped into. She has outsmarted man, and all at Sassafras Plantation seems to be running well. Why not leave it at that? Was it because the implications of the story would be too risky to sell: two women complete in their own right without men? Or did it reflect a deeper misgiving on Harris's part about a woman's ability to be whole without a man?

Miriam Ambrose as a widow has much in common with the confident, self-assured woman Harris revealed herself to be through Mary Thompson in *A Circuit Rider's Wife* and Corra Harris in life. Millicent, the pensive, second-guessing, regretful narrator, is reminiscent of the woman Harris revealed herself to be in *As a Woman Thinks*. And the Mrs. Ambrose who was self-deluded and lost in her lover is someone with whom Harris identified as the woman she was before her life-altering experience of 1899. The story reflects a time in Harris's life when she had doubts that the confidence and self-assurance of the former Mrs. Ambrose could be more than a short-lived phenomenon, when she wondered if the loneliness and disillusionment of the narrator was the greater reality for women who chose to live without men, but when she was nonetheless sure that the alternative—the latter Mrs. Ambrose—was unthinkable.

However much Harris idealized romantic love and marriage as every woman's privilege or obligation (depending upon perspective), setting sentiment aside, she had no qualms about admitting the benefits of widowhood. If she expressed misgivings about the loneliness attached to widowhood, she expressed stronger misgivings about giving up her personal liberty. She chose consciously to remain "the captain of my own fate" and to stay "a safe distance" from men who might wish to appropriate the freedom she could know only as a widow.[63] She never found a man who came close to measuring up. She was too "exacting" and not inclined to budge on her standards.[64] Given her decision to remain unmarried for the last twenty-five years of her life, one can only conclude that Harris valued personal freedom far more than the idyllic love she seemed elsewhere to venerate. Her thinking about personal liberty and the relationship between personal liberty and happiness explains in part why she chose to remain a widow. If "one must be free to be happy," a woman must be a widow to be truly free.[65] This probably accounted for the fact that though most men "resume the rank of husbands" after being widowed, "a woman clings to her widowhood." Knowing this about widowhood, Harris determined to be a "permanent" not a "temporary widow," and she gave plenty of advice to other women who decided the same.[66]

Harris's observations on widowhood align much more with her lived experience than with some of her other stated beliefs. But her insights on hierarchy were not limited to her thoughts on widowhood. Whether her disdain for woman's nature resulted from or led to one too many of those compromises is a question worth asking, if not one that lends itself to a decisive answer. From a feminist perspective one might argue that delusion and hatred of woman's nature inhere within patriarchy and go hand in hand. But again, Harris was not as deluded as some of the quoted passages seem to insist. Her compromises were made deliberately and knowingly.

Recall from the previous chapter her feminist reflections on the male (versus innate) construction of the assumed female gender characteristic of domesticity. Women were not naturally domestic, she wrote. Domesticity was a trait contrived by men for their convenience as a means of controlling women. Harris understood that in the final analysis, man's power over woman was more fundamental than even his ownership of property or control of religion. To force man to come to terms with his responsibility for the oppression of woman would involve him in an act that was "more revolutionary than if [he] were called upon to surrender his property." Surrendering his control over woman would be "like asking him to commit a personal violence against his own nature"; it would be "more awful than if he were required to surrender his religious faith [or] his system of philosophy."[67]

That "woman" was a contrivance of man was clear to Harris. Men had determined what women were and what they were not, and by claiming domesticity was their nature, had thereby justified leaving them at home where they conveniently belonged—home which was a dirty place where some of life's most irksome tasks had to be done daily and when necessary, around the clock. Harris was equally candid about the mind-numbing effects of housework. But it was on the point of housework where she lost her clarity of thinking and resorted to the most convenient of simplistic solutions—blaming the victim.

Furthermore, women who did challenge their relegated place, it seemed to Harris, were as discontented as those who accepted their fate, and some were even more miserable. "A defiant woman," Harris wrote, "is an unhappy woman."[68] The odds being what they were, and defiance being nothing more in her observation than wasted energy, Harris would find other ways of securing what life had to offer. This judgment about the cost of defiance was not limited to feminism's opponents; there were "defiant women" of Harris's day who, if they shared nothing else with her, did not hesitate to admit the cost of their defiance. Charlotte Perkins Gilman is one noted example.

Gilman, author of the haunting short story "The Yellow Wallpaper" (1892) and *Women and Economics* (1898), a classic of modern U.S. feminism, knew from experience the cost of defiance. She understood the systemic roots of legal and cultural status as well as anyone in her day, and she devoted her life to exposing it in all of its guises. But she admitted there was a price to pay. "The attitude of men toward those women who have so far presumed to 'un-sex' themselves is known to all. They like women to be foolish, changeable, always newly attractive."[69] Why, Gilman asked, should this matter to a woman who had "grown independent, educated, or wise and free"? Perhaps it should not, but in reality it did. Cultural prescriptions and all the trappings "bind us with a gentle dragging hold that few can resist" Gilman explained. "Those who do resist, and who insist upon living their individual lives, find that this costs them loneliness and privation; and they lose so much in daily comfort and affection that others are deterred from following them."[70]

Harris was not blind to women's oppression; nor was she blind to exploitation and abuse of power as its root cause. But she remained unpersuaded that public activism was a viable or effective way to overcome it. Although she was not openly defiant, she did resist the effects of oppression in her personal life through the choices she made and through the use of her pen.

"A Woman Who Writes Is Born to Trouble"

Corra Harris often reflected on the difficulties of a writing career. "It is easier to be a Christian," she wrote in 1933, "than to become a successful writer."[1] When fledgling writers asked for advice on how to get started, she tried to convince them that "literary composition is harder work than . . . sweatshop slavery."[2] Elsewhere she had written a similar sentiment to her daughter, who was still adjusting to the rigors of a writing career: "You have my prayers and sympathy this coming week . . . with your work. I hope it will go, but if it does it will be the first time in the literary history of the family that work ever took up its bed and walked off without a deadly struggle with the author."[3] A writing career was hard work, and for women it was even worse. "Now for your daughter," George Lorimer wrote. "She's younger than the rest of us, and hasn't had her share of literary disappointments yet, so we'd better train her to a knowledge that a woman who writes is born to trouble."[4] Indeed, Harris's life as a writer was filled with plenty of trouble. But in the balance, it was filled with more satisfaction and reward.

Harris had a diverse lot of admirers in the general reading public. One reader wrote that he found in her novels "flashes of genius as good as any writing I have seen outside of Shakespere [sic]." Many letters of praise came from people in the business and professional classes. One male physician from Los Angeles considered her novel *The Recording Angel* the best literature to appear "since *David Copperfield* and *Vanity Fair*." A woman doctor from California believed Harris's second autobiography revealed her ability to portray "human frailties" with exceptional dignity and grace.[5] An economics professor called her "the sanest-minded, finest witted, truest writer of the times."[6] And Milton White, an English professor from Jackson, Mississippi, wrote that he believed "future years . . . will rather increase your fame than diminish it. I believe no American author has seen more into human character."[7] Although White's opinions proved wrong, his letter no doubt heartened Harris, as it came in 1933, a year in which she faced repeated rejections to publish her works nationally.[8]

Bankers made up some of Harris's most earnest admirers. The president of the United States Savings Bank in Washington, D.C., wrote that he had "had the great pleasure of reading your various articles in the magazines from time to time." He was especially amused by *The Circuit Rider's Widow* (one of two sequels to follow *A Circuit Rider's Wife*), which was "so accurate and real that I laughed until the tears came to my eyes." More seriously moved by her philosophy than amused by her humor, the president of the Federal Land Bank of Houston, Texas, wrote: "In the warp and woof of the fabric of modern life your quaint philosophy, religious and social, so happily expressed runs like a thread of gold for all those whose privilege it is to follow your pen."[9] The bankers Harris heard from were men. After a fairly long but lighthearted letter to Harris reminding her of her "marriage" to the *Saturday Evening Post,* George Lorimer asked, "Why is it that your writing makes strong men burst into song?"[10] It was obviously a rhetorical question. Lorimer, known for his ability to gauge American popular opinion, knew well why men responded to writing that glorified traditional gender roles.[11]

Many readers believed Harris had exceptional insight into the human heart.[12] One of her most abiding admirers, editor Hamilton Holt, said so more than once. At a memorial ceremony honoring Harris a year after her death, Holt reflected on words he had published the previous decade in a review of *My Book and Heart*: "I have never met a soul in my life who could tell you so many true things about yourself that you never even suspected before, and yet you instantly recognized as so. To be sure, she was occasionally wrong, [but] . . . [h]er bull's eyes . . . far outnumbered her misses."[13]

Harris knew well her reputation for being a bad speller and grammarian and for having no regard for factual accuracy. Her daughter lectured her constantly about all three shortcomings, and her friend Bettie Rains gave up on the spelling.[14] It might have remained an inside joke, but she was at no pains to hide it. In 1934, after having worked with Harris for nearly thirty-five years, Hamilton Holt wrote, "I still marvel at your understanding. I have never especially respected your factual knowledge." Then he added, "but I have never met anyone who understands more things than you."[15] A little over two years later, in a eulogy dedicating the memorial chapel at the Valley the year after Harris's death, Holt said about the first days of Harris's relationship with the *Independent:* "In those days Mrs. Harris was the best orthologist, next to Dr. Ward, and the worst speller, next to me, of all *The Independent's* regular contributors."[16]

Harris appreciated Holt's "patience and wit in dealing with my limita-tions," she said in a speech in 1933. They were surpassed, she added, by "the liberty he permitted me to exercise in the effort to think truthfully without too much regard for mere facts which frequently belie the truth."[17] In a piece that she believed called for truth-telling, namely, setting the North straight for its "years of trying to make us [southerners] nobler men and women," Harris explained why she often sacrificed "factual knowledge": "The truth frequently makes rough copy."[18] To Harris, form or style could be more important than substance or facts; where writing was concerned, how one communicated could be more important than what one communicated.

Critics speculated on the nature of Harris's appeal. Grant Overton be-lieved her strong national identity set her apart: a southerner who identified foremost as an American. Her talent was "not so much 'literary,'" Overton wrote, "as national. Corra Harris's work could be nothing but American." He believed her distinction existed in her ability to reflect a uniquely American individualism. In a letter to her in 1933 Milton White, a professor of English at Millsaps College in Jackson Mississippi, acknowledged Harris's "nation-wide" acclaim, and believed "no American author has seen more into hu-man character" than she.[19] Her will reveals a national identity. She willed her estate first to her surviving heirs. If they were unable to keep up the estate, she wanted it to go first to the Daughters of the American Revolution before the United Daughters of the Confederacy. She instructed whichever asso-ciation accepted the offer to administer it as "a memorial to American life and civilization and whatever contribution or service my life has rendered to my Country."[20]

William Tate believed that Harris's "individuality" and "strong per-sonality" characterized both her writing and her personal identity. Harris "held center stage," Tate wrote, in person as well as "in her writings." And he added something that succinctly captures one of Harris's defining traits: "she was ever resolutely herself—not the voice of any generation, not the leader of any literary movement, nor the echo of any other writer."[21] Harris's "rebellious strain," Walter Blackstock wrote, "may have been her forte as a writer."[22] Harris was a rebellious woman whose liberty to rebel derived in large part from promoting a facade of anti-rebellion.

The rebelliousness Blackstock attributed to Harris marked her identity from cradle to grave. It developed from many sources, one of which was conflict between regional and gender identity, an experience common for southern women writers. As Anne Jones writes, "the paradox for the south-

ern woman remains that to define herself as a southerner is to accept a definition of herself that dehumanizes."[23] Certainly the effort took a toll on Harris. In much of her early published nonfiction, she foregrounds her southern
identity. Her private writings and, to an extent, her second autobiography
reveal at times intense struggles with the limitations of her gender identity, and at other times a confidence in the independence and individuality
she fought hard to develop and sustain. Like most thinking southern white
women of her generation, Harris experienced the tension between regional
and gender identity, the compounded constraints of both. It is a battle that
makes up a great deal of her life story.

Had Harris not experienced the particular constraints of gender and regional identity, had her work depended less on its "saleability," her legacy
might have been longer lasting. "Unfortunately for Harris's enduring reputation," writes Wayne Mixon, "she wrote too many facile society novels and
too few significantly social novels."[24] Blackstock writes about her novel *Co-
Citizens* what others have concluded about much of her fiction: that serious
readers "instinctively feel that she chose and handled her subject with the
consciousness of its saleability." And, Blackstock concludes, "The most de-
serving of it suggests the possibility of a growth which proved abortive."[25]

As practically all of her reviewers note, Harris's work was difficult if not
impossible to categorize. Harris offered too much realism to be classified
as a sentimental novelist, but because her subjects dealt most often with
domestic relationships, her fiction was rarely taken seriously. "Had she written more work in a caustically humorous vein, which was her forte," Mixon
writes, "her place in southern literature would be higher."[26] Even though
he dismisses much of her work as "abrasive didacticism," Mixon suggests
that *The Recording Angel* reveals that Harris came close "to writing a novel
that was broadly social rather than narrowly domestic in focus." For that
and other reasons, Mixon believes that "Harris's work, critical and fictional,
deserves closer analysis than it has hitherto received."[27]

Harris's life before and after she became a writer was governed by a strong
work ethic. For Harris, work defined life. Her work as a writer influenced
the woman she became in her maturity. Someone might easily have said
about her what Elizabeth Cady Stanton once said about Susan B. Anthony:
"To her, work is worship."[28] Likewise, Harris instructed a man hired to help
out on her farm: "When a man works, does it well, puts his heart into it,
leaves nothing undone that he ought to do, he prays the one acceptable
pray[er]. If he doesn't do his work honestly, it's no use to pray."[29]

Those closest to her knew Harris as a woman zealously dedicated to hard

work. She claimed that she came by her "mule-like endurance" from labor-
ing most of her life "under hard work sentences."[30] Indeed, she labored to
her last days. Just two months before Harris died, and while suffering the
debilitating effects of heart disease, Bettie Rains observed about her, "She
still works and I suppose she always will. . . . She is happy at work and
gets more satisfaction from working than anyone I have ever known."[31] And
Rains knew as well as anyone the futility of trying to stop her.

A successful writing career afforded Harris the liberty to be eccentric, to
indulge her naturally insular temperament the way few other livelihoods
might have. Writing became her life's work, she claimed, not by choice but
by necessity. She "took to writing as one takes to shelter in bad weather," she
wrote. The pen became the "tool of my deliverance."[32] At times she viewed
fame and success as providential, and writing as an outlet for creativity. At
other times she saw it as an inescapable burden. Then there were times when
it was neither especially stimulating nor burdensome, but simply work. "My
work is just hard work to me," she wrote her daughter, "not much affected
by temperament."[33] But work was good for the soul and could bring lasting
transformation, a "kind of luster within that cannot be taken away."[34]

The earliest years of her writing career were extremely trying. Harris was
an exceptionally prolific writer even then. "In addition to signed articles,
and a few short stories," she recalled something she and Hamilton Holt both
were fond of repeating, namely, that between 1900 and 1904 she "read and
reviewed twelve hundred books, mostly novels."[35] She was up no later than
5:00 every morning and worked most days "from morning until night,"
writing from four thousand to seven thousand words a day on any given
assignment.[36] During those years, Harris worked hard as wife, mother, and
writer. Her role as wife could be particularly difficult when Lundy was suffering with one of his depressive episodes.[37]

That sort of unrelieved stress no doubt explains her impassioned plea
to Faith in 1909 to come home and help after she graduated from college.
Harris wanted relief from some of the perennial burdens of housework so
she could channel more time and energy into writing. "For years I have
worked, worked, worked, with what weariness, what misgivings, what disappointments no one knows but myself. . . . *I am tired.* . . . *I cannot* go
on working so hard. . . . I want a chance to do something besides literary
drudgery. . . . Above all I want the chance to write a novel. I have never had
it. I have always had to do the thing that would pay the quickest."[38] She
knew she had been producing mostly "hack work" but felt she was capable
of much better work.[39] "If you will come home and give me the chance,"

she implored, "I think I could do something." She was right. In 1909, after Faith came home, *A Circuit Rider's Wife,* Harris's most popular and enduring novel, was serialized in the *Saturday Evening Post,* and the following year it was published to wide acclaim.[40]

It was not merely writing professionally that kept Harris busy. She was a prolific correspondent and, when necessary, one of the hardest-working field hands on her farm. A prominent theme in much of her correspondence and throughout the "Candlelit" columns was the unrelenting nature of obligatory correspondence. "This is the 25th letter I have written this morning," she wrote Faith during the summer in 1913, "so I must be brief." Two months later she wrote Faith that hers was the ninth letter she had written so far that morning, one of which was twenty pages long.[41] The 1910s were busy years for her in many ways. "During the spring and summer of 1914," she wrote in *As a Woman Thinks,* "I put seventy acres of the valley under cultivation, added eight rooms, and wrote a serial."[42]

The pace remained fairly constant throughout her life, even after her health declined, and at times even after she was bedridden. John Paschall recalled that in 1931, just days after he visited Harris in the Valley to "urge" her to write for the *Atlanta Journal,* she "expressed grave doubt" that she could keep up the pace of three "Candles" a week. Ten days later, however, to his astonishment and delight, she sent him twenty-four short articles, enough copy for eight weeks.[43] In 1933 she wrote Medora Perkerson of the *Journal:* "I have entertained four sets of house guests during the last 10 days not to mention callers everyday, I have written ten 'Candles,' supervised stone work in the garden, contended with tenants and a heavy correspondence."[44]

In late 1934, just months before she died, Harris published a response to a letter she received in which someone referred to hers as a seemingly "perfect life." In a reply that covered two nine-inch newspaper columns she carefully detailed a typical day in her life, which involved efforts to reply to copious correspondence, constantly interrupted by necessities of quotidian farm and home management. The piece ends with the reader vicariously exhausted from Harris's ability to relate so effectively this day in the "perfect life" of one hardworking individual, only to discover that this represents only half a day; she had only recounted events to lunchtime.[45] When Faith was distressed over work, Harris reminded her to reflect on the philosophy of her grandmother and Harris's mother, Mary White: "happiness will consist in the labor, not the achievement."[46]

Mary White taught her daughters to seek satisfaction in doing a given job, not in completing it. To work to get through with work was, to her, a sign of indolence. Harris wrote Faith about her mother's work creed at the end of one day that had been particularly tiring—she had written more than seven thousand words on a serial. "If I give it up," Harris wrote, referring to the conviction that gratification comes only after work is completed, "I should find peace in just *doing*. I remember my mother used to throw up to me that the laziest woman she ever knew was one who worked herself to death in order to sit down and do nothing. I used to do that way every time she made me work. I *hated* work so that I worked hard so as to finish it. Well, work cannot be finished, I know now, until you cannot work any more."[47] But nothing stopped her for any length of time from working. Even when she complained that she had too much to do, she knew that she "had not been working too hard, because nobody can. You are supposed to work up to your limit like every other living thing in Nature, thus meeting death on good terms according to your season."[48] If "working up to your limit" was the only criterion by which Harris judged herself, she surely met her death on "good terms."

Ironically, although the years leading up to the publication of *A Circuit Rider's Wife* were trying, Harris produced in those years some of her most significant work.[49] Her fame rested largely on her role as a novelist, but she learned a great deal about the art of fiction writing through her role as a literary critic from 1902 to 1909. Critiquing popular literature provided Harris with the opportunity to write as she was most comfortable, through the "expression of a binary relation," or comparing North with South—a method, as Immanuel Wallerstein writes, effectively used in discussing culture.[50]

As a literary critic from the South, Harris was already in a small minority. Michael O'Brien identifies five university-trained male academics, including William Peterfield Trent, the only one with a national reputation.[51] Harris, as a self-trained southern woman critic, made up an even smaller minority. Being an insider reviewing southern literature was both an asset and a liability. Talmadge rightly observes about her reviews as a whole something that was common to most of her works, namely, that "a conservative, moralistic viewpoint colored her literary criticism."[52] However, as L. Moody Simms notes, there was far more to her critique of southern literature than moralism.[53] Much of it was insightful and, for the time, courageous.[54] Throughout the decade she explained why there was such a dearth of good literature in the South.[55] Her most penetrating criticism came in 1905 when she revealed the shortcomings of *Southern Writers,* a book by William Trent that had received critical acclaim from the *New York Times,* the *Dial,* the *Nation, Forum,* and *Outlook.* Harris, however, reviewing for the *Critic,* expressed "major reservations."[56] At the time she had only three years' experience critiquing the South's literature, which makes remarkable the confidence with which she wrote.

Such confidence likely came from an experience Harris had in 1903 after publishing a review in which she proclaimed that fiction written by northerners was superior to that by southerners. Southern critics denounced her for what they perceived as a betrayal.[57] That experience helps to explain how she took on Trent with such candor and lack of restraint. Although Harris might have shared similar racial perceptions with Lost Cause advocates, she differed with them in many other ways. She might have condoned lynching, but she did not condone slavery. Regarding the antebellum classic *Uncle Tom's Cabin,* she wrote in 1906 that it was a "very good book . . . a mild one, considering the material from which the author had to choose. And it stimulated a worthy compassion for a very unfortunate class of beings."[58] By admitting in 1924 that "the South was wrong," she challenged a cornerstone of the Lost Cause.[59] In 1924 it was fairly safe if not necessarily popular to make such a statement. However, when she took on southern writers at the turn of the century, internal criticism was anything but safe, unless the reviewer wanted to live in exile.

Harris had learned quickly how "devotion to the Lost Cause became a test of loyalty to the South."[60] The cause was indeed a "war of ideas" fought with a religious fervor.[61] In 1904 she wrote that it was equivalent to committing a "sacrilege as if I had snatched a memorial wreath from a Confederate veteran's grave."[62] In "Fiction, North and South," published in 1903, after observing that the whole country was still in an "experimental stage" so far as literature was concerned and that the West would be the first area of the country to produce "great fiction," she conceded that northern literature "far surpasses" southern literature in quality, largely because of "educational advantages" in the North and the ability of northern writers to capture "the impetus of the universal mind." Southerners were too romantic, too sentimental, too idealistic—very simply, too mired in the "mind, manners and spirit of an antebellum past."[63] "Mentally," she wrote, "we are still on the defensive against the whole world, and every man born among us with a gift of romantic expression is expected to employ it chiefly to uphold the South, her prejudices and her glories, to say nothing of her misfortunes."[64] The South had a lot of "dramatic possibilities" but too little "dynamic" expe-

Fig 4. Corra Harris, 1925. Courtesy of Department of College Archives and Special Collections, Olin Library, Rollins College, Winter Park, Florida.

Fig 5. Corra Harris and students at Rollins College, Winter Park, Florida, 1930. Courtesy of Department of College Archives and Special Collections, Olin Library, Rollins College, Winter Park, Florida.

Fig 6. Corra Harris and Hamilton Holt, Rollins College, Winter Park, Florida, 1931. Courtesy of Department of College Archives and Special Collections, Olin Library, Rollins College, Winter Park, Florida.

rience to let go of the past. Although from the "vantage point of today it is not difficult to see the shortcomings" of the literature of the South of Harris's time, it was then nowhere near common knowledge.[65] In 1914, Harris was still recalling what it was like for southerner writers who chose "Southern types for his characters. When one of us does return . . . we sneak back with our tail between our legs knowing that we shall get what is coming to us for not writing better, nobler books about life in the South."[66]

Harris was noted for her disdain of realism in literature, especially references to sex, graphic portrayals of working conditions in factories, and hardships of life in general. She thought the subject of birth control particularly inappropriate in mixed company. Harris held similar views from early in her career as a critic until her death. She wrote in 1934 that "after reading 5 novels this year in which thirty-two births are dramatized I wish to go on record as being in favor of birth control in fiction." But she had a keen sense of the power of language in capturing the natural environment. She chided Mary Johnston (Virginia) and James Lane Allen (Kentucky) for failing to capture the richness of the South's unique environment. She suggested something for southern writers to ponder when developing scenes in their works: "There is a fever and a thirst in the land that predestines not only the life of the forests, but affects the temper and hopes of man." She added something that would have given a veteran realist pause: "There is a hooded, sinister silence in a Southern summer night, more depressing than all our sorrows, that Mr. Allen evidently knows nothing about."[67]

Although she criticized Allen for omitting a "sinister silence" that everyone knew existed in the South, in keeping with her contradictory nature, she criticized Thomas Dixon for the "darker undercurrents" he did expose. Harris had no respect for Dixon, neither personally nor for his writing.[68] She considered his "Leopard's Spots" (part of a trilogy from which the epic racist drama *Birth of a Nation* was made) nothing more than "a fierce appeal to sectional hatred."[69] Two months later she wrote elsewhere with even more contempt for Dixon's "The One Woman," an attack on socialism and the sexual license he believed inevitably accompanied it. Harris may have shared his aversion to socialism, but she considered depraved his use of the sexually explicit to make his point.[70]

Harris paid for her criticism of the South. She wrote about the experience of being reprimanded in "Patriotic Criticism in the South," a follow-up article in the *Critic*. Harris responded with respect but candor to the United Daughters of the Confederacy and other "club women" offended by her critique of southern literature.[71] She understood their concern and empathized with the "repulsion, resistance, and antipathy" that characterized attitudes toward outsiders. "Our strength," she wrote candidly, "consists in resenting every outside effort, however well-meant, made to modify our formula of existence." Paradoxically, however, this very "determination to make our own scriptures accounts for the social, literary, and political tragedies that occur from time to time in this section."[72]

But resistance to outsiders was not the only reason southern literature suffered. It was just as much the "club women" who stood guard over the heritage and raised the banner of southern patriotism when anyone dared not "stretch their faculties in a forty-years' perspective over the battle rim of the sixties." Such public reprimand was "destructive to the creative faculty [and] originality of expression" and explained "why so many Southern authors squat about in military cemeteries to write their novels."[73]

Four years after writing "Patriotic Criticism" Harris was more ardently blaming blind adherence to the Lost Cause for making it impossible for young "literary aspirants" in the South to publish anything but "whangdoodlism." Such retrograde thinking would have irked the veterans about whom the cause was ostensibly organized. The first thing these long-dead Confederates would do if they could come back from the dead, she believed, would be to "kick all such puerile talkers into that state of innocuous desuetude where they belong."[74]

By the time Harris reviewed Trent's *Southern Writers* she had honed her critical skills and, with proverbial "all due respect," exposed his privileging regional patriotism over "literary patriotism." She acknowledged how challenging it was to tell the truth in the South: "Everyone resents the truth, but in the South we make a battle-ground business of resenting it, which has made literary criticism too much a matter of circumspection." But Trent, having paid the price for publishing a not-so-flattering biography of William Gilmore Simms in 1892, had been too willing to retreat. She understood, having just experienced her own reprimand, but she could not let it pass that in *Southern Writers*, to make up for his past betrayal, Trent had numbered Sam Houston and Robert E. Lee among "representative 'Southern Writers'" of the antebellum era.[75]

Harris's courage is most apparent in her retort to Trent's explanation for the dearth of quality literature in the South. Trent blamed the absence of credible art on the "rural aristocratic system" in the South, not, he is careful to point out, on "mental or spiritual defects on the part of the Southern people." She replies, "conditions and institutions do not explain everything that went right or wrong in the South any more than they do elsewhere. After all, it is the people who are responsible for both."[76]

Harris believed that southerners were pathologically consumed with developing personality over intellectual or moral development. "For just as the South coveted the romance of living grandly, heroically, and a little absurdly, New England coveted 'the best gifts' along the lines of intellectual and moral development." She continues: "The South produced orators and public men rather than literary artists, not only because she needed statesmen to defend her institutions, but because by temperament the Southerner is a sort of demigod . . . and prefers to stand above the eyebrows of a crowd, demonstrating the fact in appropriate language, to writing a book."[77] Trent excused the absence of poetry with the remark that Civil War poetry was marked with an "intensity of emotion that somewhat hampers cool criticism," to which Harris responded, again as if to suggest he had a flare for the obvious, "That is the point. Everything the Southerner is or has done challenges calm criticism upon the same grounds."[78] In 1909 Harris was still troubled by the fact that even though the South was the most fertile region of the nation for literary possibilities, whether one wanted to romanticize existence or portray reality, it was still chronically "behind the times" in literature.[79] She continued over the course of the decade to point out the deficiencies in the region's fiction until she began publishing novels herself.

In the century's first decade, when Harris wrote most of her literary criticism, she had little good to say about southern writers. About the only good served by the sentimentalism and romanticism in which southern writers were mired was that it kept most of them (Dixon excluded) from "sexual perversity" and from revealing the "darker undercurrents" of life.[80] Such was understandable coming from a woman who believed that "the ultimate end of every human life is romance," who "spent the whole of my writing life trying to cover up what should not be seen, believed or suspected."[81] Even though she admitted that Upton Sinclair's *The Jungle* resulted in reform, she concluded shortly afterward that novels aimed at provoking reform would generally fail to work toward that end because the class to whom they needed to appeal for help had stomachs too delicate to digest the realism.[82]

Harris appreciated Will Harben for portraying mountain people in north Georgia with what she considered originality. She approved of Ellen Glasgow's novel *Deliverance* for being forward- rather than backward-looking, though in 1907 she seemed to agree with a reviewer who dismissed Glasgow's *Wheel of Life* as wholly unoriginal.[83] In 1908 she claimed that

J. Breckinridge Ellis's *Arkinsaw Cousins,* a novel that "contain[ed] remarkably sympathetic and wittily drawn portraits of Southern types," would have
been a success if readers had cared more for literature than for "fairy lore
about the South."[84]

Such, in essence, revealed to Harris a very large part of both the problem
and the explanation for the sad state of literary affairs in the South. She understood the workings of a market economy and lamented the fact that even
literature had became a victim of market forces. "A new novel," she wrote,
"becomes more and more a question between the author and the publisher,
and less and less a voluntary, unhampered expression of life inspired by
purely artistic motives." Furthermore, it was not so much southerners' need
to dramatize and sensationalize a past that even they knew never really existed as it was northerners' need to read about that romanticized past:

> This is why we continue to be persecuted with stories of the Civil War
> period. The reading public which is *not* the South, retains a romantic
> interest in a class of people who no longer exist, and the like of whom
> they never saw among themselves. The publishers are well aware of
> this fact. . . . All this is well enough for the people of the North if they
> are so sick for fairy lore about the South, but it is hard upon writers
> from this region who are making an honest effort to produce vital fic-
> tion. It is doubtful if any of them would recognize an up-to-date novel
> of Southern life even if such a thing were to be had.[85]

She feared that Harben, who had received far "less attention than he deserves, because he leaves out the Civil War," would be seduced by temptation and financial necessity at just about any time to "make a fool of himself" and start writing "fairy lore" for the market.[86]

In 1908, still lamenting the dearth of good literature to come out of the
South, Harris offered a further explanation. Southerners had plenty of intelligence and more than enough "dramatic material," "but *nothing,*" she wrote,
"will induce us to tell the truth about ourselves that is not complimentary,
no matter how thrilling it should prove to be." The reason was that there
was no demand, no "enlightened intelligence" among readers. And this was
because "we lost the leisure and peace of mind after the war which makes
novel readers."[87]

In the first decade of the century Harris had an awareness of the systemic
causes of the South's regressive status and the role played in this by a political economy, an inferior educational system, and the inordinate hold of a
romanticized past, among other causes. That awareness stands in stark con-

trast to the dispassionate conclusions about social conditions in the South and elsewhere that came to govern her thinking for many of the following years.[88]

Unquestionably, whatever Harris wrote about the burdens of establishing and sustaining a writing career, when these factors were weighed against her life as a whole, the benefits of success exceeded the drawbacks.[89] Having her work well received and well remunerated was deeply gratifying to her at many levels. In most of her autobiographical accounts she wrote about how the work brought affirmation. And though she claimed that happiness itself was forever escaping her, she credited writing with bringing her closer to that elusive dream than anything else. "I came nearer to what happiness must be," she wrote in 1925, "a sort of deliverance from the things that are, after I began to do creative work. Once I had a pen in my hand and the use of my faculties, the casements of all my darkness were flung wide and I escaped into a very bright, quiet, good world of thoughts."[90]

The theme of escaping to the life of the mind graces Harris's writing throughout her career. In the early years it carried her through a troubled marriage, financial hardship, and the deaths of those she loved most; later, she escaped some of the trials of declining health by writing and publishing until just before she died. In the beginning of her career she wrote editor Paul More: "In your last letter you explained that you did not wish to overtax my 'kindness' in asking for book reviews. That would be impossible. Nothing in all my life has ever afforded me half the pleasure as does this work."[91] Similarly, near the end of her life she wrote to John Paschall, managing editor of the *Atlanta Journal,* how much she appreciated the job he had given her to furnish the "Candlelit" columns: "I am joyfully indebted to you . . . for something that is worth more than any money you could have paid, that is to light this little candle on your page."[92]

Harris found writing deeply gratifying.[93] It was the closest thing to happiness she ever felt. "Many a time when I have filched a grand thought or some finer truth out of life to write down, I am too moved to do it. I get up and pace the floor . . . or I rush bareheaded out of doors in the bleakest weather to cool off this happiness, so that presently I may return and copy it into words."[94] Once Faith could appreciate similar experiences, Harris shared with her something she knew would resonate: "The mind is a wonderful thing. It works when you do not know it is working, and suddenly a miracle is wrought."[95]

At times, writing was a form of grace that helped Harris bear personal tragedy, the one constant in a life filled intermittently with loss and disappointment. "I should have been dead years ago," she wrote Faith, "slain by the griefs and terrors of life if I had not escaped into self-expression, congenial work." Work was Harris's most effective coping strategy, and she advised Faith to make it her own: "The way is open to you. Don't be afraid!"[96] "Do not bear your burdens," she wrote. "Escape in your work."[97] "The only way I could save myself," she wrote Faith shortly after the breach between herself and Faith's husband, Harry, was "*not* to think, but just to *work* from morning until night. I have done that as much for you as for myself, that I might not lose my spirit, nor my interest in life. . . . I have not and I will not allow myself to suffer."[98] Work kept Harris sane and balanced during the most trying times. It even sustained her through the shock and grief of her daughter's death, as she poignantly recalled a few years later in her first autobiography: "What I kept saying to myself was that I would get up presently and go back to work."[99] Work was the intimate companion that alone could console, or perhaps numb, her through a grief for which otherwise there would have been no relief.

Being a writer was one of Harris's favorite subjects to write about and was a frequent topic in the "Candlelit" columns. In one column she wrote that it was an all-consuming occupation that seemed at times to undermine normal "living": "One cannot live and write copy at the same time. . . . I believe I have a real talent for living . . . but I shall never be able to prove it for more than a day or two . . . so long as I am obliged to write to earn a living."[100] As long as writing is one's livelihood, she explained, "You can never choose your own duties or pastimes again. You must work at your thoughts. They hold you and compel you like voices calling to be heard."[101] "Because thoughts 'are like children born to us.' They must be developed, and shaped up into words so that the reader may enjoy them without thinking."[102] "I would give much to cast my pen far from me and follow it out and away," she wrote. "But I cannot take the day off. I must stay here and write down the things my mind makes believe."[103] "Every author knows what I mean. We become the slaves of our thoughts that must be written before they fade into forgetfulness."[104]

Harris could be philosophical about her fame and her talent. In a letter to Paschall she captured poignantly what she valued most in life. However much she identified herself as a writer, that was just a part of who she was. Although she was an exceptionally private person who dwelled much in her mind and limited her friendships, it was herself in relationship that defined her essence. "I suppose that no woman in this country is praised in the peculiar way that I am," she wrote Paschall. "But it . . . seem[s] . . . a little like cheating to take their praise seriously. For they only knew me by the words on a printed page. . . . But after all it was just words they read. And who can know a man by his words, or a woman either." She regarded the praise of anonymous readers as so much flattery, but "what has fed me and sustained me was either sorrow that lifted me out of myself, or, the inspiration I re-cieved [*sic*] from those who really knew me and believed in me.[105]

Harris wrote often about how taxing a writing career is, but she also be-lieved that anxiety catalyzed inspiration. "I have got to feel opposition as well as encouragement," she wrote.[106] Anxiety was a double-edged sword of sorts: it held her hostage, but without some sort of vexation she could not write. She wrote More that once her mind went into "an eclipse" because of "the inertia of peace and content," and "I was ready to pray for all my anxiet-ies just to get quickened again mentally."[107] In 1913, while away from home to escape domestic pressures and find some inspiration, she confided to Faith, "I came up here almost overwhelmed with anxiety over the future and with the obligations it entailed, but they have slipped from me like water from a duck's back. I am placid and serene. Though I am a little anxious about my serenity now."[108] In 1923 she wrote Lorimer about the year she lived at Ox-ford, Georgia. It was the best year of her married life and the only "rest" she had "from this awful strain," yet she saw in retrospect that such contentment threatened to make her "into an invalid."[109] Life never failed for any length of time to provide Harris with the anxiety she needed to keep her inspired.

Of the paradoxes that characterize Corra Harris, the disparity between her successful determination to be her own person, to be "ever resolutely herself," and the self-doubt she suffered about the merits of her work vies to head the list. In 1902 she wrote More about her realization that she was unprepared for a career publishing literary criticism for a national audi-ence: "For myself, I have never written anything over a three inch review of a novel that I did not actually suffer over the uncertainty of its merits. And *anybody* can convince me that what I have written is a poor thing."[110] Friends, she wrote later that year, had to put her to bed with a fever when she grew ill over realizing what a "fool" she had been for writing book reviews as if she knew what she was doing:

The day before I had spent reading over all my reviews of the past year in the *Independent*. There was not an intimation in a single one of them that the critic had ever read what the masters say of the *art* of criticism. All of them were idiotically original, impudently so, truth-ful, I *will* say that for them, but there was no foundation of information back of them. How could there be? I don't know anything! . . . "I have just discovered that I am a *fool*," I explained, between chattering teeth. "I have no sense at all for the sort of work I have been doing!" Enough to give anybody a chill, wasn't it?[111]

Moreover, not even years of success delivered Harris from self-doubt. Toward the end of her life she expressed similar sentiments, writing Medora Perkerson in 1931, "I have a despairingly poor opinion of my own work."[112] "I have never had any confidence in my copy nor in myself," she confided to Paschall in 1934. "This has made me a temperamental mendicant all my life."[113] "The smart old bareheaded woman of me who always sits in the back door of my mind, keeping [an] . . . eye upon my literary performances, never has had any confidence in me as an author," she wrote in *My Book and Heart*. "She suspects it is a trick I turn. For years her secret criticisms have embarrassed . . . me . . . like the snicker of an unfriendly audience sitting off somewhere in the dark."[114] Plagued by such self-doubt, Harris found it difficult to fathom her reputation for being arrogant about her work. As early as 1912 she was aware that "I have the appearance of being a middle aged, impudently assured woman about my work," she wrote Lorimer.[115] "The thing I cannot understand," she wrote Paschall not long before she died, "is how I produce the impression of [being] a formidable old ass, dedicated to the propogation [*sic*] of my own conceit when I am the humblest of writers when it comes to judging my own copy. I am so stricken with the consciousness of my limitations that I rewrite it over and over in a sweat of dispair [*sic*], because it never . . . [is] as good as I should do."[116]

Paschall at first found Harris's candid revelation of self-doubt difficult to believe. "Somewhat awed by the brilliancy of her mind, the wit of her conversation, the magic of her seeing and understanding and interpretation," he was "even more surprised by her littlegirl attitude."[117] His description of Harris's attitude aptly captures her relationship with some of her editors. She could be everything associated with little girls, from innocent, naive, and charming, to coy and coquette, to irascible and unpredictable. Her editors brought out the best and the worst in her.

Harris could be as self-revealing with her editors as she was with family, and sometimes even more so. She had long-term relationships with several editors. In a 1933 speech she claimed to have served "a sentence of nearly thirty-five years [of] hard labor under the wardenship of fifty-five editors all told," to "have buried about three times as many editors as will ever get the chance to bury" her, and hence felt well qualified to render an opinion on them. Harris took the opportunity to do so when members of the Emory Institute of Citizenship and of the Georgia Press Institute asked her to speak at a joint session. The event's organizer, Dr. Harvey Cox, suggested she speak about "The Feminine in Politics." She declined and instead chose editors as her topic, a subject on which she felt far better suited to speak. Although she had written volumes on women, she told the assembled group, apparently unabashedly, "Women should never discuss other women."[118]

To Harris, editors were in a class by themselves, alone in being outside the reach even of prayers. "It will not do to trust God in dealing with an editor, for the Lord is apparently indifferent to exercising His will over them when it comes to judging copy." She often referred to editors in deific terms. They were like gods "with blue pencils stuck behind their ears."[119] "I submit to editors as I do to the mercies and adverse judgments of God," she wrote Paschall.[120]

Harris never overcame her obsessive need for praise and constant feedback from editors. Her need for praise especially from editors is a common theme in her correspondence, especially with those whom she admired and respected. Perhaps no one knew her better in her last years than John Paschall. After her death he delivered a eulogy at the dedication of her memorial chapel. Shortly after she first started publishing the "Candles," he wrote to a newspaper syndicate about Harris, who was sixty-two at the time: "What has amazed and gratified us most has been the girlish enthusiasm she has evidenced over this work. . . . It pleased and flattered me that during the several years of our happy association, she showed so much conscientious concern about the quality of her work for The Journal and my humble approval of it as an editor. This attitude on her part was in no sense feigned. It was a little girl quality that characterized her whole career as an author."[121]

Harris's relationship with many of her editors can be described as being as much familial as professional. Talmadge described her relationship with William Ward, the *Independent* editor with whom Harris began her career, as that of "an unpredictable daughter" with an "indulgent, amused father."[122] She had a similar relationship with Paschall, with whom she ended her career. Unlike Ward, however, Paschall was younger than Harris. With Holt and Lorimer she had what may be considered more of a sibling relationship. She regarded them as brothers and felt a great deal of affection and admiration for them. She confided in them, especially in Lorimer, with her crises of faith and other personal issues. She found Holt's admiration of and appreciation for her and her work very gratifying considering that he held what she considered exacting standards. Her early affection and regard for

Holt surfaced in a letter to Paul More in 1904: "I do not love anyone so much as I do Mr. Holt, not you or anybody, outside my home you know. . . . You arn't [sic] kin to me, but some way he is. He is the real thing."[123]

Harris wrote More in 1901 about her feelings for the editorial staff at the *Independent*: "I think of you as the most inspiring editors [sic] and of Mr. Holt as the most merciless disciplinarian of a crude mind."[124] "Dr. Ward has the warmest, least protected heart of any of you."[125] In 1933 she wrote about Lorimer what was a common perception among periodical circles: "George Horace Lorimer is the greatest editor of his times. . . . His powers of telepathy are so strong that he never misses counting correctly the pulse beat of this nation."[126] She wrote to Lorimer on the occasion of his thirtieth anniversary with *Saturday Evening Post,* "You were the seer of hidden mind, publishing from week to week not only what men are thinking, but what they will think!"[127]

Harris had an infamous reputation for being especially sensitive about feedback—to be precise, the lack of it—from editors. And she was that way from the earliest days of her career until the end. The majority of her letters to More are filled with plaintive requests for some sort of feedback. This request while he was at the *Independent* is typical: "I must have a word of some sort from some of you . . . or I am like an actor who has lost his cue. I am out of touch."[128] During the first decade of her career, her insistence on feedback was as much to relieve loneliness as it was the need for responses to her work. She wrote More in 1903 of an awareness of what becoming a writer would cost her, namely, chronic loneliness. Not only the experience of isolation required to write but also the intellectual growth that resulted from writing had begun to alienate her from those around her: "I feel it more and more that the way I am coming up, growing, is going to make me pretty lonesome after a while."[129]

A passage from an early letter to More captures something of what became a typical effort for Harris to explain herself. In response to something More wrote about the need for her to try to balance her inordinate passion for learning and writing, she wrote: "Mr. More, sanity and poise are not my distinguishing characteristics. The chief thing about me is that I am alive, with so much vitality of mind and will that though I died a thousand times, I should inevitably 'live again.'"[130] She once responded to a generic form More sent her to reply with pertinent information, a form that she considered a substitute for more routine letter exchanges. In a jesting tone but with serious intent, she wrote that she was pondering a way to "defend myself against this epistolary injustice." She was not sure what she would do, but she assured him that "getting what I want is a fine art, and I shall get the kind of letters you write in spite of all your precautions!"[131]

Her relationship with John Phillips of the *American* magazine was not as long-standing as others, but his letters to her illustrate how the experience with Harris was common. "If I do not answer your letters with the feeling and in the spirit that you would like," Phillips wrote, "you will know it is not because of misunderstanding you but simply because of the demands of work."[132] A little later the same year, Phillips wrote in thinly veiled exasperation that he did not "know how I can make it more clear" that they were pleased with her work.[133] Holt was forever having to assure her that he and the others were very satisfied with her work and that if she thought otherwise she was reading meanings into his letters that were not there. "You are the greatest person for always thinking that my words mean something else than what I intended," he wrote in 1906. "Have I not told you a thousand times that if I am dissatisfied with you (and I have never been yet) I would tell you so plainly."[134]

Russell Doubleday of Doubleday Page & Co., after assuring her, "Of course we are interested in your books," wrote, "I hope you will not consider me unkind if I say I think you should not be so sensitive. I am afraid you are inclined to read . . . into acts and phrases, meanings that are not intended in the least and are really not there."[135] Harris frequently wrote Arthur Vance of *Pictorial Review* while she was in one of her "belligerent moods," convinced that he was trying to pull something over on her. "I am sorry you should have misunderstood our purpose," Vance wrote.[136] Once she wrote him that she heard editors were banding together in New York to underpay writers and that she had no intention of taking a penny less than she was accustomed to being paid. He wrote back wondering, "Aren't you feeling well and what kind of editors have you been dealing with lately!"[137] Another time he jestingly invited her to come to his office so they could have it out: "For once I got the best of you. . . . When you get to New York, call me up and we will have a friendly argument."[138]

Harris had close friendships as well as working relationships with many of her editors. In reply to Harris's concern that she be able to censor Charles Dobbins's biography of her being published by the *Atlanta Journal*, Medora Perkerson wrote her, "don't worry about it a minute. There are lots of reasons why we want to stay friends with you, the main one being that we love you."[139] Certainly one of the warmest friendships she had was with John Paschall. He and other *Journal* staff enjoyed many memorable visits to the Valley. In 1934, when Harris was staying in Winter Park, Florida, with Hamilton Holt over her birthday, Paschall wrote her to hurry home so they could "get the gang together and fling a beer party in the Valley that will scandalize the whole Pine Log section." He closed with his "love to the life of the party."[140]

In one of her last letters to Paschall before she died, Harris wrote about an uncharacteristic impulse that had come over her in her years of declining health. She knew she was beginning to act the way very old and infirm people act. "For example, Sunday [with many guests present] . . . I suffered an almost overwhelming temptation to . . . kiss each guest politely sidewise on the cheek or forehead." She resisted the urge because she did not like to be kissed and hence would not impose a kiss on others who might feel the same. But by then she often felt more affection than she knew what to do with. "The disposition to kiss others comes over me sometimes like a happy tune." But she knew what such emotions meant. "It indicates the same sign of emotional disintegration . . . which makes the Methodist Conference superannuate a preacher who cannot lead in prayer without beginning to sob to the Lord." She would have been embarrassed at such feelings earlier in life, but by then she realized they were a pleasant alternative. At least she had not grown mean and discontented.[141]

Harris realized some things about herself in relationship with the *Journal* in general but Paschall in particular that surprised even her as nothing short of a revelation. All her work to that time had been with book-publishing companies or national periodicals. They were not like daily newspapers. That was one thing that made Paschall different. She confided to him, "One reason I make so many tragic mistakes in dealing with you is that I never knew . . . an editor like you. The [others] . . . never are apologetic when they return copy. They give me hell and leave me sobbing in the dust of dispair [*sic*] till I take up my cross . . . and walk. Neither are they satyrical [*sic*]. They slay me with a 'blunt instrument' and let it go at that."[142] Paschall had a difficult time fathoming Harris's lack of confidence in her work. She wrote him that she was forever worrying that he was going to fire her from the *Journal* because one of her "Candles" turned into a "smoking torch" or because she said something impolitic that embarrassed the paper.[143] If she sent in a "batch of Candles" and did not hear from him, she wrote, she always thought it meant "the same thing." "I have fully expected to get my walking papers anytime, and have wondered if I should not have the courage to beat you to it by resigning before you put me out." Thankfully, a letter from Paschall fully supportive of her work brought her relief. She would not after all have to resign or "risk being jilted by a paper," even one that covered "Dixie like the dew!"[144]

Paschall told her something he could not imagine she did not already know. His response reveals the difference between her self-perception, in this case as that of "an old lamb," and the way others perceived her, as self-possessed and self-confident. Once he realized, after many pleading letters from her for some positive feedback, that she was serious, he wrote that she did not "need my praise." In fact, "I even suspect that you are getting too much already—you are getting hard to please. You ask for something 'pleasant' but you don't like it if I say 'nice'—you don't like mush and you won't have pie. I tell you that I like your copy, admire your genius and worship your sweetness and you say I am spoofing—and I don't like this 'old lamb' stuff—you are very dear to Bettie and to Trannie and to Bill and to me, and to your readers but you are nobody's 'old lamb.'"[145]

Juxtaposing her perception of herself as an "old lamb" against her friends' perception of her as a genius (among other commendable things) reveals the many sides of Harris. Four months before she died, Harris wrote Paschall about an "aha" moment she had during a casual conversation with another contributor to the *Journal*. She finally "got it" about dealing with editors. This other writer helped her to see that especially when working with editors of newspapers, news copy came first. The other "experienced newspaper writer" said that a columnist "should be thankful if the editor didn't say anything." "Somehow for the first time since I had been working for you I caught on," she wrote. "And by what I consider a miracle of readjustment, I settled down to enjoy this column myself, and to stop being a mendicant begging for praise." She hoped he would agree she was behaving much better" and was no longer hanging like a stone around your neck, begging for the ointment of a few kind words."[146]

As her nephew Al Harris confessed, and as she was even quicker to confess, Corra could be difficult at times. Her successful career afforded her the liberty to be eccentric and to indulge as much of her personality, which included a quick temper, as she felt inclined. But whatever her eccentricities, people such as Paschall recognized "the light of her genius" and found great "satisfaction" in believing that through her work she "did literally achieve her heart's desire." That desire was, she Harris wrote in a letter to him, "to die with the seven league boots of my mind on."[147] She had written to the very end. The *Journal* published posthumously a few from the stockpile of "Candlelit" columns. In those short works some of Harris's most interesting reflections on the controversial subject of religion appear.

8

From Circuit Rider's Wife
to Spiritual Pundit

In 1933, J. E. Hall, an attorney friend, wrote to thank Corra Harris for her hospitality on a recent visit he made to the Valley. He was so impressed with her private "dissertations on all that matters in life" that he suggested she "do something to humanize the Bible," to make it "more intelligible to the average person," so readers would be "relieved" of its "forbidding aspects."[1] Indeed, much of Harris's discourse, written and spoken, was filled with biblical nomenclature. Grant Overton, a literary critic who recognized Harris's national identity, also valued her literary use of the Bible. Overton wrote, "no other American writer has that homely vigor and Biblical phraseology." And Milton C. White, a professor of English at Millsaps College in Jackson, Mississippi, wrote Harris in 1933, "I believe no American author has seen more into human character and certainly none has attained a like vividness and concreteness of imagery in the portrayal of spiritual things."[2]

For someone whose national reputation during her life and more lasting legacy since then have been largely based on a novel about an itinerant Methodist minister, Harris's religious identity is undeniably central to understanding her. Although she was, as one scholar wrote, "famous for her attachment to traditional religion and piety," such a reputation belies her religious identity. In 1933 Harris admitted, "I have totally changed my conception of christianity [sic] at this point."[3] But long before then she had begun to wonder about her orthodoxy; she wrote in 1901 that she expected the very "by laws of Heaven" would have to be amended "if I get in!"[4]

Harris's reputation for conservative, traditional Christian values is understandable given the moralism that pervades her work. Harris called herself a "moral snob," often used the discourse of southern evangelicalism, believed the Ten Commandments ought to be taught in school, and preferred the Old to the New Testament.[5] In much of her fiction she repudiated the liberal theology that was challenging orthodoxy all over the country in the late nineteenth century.[6] Generally, she seemed to promote a fairly simple religious philosophy in which folk just ought to behave, and, when they failed to do so, ought to be made to suffer the consequences and be done with it. Such simplicity describes the surface of Harris's religious thought but contradicts the fuller picture. As Charles Dobbins wrote, Harris "adopted a more or less independent spiritual platform," so it is a "practical impossibility" to pin her down to any particular set of beliefs.[7]

About at least one thing, however, Harris was consistent. Throughout her life she identified herself as a Methodist, if "emeritus" or "superannuated," even though she "quit the church" soon after she started publishing.[8] If, when she arrived in heaven, God asked who she was, she would answer, "I am a Methodist," one "unconfined, outside in the Lord's pasture at large," no matter how much the "loftier saints" might protest.[9] But her Christianity reveals complexity, contradiction, and (as she admitted at times) downright blasphemy, if held to her region's definition of orthodoxy.

Corra Harris, the circuit rider's wife, was *in* but clearly not *of* the evangelical South. In thinking and behavior she was a long way from either traditional piety or the region's evangelical tradition. Although she believed in an afterlife and wrote at times (often blithely) about "working out one's own salvation with fear and trembling," she was not at all "salvation-minded" or "otherworldly." She did not believe in hell.[10] There would be no eternal damnation—neither for Roman Catholics, for whom she had deep regard, nor for atheists, for some of whom she held deep affection, nor for anyone outside or in between those two. She believed evil existed, but she did not believe in a personal devil. Her faith did not depend on a belief in the inerrancy of scripture. Even though she respected the Bible's moral authority, she claimed to read it more as literature than for instruction. Her works often suggest deism rather than evangelicalism. Whatever theological position she took, she was a naturalist. Her experience of the divine was at times personal, but more often she wrote of God as an impersonal force.

Harris would not have considered herself ecumenical, and she had an especially low regard for Gandhi, whom she dismissed as a "cracked" "Hindu fanatic."[11] But some of her writings reveal an understanding as much Eastern as Western in it emphasis on the symbiotic relationship between humans and the natural world. When she left California after a trip there in 1925, she admitted that if she had stayed longer she might follow up on a budding interest in Asian religious philosophies.[12] When she wrote about Jesus, she was more interested in his role as teacher and exemplar than as savior. At times she wrote of him as the "Way, the Truth and the Light," but she also called Christ an "illusion" and the cross a "symbol" as opposed to the basis of faith.[13] Her favorite image of God was that of Creator, the God of Genesis.[14] Harris saw no conflict between the theory of evolution and Genesis, and she thought William Jennings Bryan was wrong to "assail the theory of evolution."[15]

No matter how far Harris ventured from the region's prevailing religious ethos, she was never exiled for her departure.[16] If she received letters from many who sought to enlighten her on how to be "saved," many others were intrigued by or actually appreciated her ideas. A senior editor of the *Atlanta Journal* wrote her that he believed her "exposition of the text" on being "born again" was the best he had "seen or heard, outside of William James' *Varieties of Religious Experience.*"[17] For Harris being "born again" had nothing to do with piety, reverence, or any particular behavior, and everything to do with one's attitude toward others. To Harris, evidence of one's being "born again" was found in the ability to fulfill Christ's command to "love one another." And it was something one needed as often as one fell short of the command, and she lamented that for her personally it happened too often.

Among the influences shaping Harris's religious identity, southern culture figures prominently. No one born and raised in the South during her time could escape the influence of the prevailing Protestant evangelical ethos. It was a "social and cultural totality" that marked every facet of life.[18] There was no identity separate from it. It solidified, strengthened, and justified a caste/race, class, gender hierarchy more deeply entrenched in the South than anywhere else in the country. Because of the region's relative religious homogeneity, evangelical Protestantism was ubiquitous in the mind of most native southerners, whether in reaction or response.

Harris's religious identity was also influenced by the strong and stern religious practice of her mother, whose humorless God could be cold and unforgiving; by a father whose God by comparison was loving, merciful, and mirthful; by a husband who was "God-obsessed," a model of Flannery O'Connor's "Christ-haunted" Southerner; by the changes the southern Methodist Church underwent, particularly in Georgia, in the late nineteenth century; by Paul More, a mentor whose secular moralism seemed to validate that of southern evangelicalism; by the works of agnostics such as Anglican Matthew Arnold, whom she read avidly at More's instruction around the turn of the century; and by a life marked with tragic loss throughout her middle years.

But the most pivotal influence on Harris's religious thinking was the shift in her consciousness that occurred in 1899 when, from force of circumstance, she became her own "I am." With her own well-being and that of her family at stake, she decided to think and act for herself rather than surrender her will to her husband's, as she had done in the past. She wrote in *My Book and Heart* the "obituary of the woman I ceased to be" after that event.[19] She wrote repeatedly about the pivotal nature of the experience, claiming in 1931 that it "exercised more influence over the whole of my life than any other circumstance—more than love or happiness, than death or grief. In the deepest misfortune I was never quite sunk. . . . I had a curious confidence . . . at such times, supported by this idea of being backed by the Almighty."[20] Writing more than thirty-five years after the experience, she articulated the belief that informed it: she had "as much right as any apostle or sinner to interpret" God, the scriptures, creeds, doctrines, and so forth. She would "repudiate any idea of immortality which deprives me of the I AM sense I have of myself."[21] The decision fundamentally altered all of her relationships, including with herself.

Harris believed that God sanctioned her private rebellion against the myriad voices of restraint that kept her from being her own "I am." The resulting sense of self evolved through many stages. It informed her writing, her personality, and her behavior in ways that led people to interpret her in many opposing ways during her life and since. She struck people variously as arrogant, hypersensitive, diffident, confident, self-effacing, and humble. She provided ample evidence for each interpretation. She also had an uncanny self-awareness of her shortcomings, which disarmed many of those who saw her in unflattering ways.

The spiritual experience she had in 1899 inspired the autobiographical novel *A Circuit Rider's Wife* and ensured that Harris would spend her life pursuing over and over again the sense of empowerment and personal liberation which that event brought her. After the experience, for every time she wrote about her proclivity to be "superstitiously reverent toward authority," she wrote as well that nothing would keep her from thinking for herself, from being the "captain of my own fate."[22] In some of the changes she underwent, Harris mirrored Southern Tenant Farmers Union organizer Howard Kester, who, after his "religious populist radicalism" had run its course, "eventually return[ed] to a theology that distrusted all institutions and relied on a personal witness."[23] Her confidence in a philosophy of self-reliance is captured succinctly in an instruction she gave her daughter: "trust nothing, neither governments, nor God, but trust yourself."[24]

Harris's decision to allow nothing to intervene between herself and God illustrates Paul Harvey's point that "If white southern theology generally sanctified southern hierarchies, the belief and practice of Christians could also subtly undermine the dominant tradition."[25] Harris defied the hierarchy, though she never broke completely free from nagging guilt over the defiance. The point also suggests why no southerner living at the time, no matter how independent-minded, could be entirely free from the downward pull of the region's hierarchical ethos. For Harris, refusing to conform did not bring a life without regret. She wondered often if she might have been too independent and if such guarded independence—especially since women were not supposed to be—was the reason why happiness eluded her. Harris expressed both confidence and doubt about pivotal decisions in her life, but in the balance, when she wrote with confidence, when she wrote about times she felt fulfilled, and when she even considered herself happy, it derived from convictions she regarded as spiritually or religiously informed.

Because Harris was so closely identified with Mary Thompson, chiefly the fictional character in *A Circuit Rider's Wife*, there was confusion over Harris's Methodist roots. Unlike Mary Thompson, who grew up Episcopalian, Harris grew up Methodist. Even Edwin Mims in *The Advancing South* (1926) repeated the error that the Episcopal Church was the church of Harris's youth.[26] "Nothing could be further from the truth," Harris said.[27] She grew up in the Methodist Church and identified with it her entire life.[28] She felt far more affinity with the Arminian theology of the Methodist Church than with the Calvinism of the Baptist and Presbyterian churches, a common affinity, Anne Scott explains, of "most southern women."[29] A quote from Harris captures why women might prefer a theology with more "elbow room" in it, or one that seems to honor individuals' hard-fought battles to do and be good over a theology that predestines souls for eternal salvation or damnation ostensibly without regard for moral and ethical choices. "I have always lacked the doctrinal stamina to be a durable Baptist," she said in a speech. It is "less taxing to be a heart felt Methodist."[30] "Give me a creed, with more elbow room in it for my transient transgressions and more encouragement for believing I have a chance to save my own soul by growing my own virtues according to the Word, which I could not have if I got the notion that I was damned or elected from the foundation of the world."[31]

Two recent studies suggest relevant ways to approach religion in southern history. "Students should neither ignore nor restrict themselves to obviously holy things and sacred discourse," Donald Mathews writes, "but explore the full ramifications of the religious, both in the evil that humans do and in their capacity to survive it."[32] As a woman identified with southern Methodism, Harris thought and wrote about the subject of evil, typically asking how and why humans more often gravitated to hatred than to love in relationships with one another.

In a summary survey of women and southern religion, Lynn Lyerly makes a suggestion relevant to the influence of religion in Harris's life. She posits "a need to bridge the divide that still exists between scholars who ask what religion did *to* women and those who ask what religion did *for* women."[33] Religion did both in Harris's case. It did plenty *to* her in the sense that she might never have fully overcome the psychological damage caused by her mother's religious beliefs and the anguish she suffered from her husband's religious intensity. However, it also did much *for* her in many ways, two of which are of relevance here. Her spiritual values were the basis of her self-confidence and counterbalanced the self-doubt she suffered as a writer. She also derived acute self-awareness from her spiritual values. Harris's strongest buffer to criticism was a candid self-critique.[34] She very often confessed in published and private writings her personal biases, prejudices, "meanness," hatred, and other shortcomings. The self-effacing manner with which she wrote about herself did not reflect a lack of confidence, as some might interpret; to John Paschall it was arguably the "truest evidence of her greatness." Harris, Paschall noted, "spoke and wrote of herself and her work as naively as a child." She had an "honesty and integrity and . . . fearless mind that analyzed her own life and personality with the same frankness that she interpreted the people about her." Such self-revelation was, to him, the chief "virtue that distinguished Corra Harris."[35]

To understand the ways religion distinguished Harris requires a brief examination of the religious ethos of her day. The tenets of Protestant evangelicalism that covered the New South into which Harris was born were rooted in the Old South.[36] Writing about how they applied to women in the antebellum era, Ann Scott explains that "women communicants seem to have absorbed a common theological outlook." Although the "themes which recur in the diaries . . . are familiar to any student of evangelical religion," they are worth recalling. They include, Scott writes, an "emphasis upon prayer" and scripture reading; "constant cultivation of submissiveness"; "practicing goodness"; "raising children to fear God"; achieving "conversion"; and a "sense of one's own innate wickedness." Most women, regardless of the theology of their church, seemed to believe that "faith and works" were required for salvation, and they all seemed to believe in life after death.[37] Although these tenets were not unchallenged or unquestioned, they were so thoroughly understood that they did not need to be explained to anyone, whether within or outside the church.

Mathews explains how, once established, cultural symbols create an implicit "group awareness." They create "moods and motivations" that "flowed from 'an awareness of the group' or community establishing its integrity, solidarity, and meaning so that every white person understood what was sacred without opening a Bible, raising a prayer, or singing a hymn."[38] In the South, religion was "the pervasive ambience of society."[39]

Revivalism provided the forum for conversion, the central experience in evangelical faiths. Samuel Hill observes that William McLoughlin "makes no mention of the South" in his book on "revivals, awakenings, and reform" in the United States during the period from 1890 to 1920.[40] This was not because the South had no revivals, Hill explains, but because revivalism actually characterized the South. The North experienced an "Awakening" during those years through the revivals that made Dwight L. Moody famous, while the South had no such equivalent prophet/evangelist. Though Sam P. Jones was a noted revivalist of the time, his heyday actually predated the era (he peaked in the 1880s). The South by 1890 had more or less "fastened itself ever more firmly onto a form of religion basically characterized by revivalism. It was the standard fare of many churches and a common occurrence in most others."[41] Revivals were the norm in the South, not the exception.

The Civil War brought significant changes in every area of life, including religion, but the theological basis of southern religion did not outgrow its otherworldly preoccupation, which had positive as well as negative effects. On the positive side of change, white women found ways through the churches to rechannel energies used on the home front during the war into public roles endorsed by the church afterward. By insisting that women keep quiet in church, authorities "inadvertently provided Christian women with a road to emancipation."[42] They channeled that energy outward to causes such as the postwar South's celebrated Lost Cause. Without women the Lost Cause would never have been a cause, certainly not the successful and sustained one that it became.[43] The cause was a venue for women to think of themselves outside the exclusive constraints of domesticity. From Lost Cause monument building to education reform to interracial cooperation and many other efforts, white women headed the drive to reconstruct the South on its own terms. They may not speak out in churches or take leadership roles there, but they would do what women in the North had done in the previous eras and take their drive out of the home into the public sphere.

On the negative side, the emotionalism of evangelical Protestantism and an accompanying "segregationist folk theology" in the New South underwrote flagrantly unjust race relations and led at times to "dangerous passions."[44] Southern white evangelical Protestantism was "a religion of violence," with a "theology of vengeance" and punishment at its core.[45] Lynching became for NAACP official Walter White "the natural issue of a religion that was characterized more by passionate expression and emotional fury than by reflection."[46] In "The South's Two Cultures," Hill writes about the paradox of a region infused with a religion that teaches "love as the norm for human behavior" while simultaneously sanctioning violent racial oppression.[47] Harris embodied, as did the South's religion, some of the best and some of the worst of the contradiction and irony that set the region apart from the nation and the nation apart from the world.[48]

Because the South bore a "culturally aggressive and frequently arrogant evangelicalism," the region zealously resisted pressure from the outside to change.[49] And pressure came to all churches in the years after the war, creating what one historian called the "spiritual crisis of the Gilded Age."[50] The liberal theology responsible for those changes affected the South indirectly through southerners' reaction, or that at which they were best, "repulsion, resistance, and antipathy," as Harris wrote.[51] Church authorities erected a barrier that kept the crisis at bay from the Gilded Age through the Scopes trial in the mid-1920s and beyond.[52] While clergy (and eventually members) in most denominations outside the region struggled to reconcile orthodox views with the higher criticism that questioned biblical inerrancy, southerners mostly refused to hear the arguments. "The South . . . simply lived in a different theological time-zone," writes Hill.[53]

Generally, the region as a whole refused to give the new theology a hearing. Methodists were more tolerant than most other denominations. Vanderbilt was among the universities less "salvation-minded" and more "in touch with the wider educational scene," Hill writes, "in part because there were professors on their faculties trained in the Germanic tradition."[54] Additionally, the "absence of particularistic doctrines and exclusive pretensions" and Methodists' "active cooperation with other denominations inclined them to liberality in doctrinal matters, making them the more ready to examine critically their own creed."[55]

Harris examined all creeds critically. "I care so little for creeds, doctrines and mere mortal prejudices about God," she wrote, that "I should spew any God out of my mouth who could be defined by a creed or a doctrine."[56] She took what suited her and with little second thought left behind what did not. "Religion," she wrote, "is an intimate experience and comes according to the nature of individual men and women . . . [each of whom] must have an interpretation of the doctrines that fit him."[57]

In spite of the potential in a small minority of religious liberals, such as those in the Methodist Church, southern Protestantism remained firmly opposed to the "diversification" that characterized its northern counterpart. As a result, "Regional insulation, aberrant racial attitudes, economic backwardness, and religious orthodoxy were among those features which were changed very little."[58]

It seems incongruous to say that women moved into reform movements after the war while acknowledging that the social gospel, the praxis of liberal theology, was no more at home in the South than the higher criticism, but the South's religious "belief system" was as subject to "contradictory principles" as any other element of southern culture.[59] Expressing a commonly held view about southerners' preoccupation with otherworldliness over social reform, Wayne Mixon writes about religion in Georgia that "Many Christians, particularly Evangelicals, believed that the proper business of the church was to win souls to the Lord and then to encourage pious and moral living in preparation for the hereafter, and not to promote social reform."[60]

"The South's . . . dominant religious bodies had repudiated anything resembling a social interpretation of the gospel well before the Civil War," explains Hill.[61] And it was an ethos that remained firmly rooted afterward. It was not that southern churches were entirely otherworldly. Elsewhere Hill qualifies the characterization: "The churches of the American South have not been asocial or apolitical, rather, selective in the public causes to which they have devoted their passions."[62] Further, "Among the three leading Protestant denominations, women in the Methodist Church moved furthest in the direction of a social gospel," a phenomenon explained in part by the Arminian theology informing Methodist doctrine.[63] Southern women were able to utilize the ethos of the social gospel practiced in northern and midwestern churches by limiting the causes to those not considered a fundamental threat to the southern social order. Some of them challenged the system by engaging in suffrage activism and interracial cooperation; by

maintaining the image of ladyhood, they managed to subvert the threaten-
ing aspects of such issues.

For Harris, who had no interest in the public sphere and had a writing
career in her future, the Methodist Church, if not Arminian theology, had
begun to hold less influence on her religious ideals by the turn of the century. In 1901 she shared with Paul More changes taking place in her belief
structure at the time. At the age of thirty-two she recalled that two ideas in
the past decade had fundamentally "affect[ed] her viewpoint." One was "the
assertion that 'faith is an act of the will' made by a simple old preacher in [a]
holy roller church somewhere out in the country." The other was something
in More's last letter that had "made a profound impression upon her."[64]

More wrote her that freedom was innate in every person and that oppression was merely an illusion. She replied that she wanted to believe this
but found it difficult to do so, since her life and that of others around her
contradicted such a belief. At the time she wrote she was not far removed
from the experience of being "tenderly in touch with misfortune."[65] In time,
however, she willed herself to believe it. Within the belief was the potential
for personal liberation as well as justification for a belief in self-making. To
the extent that her success eventually validated the belief that oppression
was an illusion and that freedom was available to anyone who wanted to
claim it, Harris accepted the principle as a universal truth. That belief often
conflicted with her religious ideals as she demonstrated in her writings later
in life, particularly the "Candlelit" columns.

Later in 1901 she wrote More that through reviewing books she had come
to see that "real genius consists in holding together the conception you have,
allowing no idea of rights or wrongs from the outside to effect [sic] your
integral idea. To have the power to out last analysis and the disintegrating
influences of outside prejudices moral, or immoral."[66] As long as Harris
defined morality in terms of personal sins, as did the religious majority, her
"integral idea" was very limited. Once she began questioning the origin of
the moral order, her definition of morality expanded. She would begin to
insist that Christ's mandate to love was the fulfillment of the law and the
true measure of morality.

Harris spent the first decade of the century, the first decade of a very successful writing career, and the last decade of her married life with a growing
belief in two ideas, one encouraged and one largely forbidden to women in
her time and place: that faith was an act of the will, and that thinking for
oneself was the link to claiming one's innate freedom. As a self-described
willful child who had been forced to learn submission, she found it liberat-

ing to think that one could will faith, an essential trait for anyone raised in an evangelical environment, and that one could claim freedom, even if it meant she would have to find a way to cheat her fate as a woman.

For a while, Harris was torn between the need to believe in a personal, intimate God, the one she felt convinced responded to her prayer in 1899, and a conviction that so much of life's reality would make such a God seem merciless. Her belief in a God somewhere between the impersonal God of eighteenth-century deism and the personal God of Christian evangelicalism of her own day is revealed in a letter to More in 1902. It also reveals one of the reasons Harris had to "quit the church" to be able to write. "I am two or three days late in getting off my work this time," she wrote, and offered the following as a reason: "If you will consider that last week besides writing an editorial and reviewing nine books, I 'lead' the Women's Foreign Missionary Society meeting, went to a Baptist reception, a Methodist dinner, and a Presbyterian [luncheon], presided over the death bed of a Methodist baby and was chief comforter after the funeral. I would not be putting this in only I am proud of my record. None of it was difficult except the comforting. The mother had the orthodox notion that God had sneak [*sic*] out of Heaven and snatched her child just to punish her for something."[67] She went on to say that the baby died from overeating, an unlikely explanation, but useful for the point she was making, namely, that secondary causes, not a punishing God, were responsible for the baby's death. Another of Harris's strong suits was the ability to relieve grieving or dying people of guilt and fear of a vengeful God, as she had the baby's mother.[68]

By 1908 Harris had begun to focus on the stark differences she saw between rural and urban life, preferring the former because it allowed more interaction with nature. Her courtship with nature and the land was a theme she revisited many times in published and private writings, so much so that she was accused of pantheism.[69] She claimed that she was "closer kin to it [the land] than to thoughts, pieties or people."[70] In time she developed a spirituality based on humans' affinity with nature and the natural world as their surest link to God. Such naturalistic discourse fills many of her "Candles."

That Harris's writing career began in 1899 with a letter to the editor of the *Independent* defending the practice of lynching indicates the centrality of race and race relations in her thinking. As set as they were, however, not even racial views escaped ambivalence in her mind. A few references illustrate Harris trying to think critically about an issue covered over in the southern psyche by generations of a certitude that generally did not tolerate critical thought. Her religious values did not erode the essentialism of her ideas about race, but they did force her to try and justify essentialist thinking. In the process, she had to deal with the contradiction between democratic spiritual ideals and exclusivist practices. Several examples demonstrate the point.

In 1899, in an essay about black women, Harris accepted as a given the assumption that all black women were promiscuous but shifted blame for their reputation from them to men, both white and black. To do so was much out of character for Harris, whose approach was usually to blame the victim, especially if the subjects were women. Black women, as she wrote elsewhere about "bad women" of any color who had been compromised morally, were "not really bad, but they have been damaged or damned by forces outside of themselves."[71] Repeating the belief that black women were sexually promiscuous, she conceded that they were first "every man's victim," including the white man. Furthermore, she argued that if northern philanthropists really wanted to make a difference in the lives of the "negro race" in the South, they would spend as much or more money to educate black women as black men.[72]

In 1905, Harris came close to endorsing W.E.B. DuBois over Booker T. Washington as the rightful leader for "the negro's social and political future." If the black race stood the chance of getting ahead, it would be through education in the liberal arts, as DuBois insisted, rather than in the industrial world where Washington saw their opportunity. "When a man is a sculptor, painter or poet," Harris wrote, "people do not know how to inquire the color of his skin."[73]

A thought-provoking example of Harris's thinking about race is a 1909 review of literature in the *Independent* in which she parodies novelists writing "Messianic stories." She suggests that authors inclined toward a modernized soteriology consider exploring an "apocryphal Christ" who could reconcile race relations in the South and, for effect, have him lynched rather than crucified.[74] She intimates here and suggests more explicitly elsewhere that the black race comprehends through empathic suffering the historical Jesus much better than the white race. "During the terror of lynching," Donald Mathews writes, "African-Americans experienced suffering and sacrifice, which many of them bore through religious understanding identified with the life, death and resurrection of the Christ."[75] They "perceived that the one broken on the cross suffered *with* and not for them."[76] Even if Harris never publicly denounced lynching, if she grasped this "homiletic insight that Jesus, too, was lynched" she might have shared in the "subversion of the myths that justified lynching."[77]

The short story "Jeff," published in the *Independent* in 1912, also reveals insightful thinking by Harris on race. It is worth noting a sidebar observation about history in the story that sets her ahead of her time. In an attempt to explain why she would spend two columns setting the scene in a story in which a black family is central, she writes that "we have too much glorifying history of great people and not enough intimate literature of undistinguished men and women," an insight rare even for a professional historian of the time.[78] "Jeff" shows Harris mired in rigidly held racial views on the one hand but questioning her essentialist notions of race on the other. The story illustrates her belief that spiritual hegemony could flatten cultural, even racial, barriers when the title character transforms from profligate to redeemed hero.

"Jeff" is set in Brandon, a small, fictional town in post-Reconstruction Georgia that has equal numbers of black and white residents and where the two races live "side by side . . . upon neighborly terms of mutual helpfulness and goodwill, without ever 'mixing' socially" (there was never a reason in Harris's mind for distinct social classes or races to mix). Jeff and his wife, Moll, the heroine, are a black couple who embody many racial stereotypes but clearly challenge others. The story opens with a flashback to Jeff, Moll, their two daughters (Mary and Nannie), and two unnamed sons moving to Brandon to escape a situation from Jeff's past to which the reader is not privy. Whatever prompted the move also led Jeff to shed his surname. An experienced quarryman, Jeff immediately takes a job at Brandon's slate quarry.

The narrator describes Jeff and Moll as moral opposites. Jeff is a gambler, a drunk, and a wife-beater, given when drinking to jealous rages and violent excesses. Moll is an exceptionally "virtuous" woman even though she derives from a "race where wives so often take French leave of their marriage vows." Jeff's moral violations are accompanied by a zealous enforcement of fidelity in Moll and chastity in Mary and Nannie. He leaves his sons to their vices, which happen to be the same as his own.

Jeff's existence in Brandon is unmarked the first ten years. Then, in a newsmaking act, he risks his life to save a Welshman at the quarry. However, the obvious strength and fearlessness required for the heroic feat provokes more fear than respect from Brandon's whites, making Jeff the object of community suspicion. Not long after saving one coworker, a white man,

Jeff murders another, a black man whom he discovers is the secret lover of his elder daughter, Mary. Interestingly, however, Mary "went astray" not because of a lack of virtue, which would have been more in line with traditional beliefs—including Harris's—about black women, but because of her father's "tyranny," or his practice of "Old Testament ideas about taking care of his" women. Once he learns of Mary's pregnancy, Jeff, in a drunken rage, seeks out her lover at a church revival and murders him. No one investigates the murder, since it was black on black, and Jeff goes unpunished. But he does not let Mary off. He "sentences" Mary to pay for her sins by becoming the family's domestic servant, forcing her to add to the family's income by taking in washing from white people.

Mary's "sentence" gives Moll "liberty" to wander at will, which she does fearlessly and beyond her husband's eye, finally enjoying the silence in which she had been forced to suffer for so long. Jeff gets away with murder, but his guilt nearly drives him insane. It makes him fear Moll and defer to her because of her purity and innocence in contrast to his sin and guilt. For the remaining years of her life Moll has the edge in their relationship.

Jeff's deliverance comes one day when, while hoeing in the field, he hears God audibly forgive his sins. Although the voice is actually that of the town jokester, it makes no difference to the outcome, which is Jeff's spiritual transformation and his eventual success as an itinerant preacher thereafter. The story ends with Jeff converting folk around the region wherever he went, "blessed" by God "as if his 'call' to the ministry had not been a practical joke." "Faith is a great thing, greater than love," Harris writes. Through mirroring her pivotal experience in 1899, she extends to Jeff an autonomy similar to that for which she credited her own strong faith. "It is the one amazing experience in a man's life that can literally change it from the way of darkness to the way of light."[79]

Several points in the story, primarily those characterizing the women, counter the obvious racial stereotypes. The description of Moll mirrors that of any white woman about whom Harris may have written who was resigned to the fate of marriage. Moll has the same look on her face that had been "worn . . . by all women since the days when the first one understood what marriage really is." The reference to "all women" infers no racial distinction. In Harris's mind, gender trumped race in this case. Moll wore the same look as any woman, and "so long as that look lasts she is a virgin and you cannot really possess her."[80] Moll and her daughter sit one evening together in the sort of "silence [that] belonged to those great scriptures of sorrow and suspense to which women in every clime and of all ages have contributed so much."[81] If Harris refers to Jeff most often in relation to his race—that is, he is black first and a man second—she refers to Moll primarily in relation to her sex: she is a woman who happens to be mixed racially. And she is, as are "all virtuous women," loyal to her not-so-virtuous husband, and lives in the hopes one day of seeing him reach a higher moral standard.

Although she portrays Jeff mostly stereotypically, Harris portrays Moll, Mary, and Nannie much as she would any white women in their roles. The best she warrants Jeff are some of the traits of the "best men"—black men dedicated to the virtues identified with white middle-class men at the turn of the century. There is not the same tone of fear—either implicit or explicit—of "moral contamination" in the story that one finds in her writings at the turn of the century, such as those reacting to the editorial on the lynching of Sam Hose.[82] However, she attributes no less dignity to Moll, Mary, or Nannie than she would to any white women. When writing about the black race through the prism of religion, faith and virtue humanized the family. By having God honor Moll's virtue and Jeff's faith, Harris illustrates the central and integrated role of the two traits in Arminian theology. The story's conclusion is no different from what it might have been if the family had been white. The key in this case is not race but virtue and faith, neither of which is a respecter of persons of any race. Paul Harvey found that when "compelled to choose between Christ and culture," in most cases most southerners, even prominent black ministers, "chose culture"—that is, chose the South's racial caste system over Christ's mandate to love.[83] "Jeff" demonstrates how Harris chose both; it reveals the way someone who may at times typically choose a blanket acceptance of racial caste could come up with a different perspective when she was forced to think through the assumptions.

In "Black and White," an article she published in 1930 in the *Saturday Evening Post,* Harris wrote about race in spiritual terms.[84] She credits African Americans primarily for maintaining their spiritual values in spite of the pressures of modernity. She claims that the black race "probably" predates the white or any other race, but that insight is eclipsed by her claim that the race had neither "energy nor conceit" to build anything "that could last long enough to betray his past even to an archeologist." The black race's past and character were hidden within its "strangely elusive mental processes." Unlike the white man, who was "synthetic," an amalgam, the black man was the "one man singular that God made . . . an original script of human nature laid away in the dark archives of man."

That was to her what gave the black man the edge on whites. The black man had an acute insight into the heart and soul of the white man; to the white man, however, the black man would remain an elusive mystery. The white man could never write a biography of the black man but the black man could write "the most revealing, veracious, entertaining interpretation ever written" of the white man, a view commonly shared by many black intellectuals of her day.[85] Harris recognized what some social theorists have claimed, namely, "that a dominated group has, perforce, a much clearer picture of those who dominate than the other way around."[86] "Black and White" reveals that Harris differs from many of her contemporaries who maintained that the races knew each other through some common bond of mystical understanding in which both recognized and accepted the white-over-black hierarchy. "I knew a hundred of them on the old plantation, but I have never been able to recite the negro," Harris wrote. "They were all like a secret near knowledge of me, myself, which I could not put into words."[87] Harris at least was not sentimentalizing an illusionary bond between the races the way women such as Rebecca Felton, Mildred Rutherford, and others were through their promotion of "mammy lore" and their insistence that a deep, abiding affection was the basis for race relations in both the Old South and the New.[88]

Through "Black and White" Harris hoped to appear open-minded about race, as one whose "prejudices have died down," no longer having any "crow to pick." The article is more an indictment of modernity than it is a statement of what she sees as the differences between the races. She asked what it meant if the more highly evolved of the two races was the more spiritually bankrupt. The white man had more material wealth and for that reason the largest measure of control, as well as the greatest measure of responsibility, but he had sold his soul to acquire it. He had sacrificed spiritual for material values. The white man became a worrisome busybody trying to make "darker color[ed] people" throughout the world "over in his own image." Moreover, the white man, not the black man, had produced "mass problems simply by thinking in terms of his own greatness."[89] Harris's religious ideals did not rid her entirely of essentialist thinking with regard to race, but neither did they lead her into the sort of paternalistic thinking that governed many of her contemporaries.

Four of Harris's writings during the 1910s, the decade of her most widespread fame, illustrate the evolution of her religious thought during the period: her report on a visit to a New York dance hall, or "trottery"; her observations of life in New York in the middle years of the decade; her published reflections on the Methodist Conference in 1918; and her private correspondence over the decade.

If "Jeff" reveals the role religion may have played in challenging racial stereotypes in Harris's thinking during the 1910s, "The Turkey Trot," published in 1913, reveals her thinking about morality and the "sin" of dancing. Harris visited a "trottery" in New York with several "distinguished" friends. She described the Turkey Trot as a natural but orgiastic indulgence, mostly by women but also men, taking advantage of the liberties modernity brought and, in the case of women, reacting to "the ancient bondage of their sex." The Trot to her was not a dance but simply humans responding to a primal rhythm, a beat, in a way that required no talent, no art, whereas real dancing required both. "The Turkey Trot is a form of amusement designed for primitive people by primitive people before they discovered the danger of being too natural," Harris wrote. It was merely the human body letting itself go, and even if that was not immoral, it was indecent, and hence could lead to immorality. There was no way for a woman to dance the Turkey Trot and keep her skirt below her knees.

What seemed to bother Harris most about the dance was that it resulted in "social confusion" because it brought together people of all ages and "from every walk and condition of life." In her mind that was a recipe for trouble, even if, surprising to her, no such trouble took place on this occasion. She was offended by the sight of so many older women with younger male partners, and by seeing both mistresses and their servants together at the same "trottery." "Democracy is a good thing," she wrote, "but a dancing democracy is not."

Harris understood the historical and socially constructed origins of morals. God did not make morals; man did to be able to live with God's natural laws. "Nature is never moral," she wrote, "but because we have discovered that Nature punishes immorality we have been obliged to invent morals. They are not natural, but they are necessary." Later she would question what it was about morals that was unchanging, and she would decide it had less to do with sins as defined by southern religion than she was able to fathom in 1913. The dance itself did not "indicate wickedness," she wrote, but it did create circumstances for poor and rich that invited sin. The dance led to a "condition" that distracted the poor from the straight and narrow and led to "ennui on the part of the rich and idle."[90]

During the mid-1910s Harris spent weeks, at times months, in New York City (mostly on assignment), made observations, and wrote reflections on the differences between New York and the Valley. Most of the works are on the glories of rural, "natural" living versus the "unnatural" conditions people suffered in cities. In the first of a series of these articles, she wrote about the glories of nature. Although she was "no Pantheist," she believed that nature and God's spirit were one and the same. "God is the spirit of nature." "*Nature* is right. She never sins, nor comes short of the glory of God. And Nature never built New York. This city was built by greed, by cruelty, by vice, by imposing the strength of the strong upon the helplessness of the weak."[91]

In this article she shares her conversation with a reformer in New York who believes his and other reformers' plans for uplifting the impoverished of New York are superior to the money and plans of those of "all your churches put together." She admits that although New York reformers may have access to more money and knowledge than the poor mountain churches in Georgia, the spirit of community the people in the Valley share is their strength. She tells the story of a typical ignorant preacher who had received his "call" from God. He and others like him, some of them experiencing possibly no more actual divine audibility than the protagonist of "Jeff," go into the ministry—not to recite or fulfill the Nicene Creed but to help their neighbors. The genuine humanism it reveals would have scandalized Paul More and warmed the hearts of the "humanitarians" he loathed.

If this young hypothetical preacher's beliefs could be reduced to the "sentimentality" of a creed, it would go something like this: "I believe in man, the brother of man, born of every woman, who has suffered crucifixion in all times, who has been dead and buried in every generation, who rises again from the dust to live and to suffer, and to make intercession with man for man till the end of all time."[92] Harris reveals here an awareness of human connectedness and interdependence that will be tested by a strong disregard for organized labor during their struggles throughout the 1920s and into the depression.

In 1916, the *Independent* published "Politics and Prayers in the Valley," in which Harris writes about how and why people living in the country were, she believes, better people. They have no choice but to live by faith. And not just faith in God, but faith in each other. She writes stories about mountain people devastated by harvest failure, women devastated by the death of their husbands. One woman in particular, "Sister E.," pregnant with her eighth child, has lost her husband. When Harris asks her how she will get along, she answers that she "reckoned the neighbors would look after her. And they did. Such sublime faith in your fellow man is faith in God."[93]

Harris's candid reflections on the Methodist episcopacy as demonstrated at the General Conference in 1918 make tame by comparison her novels noted for the same. The *Atlanta Constitution* published a report she wrote on her attendance at the conference that year to discuss, among other controversial issues, laity rights for women.[94] She heard about the proposed "radical changes" but, based on her long experience, believed it was a pipe dream to think the bishops would allow such reforms. Bishops were "tyrannical" "autocrats" whose powers ought to be reduced for the benefit of the church at large and for their own spiritual health.[95] She predicted that the laity rights for women would not go through. Even though reaffirmed over the bishops' veto, the issue required three-fourths of the members of the annual conference to ratify it. She believed it would take "something much more than courage" to make the voting clergy "vote bread out of the mouths of his wife and children in order to win a reform in the laws of his church."[96] Harris applauded a measure that passed without needing further ratification, namely, lifting time limits on preachers. It would affect positively and immeasurably the lives of circuit riders and their families.

At the close of the 1910s, Harris faced grief over Faith's death, and religious doubts rose to the surface. Because George Lorimer was the son of a "strong-willed clergyman," Harris often confided her feelings about religious subjects to him.[97] A letter she wrote to Lorimer on May 18, 1919, shortly after Faith's death, reveals what her autobiographies and other published accounts of her reaction to the loss do not: that the reportedly eerie composure people saw in her in the days after Faith's death was not the whole story.[98] Once grief set in, Harris was overcome with doubt and disillusionment. "I am an agnostic in the face of death," she wrote. "I do not know where Faith is. If one could only know. . . . It is no use for anybody to rebuke me with God, and His mercies. I know all about God that anybody knows. But there is very little in His word about what happens to those who pass through the grave."

She wrote about her inability to pray, as Harry and his mother were praying, "that Faith might live." All she could pray, she wrote Lorimer, was "a frightful submission to 'Thy will be done.' It is a way I have of putting the responsibility where it belongs." She continued with the willed confidence of a bereaved person determined to make God accountable. "But I ask you this, how will God square accounts with me? I mean however in the great scheme of things can it be made straight, the awful balance? All my life I looked for peace. I wanted often not to do right, but I did the best, better than nature made me, so that when the time came I might be ready and clear for happiness. And now I shall never know that dear happiness."[99]

She wrote that she was willing to wait it out, to hold on to the hope that through death Faith might have "escaped something awful here," that time would heal the wounds and she would see clearly. She was willing to wait, but for the time, she wrote, it seemed to her that she had merely spent "these terrible years in which I have won everything that I did not so much need, and lost literally everything that I need and love." She wrote that if, when she got to heaven, she did not find her beloveds happily spending eternity, if she did not find "Faith writing Paradise copy," "Lundy preaching to the saints and . . . free from his sins," and "little Lundy a full grown archangel," she would hold the "unjust Steward of that place" fully accountable and let loose with her best "immortal powers of invective."[100]

But Harris regained her faith after her daughter's death, as she had after her husband's death. Her faith reemerged in a different form or with a renewed perspective. She "did resume intimate relations with her soul" after each loss, she wrote in *As a Woman Thinks*, "because once you have adopted the ideals of a spiritual life you are meanly impoverished without them."[101] Much later, in a letter to a grieving friend, she reflected that even when she was acutely aware that "none of the things that have happened to me that hurt the worst could have possibly happened if he [Lundy] had lived," she also knew that the losses had made her a better, stronger, more productive person and had led to her "greatest private personal victory." She would not otherwise have learned to "stand on my own feet and do what I have done without their presence or support."[102]

Harris continued to travel and write during the 1920s. Her religious reflections are recorded in the three autobiographies she published over the decade and in a long letter she wrote Lorimer in 1925 reflecting on reader response to *As a Woman Thinks*. As a result of that response she was considering a third autobiography. Readers were concerned about her. A constant theme in *As a Woman Thinks* was how happiness had eluded her. She proposed to Lorimer that she would write an upbeat book about happiness after taking a long trip for the sole purpose of finding the source of happiness for humankind. Wanting to explore different places and different people, she planned to start in California and make it abroad to the Far East, but health problems kept her from making it past California, where she spent much of her time confined either to a bed or, at best, a hotel. She never got to test the theory of happiness she suggested to Lorimer, which consisted largely of maintaining a positive outlook on the innate goodness of humankind and claiming the inalienable right of all humans not just to "pursue happiness" but to be happy.

Harris's ideas about human nature did not so much change over time as they shifted in focus from positive to negative. In 1908 Harris wrote about the novelist's ability to "prove" that "in the mathematics of morality" good generally overcomes bad.[103] But the following year, in an article on politics in Tennessee, she questioned whether human nature was more good or more evil. It was the "one permanent, disaffected, invincible thing," "the Unchanged and Elemental," but "which way it tends"—whether toward good or evil—she was not sure. With typical tongue-in-cheek, she suggested that Tennessee politics would provide a good proving grounds.[104]

When Hamilton Holt asked her to lecture on the subject of evil in 1930, her reflections on human nature were negative. But a letter to Lorimer in 1925 captures the view that prevailed in the balance. "People are really good," she wrote, and "if you can wheedle them up out of their limitations and meanness, they *are* good and they *are* happy, and you can trust them!" She wanted to discover that there was no reason to fear anyone, and to believe that if people could cultivate "such power of faith in the deep lasting goodness of people," such faith itself would keep one from disappointment.[105] Faith in the goodness of people, she suggested, would bring about such goodness. If one looked for the best in people, that was what one would find. The letter to Lorimer in the middle of the decade reflects Harris's spiritual goals and aspirations. The three autobiographies capture Harris dealing in her maturity with religious ideas she had crafted eclectically from any number of sources, including her personal experiences.

Harris knew she was a bit short on meekness, which is hardly surprising for someone who preferred the Ten Commandments to the Beatitudes.[106] She knew she had a difficult time seeing shades of gray, that she had a "somber old Scylla and Charybdis mind," and that she was frequently unable to see beyond her prejudices.[107] Some apparent contradictions resulted from her insistence upon remaining as open as she knew how to be where ideas were concerned, including religious ideas. "I am free lance when it comes to religious faith," she wrote, "and can be convicted of many contradictions by any kind of smart Aleck."[108] Because she refused to be bound by logic, she admitted, any "materialist" could tear apart her arguments on religion. She was "short on logic and consistency, artlessly claiming the Providence, either personal or impersonal, according to the kind I need on that page to convey my thought."[109] This comment, as Charles Dobbins contends, seems indefensible when taken out of context.[110] However, when the context of one's life is so walled about by contradiction, the statement is no more or less misleading than any number of passages from Harris without further scrutiny.

One of her chief struggles during the 1920s concerned the role of morality, virtue, and piety in one's relationship to God, to others, and to an afterlife. Harris often conflated these constructs, insisting they were essential on the one hand and then wondering about how essential they were, since they could be costly and the payoff dubious. She often insisted that morals were essential but that one could overdo it with virtue and piety. Then she wondered what difference it made when one realized that morals were invented by man to protect himself and his personal property (chiefly his women, she admitted elsewhere).[111] And righteousness was "like bones in your body, necessary, but not good-looking."[112] Moreover, she wrote in *The Happy Pilgrimage* that evil came from outside humans, not from within. It was an interesting observation considering that three years later, when she lectured on the subject of evil at Rollins College, she would write very differently about the origin of evil in relation to human nature.[113]

One of Harris's most thought-provoking passages on the subject of morals and morality is found in a letter to Lorimer in 1925. The passage spells out how her thinking on the human construction of morality and gender was developing: "I used to think morals could not change or be changed and still remain morals. But they do, from age to age. Now if there is such a thing really as morals they cannot be moved to the left or the right they are *fixed*. So what are morals? Conveniences, superstitions, adjustments to the order of these times or some other times? Or are they fixed principles which have something to do with happiness as the orbit of the earth determines it[s] course and motions?"[114]

Considering her moralistic tone in so many other places, her queries on the subject of morals as they apply to women are surprising. In 1931 Harris wrote that the Old Testament was better suited to women than the New Testament, which was too "ascetic and sacrificial in its effects on feminine character, since we are already inclined to be martyrs and sacrificers."[115] "And why," she asked in a letter to Lorimer, "should morals be confined to just chastity in women? And if she is not chaste all the other morals cannot preserve her from our contempt."[116] As she frequently said after making what she considered a more or less profound statement, "but let that go." Harris fully perceived the moral double standard.

Although her post as "Professor of Evil" was mocked widely, Harris reveals in her recorded lectures and writings on the subject during 1930 an understanding that moral violations associated with the flesh were not nearly as consequential for the individual or for society as those of the heart. The point is captured in the title to an article in the *New York Evening Post*: "Corra Harris Describing Her Novel Experiment at Rollins University, Gives Sex a Minor Role in Dark Drama." There were to Harris any number of evils. She listed ambition as something to avoid. But the worst "evil" in her mind was jealousy. Asked to define evil, she had a difficult time but concluded it was "going contrary to the voice of conscience . . . [or] mental dishonesty."[117] In the midst of a culture obsessed with sins of the flesh, Harris reveals herself ahead of her time by focusing primarily on the role of a pure heart.

Even though she questioned at times the origin of existing morals, Harris never doubted her own morality or the need for morality in society. But her interpretation of morality began to expand. She once maintained a measure of virtue and piety as a wife and mother. "Since that time I may have grown in the world's regard, but it does not feel the same. . . . Now I am good only by habit, not by valiant choice."[118] Harris wrote in her final autobiography that she was tired of striving to "stay in the strait [*sic*] and narrow way" and wanted to find "a broader, more circuitous route."[119] She longed in her later years to be able to stop thinking so much, especially about "what was right in the first place and what was wrong in the second place. I do not want to think at all, merely to live."[120]

Harris, the reputed traditionalist, reveals open-mindedness on interpreting scripture in her autobiographies. "I have always reserved the right to believe in the Scriptures intelligently. So far as I am able to judge, stupid faith is as dangerous and belittling to the soul as a false doctrine."[121] Intelligent belief was not the same as literal belief, however; she never believed "with the literal humble mind of the obedient spirit."[122] She had special advice for a widow inclined toward a literal interpretation of the Bible: she ought "to shed her widow's veil and be born again mentally . . . to study something besides the Scriptures, and get stout secular doctrines for dealing with a vastly competitive and acquisitive world. Clinging to the cross is nothing to the way she must cling to her own good sense. The Lord encourages us to cling to that symbol of faith, but it is no use clinging to the world that way."[123] The Bible, especially the King James Version, which was "frightfully modern when it was first published," had a "lot of queer places" and "contradictions." For that reason, folk with "childish faith" ought to be able to hold on to their faith "no matter what the Bible says."[124] In the chapter "Living in a Book" in *As a Woman Thinks,* Harris wrote about how she utilized the scriptures in her own way regardless of what the church or any other institution taught.

Harris wrote frequently about prayer. It was something anybody "must believe in" if he or she expected to "succeed."[125] At times she was convinced that a personal God answered personal prayers, and at other times she thought it silly to ask God for specifics. In *My Book and Heart* she recalled how she had held God to his promises and had asked for very specific help, and that he had honored her faith. But in *As a Woman Thinks* she tells the story of a widow who wrote to ask her to pray that she might make wise investment choices. "Imagine the Lord babbling in wildcat oil speculations," she wrote. She would offer a countering prayer: "Teach us some sense by not answering such prayers. . . . Maybe in time we shall learn that the Maker of all laws will not break one natural or moral law to save us from either death or bankruptcy. It is no use to call upon God like a fool to save you when He has endowed you with the wit to save yourself if you will only use it."[126] She never stopped praying, since it had become a "vagrant habit," but she knew there really was no need to pray, that God would do right by her whether she prayed or not.[127]

Harris knew she had a "lively temper," a "turbulent disposition," and an "acid" tongue "unbelievable in a . . . Christian woman." She could be especially difficult to hired help. "I have no conscience about a person's job," she told one domestic employee. "When I hire them—I pay them and they must do everything I demand of them and that will be a plenty I tell you."[128] She paid well, however, and so she wondered sometimes why she never seemed able to live down the reputation of being a "formidable old ass."[129] "I can't figure out how it is that I seem to be perpetually on the defensive. It is undignified and indicates a misconception of me that is beginning to irritate me," she wrote her nephew Al Harris in 1927.[130] In a eulogy for his aunt, that same nephew said, "Any one who knew Aunt Corra well knew that when the psychological time arrived for her to explode, she exploded."[131] Witnessing to the sacred nature of personal liberty to his aunt, he confessed to being present for any number of her "belligerent moods," which he called "declarations of independence." About his aunt's volatile temperament, he wrote, "The facts of life left her undisturbed. The fancies of men's minds were violent stimulants to her."[132]

She was careful not to lose her temper in public, though, and generally she found it uncontrollable only when she was ill with a fever. Harris just knew that if the hospitals where she stayed had kept charts on her "behavior as well as my temperature," the files would read like those of a "damned soul." Reflecting on her appendicitis operation "years ago," she recalled that she ran off two nurses from a hospital in Nashville. More recently, ill with "2 degrees of fever," she had "set upon . . . a very fine old physician . . . like a pack of hounds."[133] Then there were times when she could not afford the luxury of a tantrum. She wrote John Paschall that she was a bit peeved about having to entertain some ladies coming for a tea party, since it would take up the time she would otherwise spend "lighting another candle." But "I can't even afford to get angry, because to do so shortens my breath and raises my blood pressure."[134]

But such nonvirtuous traits could be useful. Even though Harris knew they were not virtues, her "temper and tenacity" had fitted her far better at times for the "good fight" she had been called to make in life than most of the conventional virtues she had acquired.[135] It was one reason why she wondered if virtue was not a bit overrated. In any case, Harris knew her capacity for a temper better than anyone, and readily admitted it.

Harris could have found no better way to end her writing career or her life than the "Candlelit" columns. They illustrate succinctly the ways she grew intellectually and spiritually and how she managed to resolve some issues and come to terms with others that had troubled her throughout her life. They also show the strong hold of the South's conservative politics and the disconnect between the region's religion and politics. It would be practically impossible to summarize the nearly five hundred "Candles" the *Atlanta Journal* published during the last three and a half years of Harris's life. They cover a wide variety of issues and situations. A few deal with subjects such as marriage and family, and a few more were "answers to correspondents," but most are devoted to politics and religion. As always, on both subjects they are replete with contradiction. She does not waver, however, on a belief that God's most direct way of relating to humans is through nature. Nothing stilled her mind more resolutely than communing with God through the natural environment, most especially the hills around her Valley home. And for every diatribe against New Deal politics and the "shiftless" poor, she published one or more "Candles" on the goodness of both God and humans and on the need to do whatever it took to love one's neighbor as oneself.

Harris was, by her own admission, verbose. After a long letter to Lorimer, she wrote in a postscript, "I'd like to be brief, but I cannot manage it."[136] In one of her "Candles" she wrote, "It is one of the griefs of my life that I have such a fatal facility of expression, because the ablest men who know how to economize in words get better results by using them sparingly."[137] But on occasion she could be brief. A few one-liners or quotable terse excerpts on religion in her last years illustrate such ability. They also encapsulate her eclectic, unorthodox theology and sharp wit. "I have never believed it [orthodoxy] essential to salvation, although I am as determined as any saint to be salvaged." "I don't give a hang for salvation. I believe its [sic] going to bore me." "I do not believe in death." "I do not believe the Lord's works are perfect." "I regard the immaculate conception as the name of a merely doctrinal contention." "The whole of life is made up of illusions . . . wisdom consists . . . in choosing one's illusions wisely." "What difference does it make whether a man believes in eternal life or not?" "The kingdom of heaven is not a place but a state of mind." "There is no such thing as time." "If I could conceive of God, that would be reason enough for not believing in Him." Although "the ablest critic of life and letters among us," "Mr. Mencken so obviously belongs . . . to the school of the Antichrist." "[I am] a hard-boiled child of God." "A cure for hatred . . . is to look upon your enemy when he is asleep." "No wrong, however grievous, justifies hatred." "An atheist is a good man, only a little hard of hearing in his relations to the Lord." "It is not our sins that destroy us, it is clinging to our sins, instead of . . . leaving them behind us."[138]

Another "Candle" excerpt captures her mixed feelings about the application of scripture. As unorthodox as she became in her thinking, Harris could struggle with scriptural passages that she thought sounded good but nonetheless ought not to be obeyed. She found it impossible to keep Christ's literal command to turn the other cheek. "It is folly to try and defend your name and fame from an enemy," she wrote. "But whatever you do, don't turn the other cheek. It is scriptural to do so, and may lead to more meekness of spirit, but it is certainly diminishing to one's self-respect."[139]

If her antebellum sisters most often referenced in their diaries and journals the verse found in Jeremiah 17:9 (KJV): "The heart is deceitful above all things, and desperately wicked: who can know it?" Harris most often prayed the psalmist's plea, "Create in me a clean heart, O God; and renew a right spirit within me."[140] This plea is found repeatedly in her reflections on religion in the last few years of her life as the most important of all aspirations. Nor was the assurance that God had answered her prayer for a clean heart a onetime experience. The experience of feeling cleansed was, for her, synonymous with being "born again," and all humans needed it just as often as they began to think ill of their neighbor. It was a "perpetual process." She often, if not often enough to satisfy her, made it to the high ground and penetrated the thin "veil of mystery" between spirit and flesh, but she had a difficult time "holding" the note or lasting very long in that "altitude of spirit."[141] "I do see God sometimes in inspirational revelations," she wrote, "but am perfectly sure I cannot remain that 'pure in heart' for long, and that presently this ineffable vision will fade from . . . my mortal mind."[142] She did not worry about whether she would get to heaven; she believed everybody was going to get there.[143] But she was not sure what God was going to do with her about her two vices, smoking cigarettes and indulging a "famous temper."[144]

Several themes emerge in Harris's "Candles." With regard to the causes of the depression and resulting poverty, and in spite of evidence to the contrary all around her, they reveal Harris persistently unable to see beyond meritocracy and continuing to believe in poverty's personal rather than systemic causes. With regard to religious thinking, however, they show her at her most original and, some would argue, her best.

It is in the "Candles" that Harris most explicitly reveals a naturalistic spirituality. She admired and envied people such as her mountain neighbors who were able to live in the moment, not worried about the past or the future. One woman she knew did so because she "had no philosophy of life, but simply lived it with her feet and hands."[145] She was the classic "doer of the word." In a conversation with this woman Harris learned more fully something she had known her whole life. The mountain woman had faith in life as it was revealed through nature: the sense of "life everywhere, growing, striving, all of it in a good humor, fearing nothing," and learning to be at home with change. There was something reassuring about the predictability of the seasons. It was the foundation of her belief in Christ's claim to be the "same yesterday, today and forever."[146] Whatever the vicissitudes of life, the predictability of the seasons and other natural phenomena governed this woman's indomitable faith. Something about the woman's soliloquy fitted Harris for the days ahead when she would be confined to bed with illness. And they may explain a passage from a letter to Paschall in which she reflects, "life is the big thing—not love, nor praise, nor fame—all those things pass away, come again and go again, but life is more than they, more than charity, stronger than death."[147]

God, Harris wrote, had "created so much material out of nothing, coordinated it, shaped it, filled it with so much life that nothing is dead or can die, not even the smallest atom."[148] For one of the "Candles" she held a dialogue with herself in which she asked "How old are you?" and answered with a soliloquy on the relationship between consciousness, matter, space, and time: "Before ever there was flesh to clothe me I lived in the heart-leaves. . . . I have been the dust of the earth, the grass, the leaves of the forest, the flowers of a poisoned vine. . . . I have been what is now stone and was ice, my fossils lie deeper than gold in the earth."[149] When asked about the scriptures, she answered that they, like humans, were "full of contradictions." When asked "about Christ," she answered, "God may have other Words for other worlds, but for this world the Word of God is Christ."[150] Her concession that God might have "other Words for other worlds" reveals an openness out of character for southern Methodism.

Her deistic thinking on the role of prayer is captured in a personal letter Harris wrote just weeks before her death. She wrote Paschall many times about how much the opportunity to write the "Candles" meant to her. Most of these letters are both chatty and witty, so what she wrote has to be read in the light of the friendly, lighthearted nature of their relationship. "Nobody but a fool fanatic of a christian [sic] ever thought that he recieved [sic] an answer from God to prayer," she wrote in 1935. "The good God is too busy to carry on a social correspondence in charity. His duty is to make the whole thing work, as your duty is to make the *Journal* cover Dixie like the dew."[151]

There were times when Harris thought about how her being a woman affected her spirituality. She knew what it was like to be respected and honored, but she did not know what it was like to be adored; only beautiful women did. She thought if given the opportunity she would take beauty over so much virtue just to have the experience of being adored.[152] She wondered near the end of her life if women had not been duped by the social expectation that they be "good." "The real trouble with women," she reflected in 1934, "is that most of us do turn out to be merely good, say along in our thirties; after the dust of romance has cleared from our visions and love proves to be a yoke instead of an illusion." Women who turned out to be good were "not enhanced, but impoverished by their virtues." Their husbands and children might respect them, but no one recognized their "services and devotion." "At best," she wrote "they are hallowed, but not praised, usually earning very short epitaphs."[153] It seemed unfair that women who were not so good were the ones who inspired men to write poetry and song; those women seemed, in the end, to be the happiest.

Harris was at her best when pondering things of the spirit. She might have seemed heartless and dispassionate, especially during the Depression, but in print she held herself accountable when she fell short of Christ's command, "Little children. . . love one another."[154] Love was one thing that "settles everything, keeps everything and forgives everything. It is the final atonement we must make for what we are."[155] To Harris, everything in life—from fate to happiness to hatred—was transient except love.[156]

At times, Harris wondered about her lack of orthodoxy. In her writings during the 1910s she defended herself against the charge of pantheism, but by the time she was writing the "Candles" she did not care what word people used to describe to her ideas. She might allow her thoughts on subjects such as politics to be censored, but she would not compromise her "spiritual candor."[157]

Harris wrote in 1932 about a young forestry worker who consulted her about a spiritual concern. He felt "removed from God." He assured her he was moral and that he did not smoke, drink, curse, or misbehave toward women—none of which really interested her. She asked him simply, "Do you digest your food?" To which he answered, yes. Then she assured him that "whether he is a good man or a bad one," anyone who worked out in the natural world as he did was as close to God as a person could get.[158] Reliable knowledge of God did not come from a book, not even from the Bible, but "from within," where the "oldest altar" of time existed.[159] There was nothing in their conversation about Jesus, repentance, eternity, or other elements of evangelical necessity.

Harris's instruction to the forestry worker was no more unorthodox than her suggestion in 1934 that "the engineer who labors twenty years to make a heathen city sanitary with a sewerage system is no less a Christian missionary than the other one who endeavors to convert them to Christianity."[160] "I am not spiritually abashed at such speculations," she wrote, "having no word-bondage of faith. . . . But it does make me feel guilty of not being orthodox."[161] Not guilty enough to change, however, and hers was always a short-lived guilt.

Shortly after the "Candle" with the story about the forestry worker appeared, she heard from a "saint" who wondered if she had been "saved"; wanting to show her the way, the reader admonished her to stop leading "many away from the Cross." Slightly annoyed, Harris took the opportunity to expose what she regarded as the hopeless self-righteousness of zealous evangelicalism. She knew that she could quote more scripture than many an "addled saint" and that only the pure in heart who could see the best in others, "even the worst people," could see God, not the "egotist" full of his or her own piety.[162]

Harris admitted that the "second great commandment"—to love one's neighbor as oneself—was the most difficult commandment of all, especially for one as "positively verdant with transgressions" as she.[163] Because human nature was so "terrifyingly uncertain" that it left good, honest folk "teeteringly balanced between his nobler spiritual powers and [their] lower nature," fulfilling that commandment could be quite difficult.[164] A quote on her effort captures Harris's typical self-admonishment: "I have spent nearly fifty years striving to outlaw the critic in me, only to find that he frequently gets up before I do and never retires at all so long as I am sufficiently wakeful to think. Seems to be constantly engaged in the effort to build me up too much at the expense of my fellow men and women."[165] It was because of this internal critic that she often needed to pray for a clean heart and a right spirit.

Sometime in the early 1930s, when Harris began to feel that her days were numbered, she began to write about the benefits of age. As a younger woman she feared growing older and experiencing the limitations that age inevitably brought. Once it arrived, however, she found age less frightful, if sometimes lonely and confining. But she found the loneliness and confinement could evoke her deepest insights. For her, age had brought a sense of kinship with all humans. "I know for certain," she wrote in 1932, "that I am closer kin than I realized to the best and worst of them, and feel neither pride nor embarrassment in the relationship. We are one, the human race."[166] She had written in *Happy Pilgrimage* that all people were "repetitions of each, playing our roles in different scenes and under different circumstances."[167] A "Candle" she titled "Not to See through the Glass Darkly" captured the essence of her spirituality in her last years:

> I always know when I am drifting backward out of sight and sense of God when I begin to see the evil instead of the good of other people. Sometimes for days I am cursed with this darkness, I am lost and damned and undone because by some fury or bitterness of my mean original nature I see how bad people are and not how good. I lose the sense of their grace and sweetness and I am alone in this world; because for a moment, or, for a day, I have ceased to be the friend of man. Then do I begin to pray to escape and to be restored to my right mind. This is not like praying for righteousness, nor for a few more virtues, nor for some mortal desire of my heart; but for the power to behold again the glory and loveliness of mankind.[168]

Human beings could penetrate that thin "veil of mystery" that separated the divine from the human; they did not *have* to see through the glass darkly if they could focus on the potential people had for good rather than bad.

Although this was not a new insight, Harris had found it very difficult to integrate. By the time of that "Candle," however, she had "not so often" found herself "lost in the dark"; she was better able to "hold this point of view" than she had been in the past. Harris's works demonstrate that she was both more and less than she appeared to be during her life and since. She was trapped at times in dispassion, antipathy, and ignorance, but she recognized that many of her shortcomings were the result of a faulty belief system. And she struggled to overcome them rather than give in to the disillusionment that often accompanied the exposure of one's beliefs. Had she lived longer or integrated her insights into her thinking earlier, her legacy might be a literature that was more socially and politically critical. As it is, she leaves history the record of a woman who made a "profoundly true" discovery, namely, "how exactly alike we all are inside."[169]

In the last months of her life, Harris's correspondence with friends such as Marjorie McClain and John Paschall is filled with mirth and merriment, despite her confinement and ill health. In one letter she asked McClain to visit soon and bring "a quart of good gin and . . . whiskey" to go in an "18 pound fruit cake" Trannie baked. They laughed about always having to get liquor in for guests "bootleg style."[170] She jokingly implored Paschall, who had long since grown accustomed to her insatiable need for editors' approval, "Dear heart, you really are good to me, but try to be better, if you can."[171]

Her own heart, Harris wrote McClain a few months before she died, "has turned to the asp in my bosom."[172] But that did not matter so much. "Physically I feel like a sick kitten on a hot brick. But mentally I am in a state of high meridian serenity. Feeling that courage I have felt before in the presence of the inevitable. And a truly devilish satisfaction in the record I have made in useing [*sic*] up all the horse power of life and energy in doing my own will and my own work."[173] Many of those letters provide evidence that, in the last months of her life, Harris was learning how to "hold" the high note of some belief that supported her spirit even as her body gave in to decline. In the end nothing in life was more vital to Harris than being able to do "her own will and her own work." Paschall shared at her memorial service what she wrote him about how gratified she was to be able to write her column for the *Journal*. Thanks to the "Candles," she could "die with the seven league boots of my mind on."[174] She wrote until just days before her death; there was enough copy to continue publishing her famed "Candles" for weeks afterward.

Harris suffered from cardiac asthma and had numerous heart attacks between the spring of 1925 and her death in 1935. She had a massive heart attack on January 27, 1935, and died on February 7 at Emory Hospital in Atlanta. Among other dispositions covered in her will, Harris left a monetary sum to Bettie and Trannie Rains. She willed that her estate be divided among her three nephews, Al, John, and Fred Harris, and that a trust be established to keep up her Valley home as a memorial. She provided that either or both of the Rains sisters could live in the Valley home rent-free as long as they remained unmarried. Neither did, however. As Faith defied her mother's wish that she not marry, so did both Bettie and Trannie Rains. The Daughters of the American Revolution and United Daughters of the Confederacy declined responsibility for keeping up the memorial. After the trust failed to cover expenses to keep up the property, Trannie Rains Smith purchased it in 1949.[175] In 1996 Marietta philanthropist Jodie Hill purchased the Valley property and began restoring it to the way it was during Harris's lifetime. Hill, together with Marilee Henson and the Corra Harris Garden Club (formed in April 2000 and reportedly the largest garden club in the state), promote the memory of Harris and her works.[176] The Valley is used today for weddings and other formal occasions.

Corra Harris endured, and through intellectual, psychological, and spiritual innovation she dared and often beat tremendous cultural and social odds. Whether or not her literature merits revisiting, her life and legacy certainly do.

Notes

Abbreviations

AWT   *As a Woman Thinks*
CCAJ   "Candlelit" column in *Atlanta Journal*
CH   Corra Harris
CHC   Corra Harris Collection. Hargrett Rare Book and Manuscript Library, University of Georgia Library, Athens
CRW   *A Circuit Rider's Wife*
CWHP   Corra May [*sic*] White Harris Papers. Manuscript, Archives, and Rare Book Library, Emory University, Atlanta
FH   Faith Harris
FHL   Faith Harris Leech
GHL   George Horace Lorimer
HH   Hamilton Holt
HP   *The Happy Pilgrimage*
JL   *The Jessica Letters*
LP   George Horace Lorimer Papers. Hargrett Rare Book and Manuscript Library, University of Georgia Library, Athens
MBH   *My Book and Heart*
"MBH"   Serialized version of *My Book and Heart*
PEM   Paul Elmer More
PEMP   Corra Harris Correspondence 1901–1935 from the Paul Elmer More Papers in Princeton University Library, cataloged PS3515.H313 Z5 A4, 1961a, at University of Georgia Library, Athens
RA   *The Recording Angel*
WACP   Warren Akin Candler Papers. Manuscript, Archives, and Rare Book Library, Emory University Library, Atlanta

Preface and Acknowledgments

1. Bettie Rains to Marjorie McClain, January 1, 1969, CWHP.
2. CH, "Who's Who—And Why," 23; see also CH to FHL, August 29, 1913, CHC.

Chapter 1: Introduction: The "Contradictory" Legacy of Corra Harris

1. W. F. Bigelow to CH, August 21, 1931, CHC.
2. CH, "Fiction, North and South," 273.
3. CH to Mrs. Strong, April 22, 1922, and CH to Medora Perkerson, September 14, 1931, CHC. She wrote that the best of her writing was "poor stuff considered from the literary point of view." *HP*, 7.

4. Al Harris, speech at dedication of memorial chapel, June 5, 1936, CHC.

5. HH to CH, October 19, 1906, February 11 and 13, 1909, CHC. For an example of the sort of response Harris received see John C. Spangler to CH, October 7, 1906, unsigned letter to CH, October 18, 1906, and Joel Chandler Harris to CH, October 9, 1906, CHC.

6. PEM to CH, December 17, 1906, CHC. Paul More, one of Holt's coeditors and one of Harris's most influential mentors, was decidedly not a liberal thinker. More considered Holt a radical. More wrote Harris about Holt: "Take it all in all, our friend Holt is the mildest-mannered cut throat that ever herded with Socialists and anarchists." HH to CH, October 26, 1906, CHC. In the years of their early association Holt would have been considered a "radical" compared with Harris's "extreme reactionary conservative" views.

7. HH to CH, October 26, 1906, CHC.

8. See Holt, "Circuit Rider's Wife," 871. Parts of the article from 1924 (Holt, "A Circuit Rider's Wife in Literature") show up verbatim in his speech he delivered in 1936 at the memorial services.

9. John Paschall, speech at dedication of memorial chapel, June 5, 1936, CHC.

10. CH, *MBH*, 12; M. M. Marshall, "Every Women"; CH, "The Walking Delegate Novelist," 1913; Jack London to CH, September 17, 1906, CHC (excerpts from correspondence between Harris and London can be found in Ennis, "Circuit Rider's Wife"); Harvey Wickham to CH, December 6, 1926, CHC; CH to GHL, October 12, 1912, LP; Alfred Gibson to CH, June 11, 1931, CHC.

11. Dobbins, "Corra Harris," 76. Though Dobbins was writing here specifically about Harris's religious ideas, the sentiments reflect his conclusions about her in general.

12. CH, *MBH*, 12.

13. CH to HH, April 23, 1931, CHC. She admits to her contradictory and inconsistent nature in many places. A letter to Paul More captures her awareness most succinctly. After writing a very unflattering image of what she perceived having her own children would do to her daughter, Faith, Harris confessed to Paul More that she knew her opinions where her daughter was concerned were "very inconsistent with the doctrines I preach about marriage, etc.—But who on earth ever made a doctrine for his own consumption? None but a fool or a crank!" CH to PEM, October 14, 1907, PEMP.

14. Mims, introduction to *The Recording Angel.*

15. Cash, *Mind of the South*, 115.

16. Brinkley, "American Conservatism," 409.

17. CH, "Answers to Correspondents," *Atlanta Journal*, October 3, 1934; Talmadge, *Corra Harris*, 6, 122–29.

18. HH to CH, October 26, 1906, CHC. For a treatment of Holt's role in establishing the national reputation of the *Independent* and for the reach of the magazine, see Hitchens, "Peace." Also see editorial, *Independent*, January 3, 1907, 51. Quote on the *Independent* as "the best weekly in the country" from Dakin, *Paul Elmer More*, 87, 98.

19. CH, *HP*, 174.

20. For an example of such critiques see CH, "Heroes and Heroines in Fiction" and "Neurotic Symptoms in Recent Fiction." Harris published in the *Independent* throughout the 1910s with increasing insight into the ill effects of the New South creed and Lost

Cause mythology on southern literature. The quote about Dixie as a time and place that "never existed" came from a later article, "The South," 177. Harris's most direct criticism of the Lost Cause is found in "Patriotic Criticism in the South."

21. For critiques of Harris as southern critic, see Ayers, *Promise of the New South*, 105, 168, 173, 335; Mixon, "Traditionalist and Iconoclast"; P. Schmidt, "Harris's *The Recording Angel*"; Simms, "Corra Harris on the Decline of Southern Writing," "Corra Harris, William Peterfield Trent, and Southern Writing," and "Corra Harris on 'Literalism' in Fiction."

22. CH to FHL, June 22, 1917, CHC. When two male instructors from the University of Georgia visited Harris in the 1930s to offer "some liberal views on the Negro question, she set them right with a lecture they still remembered thirty years later." Talmadge, *Corra Harris*, 141.

23. Bradbury, *Renaissance in the South*, 9. See Baym, *Woman's Fiction*, and Tompkins, *Sensational Design*, for examples of some who have rehabilitated the genre.

24. Bingham and Underwood, *Southern Agrarians*, 6, 15, 16. Kreyling and Yaeger are among literary scholars showing concern for the political implications of the Agrarians' writings.

25. See Inge, "Fugitives and Agrarians," for more on the relationship between Fugitives and Agrarians.

26. On the Southern Renaissance and the role of the Southern Agrarians see Bradbury, *Renaissance in the South*; Conkin, *The Southern Agrarians*; Danbom, "Romantic Agrarianism"; Grammar, "Reconstructing Southern Literature"; King, *A Southern Renaissance*; Kreyling, *Inventing Southern Literature*; and Singal, *The War Within*.

27. Cobb, *Away Down South*, 117, 121.

28. Julius Rowan Raper also credits the Harlem Renaissance with helping "prepare the soil" for the Southern Renaissance. *Glasgow's Reasonable Doubt*, 87n14.

29. Bingham and Underwood, *Southern Agrarians*, 6, 15, 16.

30. A. G. Jones, "Women Writers," 278; Fought, *Southern Womanhood and Slavery*.

31. For studies examining women and the Agrarian movement, see Caldwell, "Glasgow and the Southern Agrarians"; Manning, "Agrarianism, Female-Style."

32. Bradbury, *Renaissance in the South*, 3.

33. Manning, "Southern Women Writers," 243–44. Hall utilizes Pierre Bourdieu's work defining an intellectual field as one that stretches well beyond the "tradition of 'formal readings'" to include a "semi-autonomous 'space of possibilities.'" Hall, "Women Writers," 9.

34. Manning, "Southern Women Writers," 243–44.

35. "The material history they examined, the imaginative perspective from which they viewed it," writes LeRoy-Frazier from her analysis of Kentucky/Tennessee author Caroline Gordon, "and the literary and cultural conclusions they drew often differed radically from what has come to be perceived as the quintessential Southern Renaissance confrontation between old and new." "Saving Southern History," 62.

36. Manning, "The Real Beginning," 40. Anne Firor Scott writes about the value of women's "fiction of dissent" in "Women in the South," 31.

37. Manning, "Southern Women Writers," 247.

38. A. G. Jones, *Tomorrow Is Another Day*, 45.

39. Chopin, *The Awakening*, 893.

40. A. G. Jones, *Tomorrow Is Another Day*, 24–45.

41. Quoted in ibid., 278.

42. Manning in "The Real Beginning" cites Clara Juncker, "Grace King: Feminist, Southern Style," 48.

43. A. G. Jones, *Tomorrow Is Another Day*, 235.

44. J. W. Scott, *Only Paradoxes*, 3, 5, 11.

45. A. G. Jones, *Tomorrow Is Another Day*, 275.

46. Ibid., 275–77.

47. J. R. Raper, "Ellen Glasgow," 128.

48. Glasgow, *The Woman Within*; CH, *MBH* and *AWT*.

49. CH, "Patriotic Criticism in the South," 549. Harris was writing about Glasgow's novel *The Deliverance* (1904).

50. Kaufman, "Ellen Glasgow," 48. Anne Jones writes about internal conflict, paradox, and irresolution in Glasgow's life and writings in *Tomorrow Is Another Day*, 260–65.

51. Skaggs, "Ellen Glasgow," 336.

52. CH, *AWT*, 247.

53. A. G. Jones, *Tomorrow Is Another Day*, 236.

54. Skaggs, "Ellen Glasgow," 342.

55. A. G. Jones, *Tomorrow Is Another Day*, 265.

56. CH, "Robin Hood Roosevelt," CHC.

57. Glasgow, *The Woman Within*, 241, 271, 295.

58. Glasgow, *The Freeman*, 13–14.

59. Glasgow, *Barren Ground*, 269.

60. CH to FHL, 1916, box 7, folder 9, CHC.

61. J. W. Scott, *Only Paradoxes*, 3–5, 11. Scott explains why "paradox, contradiction, and ambiguity" have been and remain central defining elements in women's struggle for equality.

62. Woodward, *Origins of the New South*, 142–74.

63. For different views of the Progressive Era see Hofstadter, *The Age of Reform*; Kolko, *The Triumph of Conservatism*; and Abrams and Levine, *Shaping of Twentieth-Century America*. Other general works on the era include Hays, *The Response to Industrialism*; Wiebe, *The Search for Order*; and Hawley, *The Great War*. For a look at the competing ideologies, see Conn, *The Divided Mind*; Lears, *No Place of Grace*; and Susman, *Culture as History*. For a treatment of the complexity and paradoxical nature of labor reform for women see Kessler-Harris, *Out to Work*; and Woloch, *Muller v. Oregon*.

64. Singal, *The War Within*, 36.

65. For the active role women played in the Lost Cause see Whites, "Stand by Your Man," 137.

66. For works on the art and practice of writing biography and the questions postmodern analysis has brought to the genre, see Alpern et al., *Challenge of Feminist Biography*; Ascher, DeSalvo, and Ruddick, *Between Women*; Carol Brightman, "Character in Biography," *Nation*, February 13, 1995, 206–10; Hall, "'You Must Remember This'"; Iles,

All Sides of the Subject; Nye, *The Invented Self*; Painter, "Writing Biographies of Women";
Parini, "Biography"; and Stanley, "Biography as Microscope."

67. Parini, "Biography," A72.

68. Twain, *Complete Works*, 1:2.

69. CH to George Fitzpatrick, October 6, 1933, photocopy provided by Mr. Jodie Hill
of Marietta, Georgia.

70. CH to GHL, November 3, 1923, LP.

71. The Corra Harris Garden Club started in 2000 in Cartersville, Georgia, boasts the
largest membership of any garden club in the state. Visit with Marilee Henson, president
of the Corra Harris Garden Club, and Jodie Hill, current owner of the Harris home place,
In the Valley, July 29, 2006. Hill bought the property in the mid-1990s and restored it as
nearly as possible to what he could ascertain was the state it was in when Harris died in
1935.

72. CH to HH, April 23, 1931, CHC.

73. CH, untitled "Candlelit" column, *Atlanta Journal*, August 19, 1932. Dobbins wrote
a master's thesis at Columbia University about Harris in 1931. CH to Medora Perkerson
June 15, September 14, 1931, and Charles Dobbins to CH, June 18, 1931, CHC, reveal some
of Harris's discontent. Chiefly, she was not happy that Dobbins exposed family secrets
about her husband's suicide attempts and revisited her works from the "hot days of my
youth on the negro question." However, once the biography came out in the *Journal* and
was "so well received," Harris wrote Perkerson that "The thing is not so bad, really credit-
able, especially the quotations from the works of Corra Harris." Afterward she felt "a bit
ashamed of my resentment" at what she initially regarded as his betrayal. CH to Medora
Perkerson, September 14, November 21, 1931, CHC.

74. Al Harris, speech at dedication of memorial chapel, June 5, 1936, CHC.

75. Edwards, foreword to *CRW*, xxvii.

76. Hall, "'You Must Remember This,'" 441–42.

Chapter 2: Family and Tragedy in the Development of Corra Harris

1. CH to GHL, May 18, 1923, LP.

2. Biographical details are taken from CH's *MBH*, *AWT*, and "Memories of an Early
Girlhood"; Talmadge, *Corra Harris*; Dobbins, "Corra Harris"; Reeves, "Corra Harris";
and Mundy, "Philosopher of the Heart."

3. For the sake of clarity, first names are used in this chapter and the following when
confusion would result otherwise.

4. For Ward's editorial see *Independent*, May 4, 1899, 1252–53; Harris's response is "A
Southern Woman's View." Mathews, "Lynching," 161–66.

5. For contemporary attitudes toward lynching see Brundage, *Lynching in the New
South*; Clinton, "Bloody Terrain"; Dittmer, *Black Georgia*; Hale, *Making Whiteness*; Hall,
Revolt against Chivalry; Hodes, *White Women/Black Men*; Litwack, *Trouble in Mind*; Moses, *Lynching and Vigilantism*; A. F. Raper, *Tragedy of Lynching*; and Williamson, *Crucible
of Race*.

6. See HH to CH, June 29, 1899, CWHP.

7. In 1951 Twentieth Century Fox made her most popular novel, *A Circuit Rider's*

Wife, into the feature-length film *I'd Climb the Highest Mountain*. Lamar Trotti wrote the screenplay and produced the film, which starred Susan Hayward, William Lundigan, and Rory Calhoun. The film was released on video in the spring of 1995. In 1920 her novel *Making Her His Wife* became the movie *Husbands and Wives*.

8. For biographical works on Harris and for critiques of her works, see Talmadge, *Corra Harris*; Coffing, "Corra Harris and the *SEP*" and "Southern Womanhood"; Dobbins, "Corra Harris"; Mixon, "Traditionalist and Iconoclast"; Mundy, "Philosopher of the Heart"; Reeves, "Corra Harris"; P. Schmidt, "Harris's *The Recording Angel*"; Simms, "Corra Harris, William Peterfield Trent, and Southern Writing," "Corra Harris on the Decline of Southern Writing," and "Corra Harris on 'Literalism' in Fiction"; and Tate, "A Neighbor's Recollections."

9. CH, *AWT*, 14, 21, 31.

10. Mary White and Tinsley White were models for two descriptive essays written early in Harris's career: "The Southern White Woman" and "The Confederate Veteran."

11. CH, "MBH," September 1, 1923, 3, and August 22, 1925, 112. The biographical information here comes from Harris's first two autobiographies and "Memories of an Early Girlhood" and from Talmadge, *Corra Harris*. Talmadge records that the farm had been lost by the time of Mary White's death in 1888 (16).

12. CH, "MBH," September 1, 1923, 5.

13. CH, "Address at Rich's"; CH, "Maneuvering toward the Kingdom of Heaven."

14. CH, *AWT*, 31.

15. Ibid., 31, 38.

16. Ibid., 31.

17. Ibid., 32; CH, "Memories of an Early Girlhood."

18. CH, "Memories of an Early Girlhood," 1073.

19. CH, "MBH," September 1, 1923, 4; CH, "Memories of an Early Girlhood," 1073; CH, *AWT*, 14.

20. CH, *AWT*, 31, 38.

21. Ibid., 32, 35–36.

22. Ibid., 32, 33.

23. CH, "Memories of an Early Girlhood," 1073.

24. CH, *AWT*, 35.

25. Ibid., 33, 38.

26. CH, "Memories of an Early Girlhood," 1073.

27. CH, *AWT*, 35–37.

28. CH, "MBH," September 1, 1923, 4.

29. A. F. Scott, "Women, Religion, and Social Change," 112.

30. CH, "MBH," September 1, 1923, 61–62.

31. Ibid., 62.

32. CH, *AWT*, 38–39.

33. Ibid., 59.

34. Ibid., 45.

35. Harris claimed in a letter to Paul More that she "once studied medicine, and

decline[d] a medical education at Ann Arbor because the man who offered it put in the proviso that I should marry him." July 25, 1901, CHC.

36. CH, *MBH*, 74.

37. Talmadge's version of Corra's role in the troubled marriage is challenged somewhat by the observations of Harold W. Mann in a biography of Bishop Atticus Greene Haygood, a close friend and mentor of Lundy Harris's. Mann writes that it was a "satisfying marriage" that allowed Lundy to "regain composure" from his youthful indulgences (159).

38. See Owen, *Sacred Flame of Love*, especially chapter 7, and 151.

39. Owen, chapter 7 and 151.

40. Talmadge, *Corra Harris*, 7.

41. Corra wondered at times what shaped Lundy's thinking. She wrote Paul More that Lundy relied primarily upon three sources for his wisdom: the Bible, Shakespeare, and the dictionary. February 10, 1904, PEMP.

42. CH, *MBH*, 199.

43. Talmadge, *Corra Harris*, 9.

44. CH, *MBH*, 57.

45. Quoted in Bartley, *Creation of Modern Georgia*, 116.

46. In a speech delivered sometime in 1933, Harris talked about the differences between her life and that of Mary Thompson, the protagonist of *A Circuit Rider's Wife*. CH, "Address at Rich's."

47. "Underpaid American Parson Is an Accusing Figure," *Philadelphia Public Ledger*, September 25, 1910.

48. Carter, *Spiritual Crisis*.

49. CH to GHL, May 18, 1923, LP.

50. "Underpaid American Parson."

51. Ibid.

52. CH, *MBH*, 114.

53. CH, *AWT*, 183.

54. CH, *MBH*, 175, 166, 177, 184, 227, 240.

55. For a treatment of the social attitudes of Georgia Methodists, see Owen, *Sacred Flame of Love*, 149–87.

56. "Underpaid American Parson"; Harris, *MBH*, 175; Talmadge, *Corra Harris*, 7; CH to FH, February 24, 1909, CHC.

57. Talmadge, *Corra Harris*, 17–26.

58. Ibid., 22.

59. Mathews, "Lynching," 170–71. Mathews suggests that the reputation of racial progressives such as Haygood and Georgia governor William Northen can be misleading. Each "represented the intelligence, piety, and manners of the Christianized masculine South," and both spoke out against lynching. "Yet," Mathews finds, "at some critical, mysterious, and charged moment in which the canon of immaculate protection and the madness of righteous provocation short-circuited the meditation of these generous Christian men on issues of sexual identity, anomalous black men, and white masculine

duty, their sense of honor and justice collapsed into the simple belief that lynching was just and, therefore, a Christian duty" (171).

60. Mann, *Atticus Greene Haygood*, 183; Owen, *Sacred Flame of Love*, 159; Hauk, *Legacy of Heart and Mind*, 29–37.

61. "Ignoramus" to CH, December 13, 1934, CHC.

62. Talmadge, *Corra Harris*, 7; CH to FH, February 24, 1909, CHC.

63. CH, *MBH*, 79.

64. CH to W. F. Hunt, December 17, 1910, CHC.

65. CH, *MBH*, 177, 184.

66. Undated newspaper clipping, box 110, folder 19, CHC.

67. Talmadge, *Corra Harris*, 22–25, quote on page 23.

68. Ibid., 11.

69. CH, *MBH*, 173.

70. Talmadge, *Corra Harris*, 22–25.

71. CH to FHL, March 6, 1918, CHC.

72. CH, *AWT*, 115–16.

73. CH to Sarah Antoinette Curtright Candler, September 18, 1898, WACP.

74. CH, *MBH*, 175.

75. John Paschall, speech at dedication of memorial chapel, June 5, 1936, CHC.

76. CH, *MBH*, 177.

77. Ibid., 183.

78. Ibid., 183–84; see also CH, *AWT*, 82.

79. CH, *MBH*, 175.

80. CH to PEM, June 17, 1901, PEMP.

81. Harris's experience is reminiscent of that of the medieval Spanish mystic Teresa d'Avila. According to bell hooks, Avila "felt her rebellion against male authority sanctioned by grace" and afterward believed "'the authority of the heart [overrode] that of the mind—even when the heart [was] a woman's and the mind's a man!'" hooks, 110. hooks is quoting Mary Giles in "The Feminist Mystic."

82. CH, *AWT*, 183.

83. "Underpaid American Parson."

84. Talmadge found the poem on the back of a letter to Corra, 23–24. The poem was published in the *Independent* on November 11, 1909.

85. Talmadge, *Corra Harris*, 24–27.

86. Bill Winn, "'Aunt Corra' Harris: Almost Forgotten, She Was Once Famed as a Writer," *Atlanta Journal and Constitution*, February 4, 1968.

87. "Underpaid American Parson."

88. CH, *AWT*, 182.

89. CH to Arthur T. Vance, October 20, 1920, CHC.

90. CH, *MBH*, 114.

91. CH, *AWT*, 115.

92. CH to PEM, April 9, 1903, PEMP.

93. CH to PEM, August 24, 1903, PEMP.

94. FH to Lundy Harris, January 31, 1909, CHC.

95. For an example of the kind of advice Corra gave, see CH to FHL, n.d., box 1, folder 14, CHC.

96. See FHL to CH, June 7, 1916, CHC.

97. Talmadge's interpretation of the mother-daughter relationship reflects his attempt to simplify a number of complex variables. His account reads as though they were poster candidates of co-dependency—a daughter's neurosis enabled by a mother's need for control. Although their relationship did contain elements of co-dependency, there is ample evidence that in the balance it was healthier than it was dysfunctional.

98. CH to FHL, June 7, 1916, CHC.

99. In "Women and Southern Religion," Lynn Lyerly argues that women's role as mother empowered them more than their role as wife: "In the exaltation of motherhood southern women of faith again faced a contradiction: a proper mother was strong, influential, and authoritative, while a proper wife was submissive and subservient. For Protestant women in the late nineteenth century, these domestic ideals had import in church polities, for while women were prohibited from speaking to mixed assemblies and from having authority over men, they were encouraged to teach and evangelize among women and children. This implicit and almost sacred decorum resulting from the example and dignity of accomplished Christian women gave women a power neither formal nor ineffectual" (264).

100. CH, *AWT*, 115.

101. Ibid.

102. Ibid.

103. The bulk of Corra and Faith's correspondence illustrates the point. Their letters from the last two years of Faith's life especially illustrate the mutuality and maturity of their friendship. For particularly poignant letters see FHL to CH, February 20, 1917; CH to FHL, April 8, 1918, CHC; CH to GHL, May 18, 1919, LP.

104. Corra was known for being inept at making friends. As a schoolgirl she was considered "a little 'queer' because she made no close friends." A half sister recalled after her death that "it was not easy to get close to Corra" (Talmadge, *Corra Harris*, 6, 101). She was aware of her lack of sociability and expressed concern about it on occasion. "I am not temperamentally fit to go among strangers," she wrote Adelaide Nealle (February 15, 1914, CHC). And to Faith she confided after having successfully entertained a crowd of guests one evening: "Pinkie, my dear, I shall never, never be able to live with people again, not those of the world. They seem so *trivial, so gullable!* . . . I am anxious, seriously anxious about myself. Is the trouble with me? Have *I* become cynical, hard, suspicious? Or, is . . . [everyone else] a fool?" (October 7, 1918, CHC). After Faith and Corra's sister, Hope, died, Corra developed close friendships with the Rains sisters. But she admitted in a letter to Marjorie McClain that her relationship with the Rains sisters was based at least as much on money as affection, though letters among the three of them demonstrate an affectionate bond (April 17, 1929, CWHP). She continued a friendship through correspondence with Adelaide Nealle, and she made friends with Medora Perkerson of the *Atlanta Journal* and with Marjorie McClain of Atlanta, who was with her when she

died. A letter from Talmadge to McClain indicates his understanding that McClain was closer to Harris at her death than anyone (1968, CWHP).

105. HH to CH, November 12, 1906, CHC.

106. In addition to a number of works of fiction in which Harris denigrates women's clubs, see FHL to CH, June 5 and November 17, 1916, and CH to FHL, January 13, 1917, CHC. For a treatment of women writers' opposition to women's clubs and activism, see Roth, *Matronage*, 104–5.

107. FHL to CH, August 30, 1918, CHC.

108. CH to FHL, n.d., box 14, folder 1, CHC.

109. CH to PEM, October 14, 1907, PEMP.

110. CH, "Be Sweet, Clever Maid," 1007–8.

111. FH to CH, October 17, 1910, CHC. Similarly, her will indicated that she wanted Bettie and Trannie Rains, her surrogate daughters, to remain unmarried. Talmadge, *Corra Harris*, 149.

112. Quoted in Wade, *Francis Newman*, 21.

113. CH to FH, March 22, 1909, CHC.

114. CH to PEM, October 14, 1907, PEMP. Corra told More that it made her weary to think about grandchildren, both for herself and more especially for Faith: "They seem to stand and threaten Faith, . . . [and] destroy her before my very eyes! Good Lord preserve me from grandchildren!"

115. Corra turned out to be as prophetic about her daughter's marriage as her own mother had been about Corra's. Although she expressed little by way of regret about her role as mother, she did claim to have been blinded in her actions toward Faith because of her concerns about her marriage. "My one transgression against you," she wrote Faith, "has been in trying to save you from the consequences of your marriage." CH to FHL, n.d., box 7, folder 9, CHC.

116. Talmadge, 52–53.

117. CH to FHL, January 13, March 17, 1917, CHC.

118. CH to FHL, January 13, 1917, CHC.

119. Ibid.

120. CH to FHL, May 4, 1917, CHC. Among the "few duties" Harris had left to perform, the most important were caring for her father, who was in the Confederate Soldier's Home in Atlanta, and aiding her sister, who had serious health problems.

121. FHL to CH, March 15, 1917, CHC.

122. Bettie Rains Upshaw to Marjorie McClain, January 1, 1969, CWHP.

123. FHL to CH, February 20, 1917, CHC.

124. Although correspondence between Corra and Faith makes it clear that many of Faith's medical problems were gynecological, Faith wanted the information kept private. "But *please*, Mama, do me this kindness. I have a horror of the gossip of women back and forth when another woman goes to a doctor especially if its anything to do with female organs. If people ask you about what's the matter or anything *please* say I have something the matter with my stomach or my liver or anything just so it isn't distinctly female. This may be morbid but I can't help it. I'd like to survive the gossip of a doctor's examination which is more than most women do!" (FHL to CH, June 7, 1916, CHC). Corra was dili-

gent in obliging. In a letter to GHL just after Faith's death, she wrote that Faith had "some mysterious attacks, apparently acute indigestion," from which she had "suffered since she was eighteen years of age" (CH to GHL, May 18, 1919, LP).

125. Talmadge, *Corra Harris*, 85. For Corra's [response] see August 1916 Notebook, box 99, folder 3, CHC.

126. CH to FHL, January 13, May 4, 1917, CHC.

127. FHL to CH, August 3, 1918, CHC.

128. FHL to CH, March 15, 1917, CHC. Shortly after receiving this letter from her daughter, Corra managed to get Faith to agree to allow her to set up an account for her in case of emergencies.

129. FHL to CH, August 3, 1918, CHC.

130. FHL to CH, March 15, 1917, CHC.

131. CH to FHL, March 31, 1919, CHC.

132. Ibid. Corra was able to convince Faith that the quality of life for all of them ultimately depended on Faith's success in the literary world. To be successful in a writing career, one had to have more than the mere essentials of life: one had to be relieved from "household drudgery." At the very minimum Faith had to have help with meals. Addie, a longtime servant of Corra's and a favorite of Faith's, helped. When Addie's services were needed back in the Valley, Corra made other arrangements, as she did one spring when there was a turnover there in the domestic staff. "In exchange [for 'lending' Addie back to her] I will pay for Harry's meals down town, on the sly of course!"

133. CH to FHL, n.d., 1916, box 7, folder 9, CHC.

134. HH to CH, November 12, 1906, CHC.

135. CH to FHL, November 3, 1918, CHC.

136. Editors from *Cosmopolitan* wrote asking her to consider writing a novel (editors from *Cosmopolitan* to FHL, January 13, 1919, CHC). Many letters from Faith to Corra in late 1917 and throughout 1918 illustrate an uncharacteristic self-confidence on Faith's part. She wrote that she, not Harry, would decide how and with whom she would spend her time, what she would do with her money (which would include relief from domestic chores), and where she would spend Christmas. "Hereafter the 23rd and 24th of December are going to be spent with you," she wrote her mother. "I shall tell Harry that those days hereafter are yours. I have done my best these past two years. I think now I deserve a little lee way. At any rate I shall take it" (December 19, 1917, CHC). And, "Its [*sic*] one pleasure that has come to me with this work—the ability to be financially dependent upon myself. You know from your own experience what freedom of spirit that gives one. That seems a little mean in me to say when I know how willingly and generously you have always given and I have taken it knowing that but still there is nothing that has given me so much peace of mind as to know that I may be able perhaps all of my life to make enough money to smooth off sharp edges of life myself. You have done it for me hitherto (August 30, 1918, CHC).

137. CH to FHL, July 24, 1917, CHC. Corra had believed since her daughter's years in college that Faith had "more genius" for writing "than you'll ever have for any other relation in life." CH to FHL, Summer 1910, box 1, folder 14.

138. *From Sun-up to Sun-down* was serialized in *Country Gentleman*, 1918.

139. See FHL to CH, June 7, 1916, CHC. Bettie Upshaw Rains blamed Harry and Corra "for pulling poor Faith to pieces between them. That and the fact Corra Harris pushed her so hard to write was the cause of the ulcers that caused her death" (Rains to Marjorie McClain, January 1, 1969, CWHP). Whether Faith was having medical symptoms she was keeping from even her mother is not clear, but Corra believed after her death that Faith had had a premonition of what was ahead. On her last visit to the Valley when the mail arrived and there was no letter from Faith, Corra "told her that was the only trouble I had when she was with me. I did not get her daily letter. 'If I were in Paradise, Faith, I would miss your letters,' I said, laughing. Now I remember that she did not laugh, that she looked at me strangely. Without knowing it we have a precience [sic] of things to come" (CH to GHL, May 18 1919, LP).

140. Talmadge, Corra Harris, 101–2.

141. CH to GHL, May 18, 1919, LP.

142. Ibid.

143. Ibid.

144. Glasgow, The Woman Within, 188.

145. CH to GHL, October 12, 1920, LP.

146. CH to GHL, October 2, 1917, LP.

147. CH to FHL, July 28, 1913, CHC.

148. Ibid.

149. Ibid.; see also CH to FHL, June 26, August 4, 1913, CHC.

150. CH to FHL, July 12, 1917, CHC; CH to GHL, May 18, 1919, LP.

151. CH to GHL, December 28, 1919, LP.

152. CH to GHL, October 12, 1920, LP.

153. CH to GHL, June 21, 1921, LP.

154. CH to GHL, July 6, 1921, LP.

155. CH to FHL, October 8, 1916, CHC. Corra had no patience for "neuresthenic" people. Nor in her mind was the condition limited to women. She was convinced that Faith's husband, Harry, labored "beneath a pathological condition known as neuresthenia, motives that are hereditary, practiced by his father upon his mother, and as strong as instincts." CH to FHL, February 1917, box 7, folder 13, CHC.

156. CH to FHL, March 7, 1918, CHC.

157. CH to GHL, June 21, 1921, LP.

158. CH to GHL, September 8, 1925, LP.

159. Ibid.

160. See Talmadge, Corra Harris, 122–29; and letters from CH to Bettie and Trannie Rains in the spring and summer of 1925, CHC, and between CH and GHL in late 1926 and 1927, LP.

161. CH to GHL, June 21, 1921, LP.

162. Quoted in Talmadge, Corra Harris, 102.

163. CH, "Discussion on Evil"; see also Talmadge, Corra Harris, 130–37.

164. CH to W. Lyon Phelps, n.d., box 54, folder 9, CHC.

165. William Tate believed "these columns might well be among her best writings, for the vignettes or short essays—pervaded to a marked degree by pungent remarks

and cryptic characterizations or dialogue—show her at her stylistic best." "A Neighbor's Recollections," 10.

Chapter 3: The Influence of Paul Elmer More

1. Talmadge, *Corra Harris*, 33–34.
2. CH to PEM, May 23, 1901, PEMP.
3. Literary editor Edwin E. Slosson, whom Harris did not like, believed there might be more to the relationship between Corra Harris and Paul More than a literary partnership. In a review of *The Jessica Letters*, Slosson expressed doubt that "the passions and tenderness in some of the letters are fictitious." Talmadge believed Slosson's "insinuation was off the mark." He admitted that Harris admired More more than the other editors—while Harris "respected" both William Hayes Ward and Hamilton Holt of the *Independent*, she "revered Paul Elmer More"—yet he believed there was nothing to justify Slosson's "accusation" (Talmadge, *Corra Harris*, 33–35). One definitely finds the same "passions and tenderness" in Harris's letters to More as in Jessica Doane's to Philip Towers. At least about Corra Harris if not about Paul More, Slosson's observation reveals more insight than "insinuation," and here Talmadge is likely the one off the mark. Harris actually admitted in a letter to More, "I can be Jessica alright because I *am* Jessica" (June 27, 1902, PEMP). In any case, evidence does not reveal occasion for any type of relationship outside correspondence. Harris visited the More household on occasion when she made trips to New York. In a letter to More dated March 21, 1903, she refers to a visit made the previous summer (PEMP). And in a letter dated February 10, 1904, she wrote More reflecting on the experience of meeting his wife, infant daughter, and sister (PEMP).
4. CH to PEM, July 19, 1901, PEMP.
5. CH to PEM, December 13, 1901, February 24, 1909, PEMP.
6. CH to PEM, May 23, 1901, PEMP.
7. CH to PEM, December 13, 1901, PEMP.
8. Dakin, *Paul Elmer More*, v.
9. PEM, *Aristocracy and Justice*, 135–41.
10. PEM, *On Being Human*, 7–8.
11. PEM, *Aristocracy and Justice*, 144.
12. PEM, *Pages from an Oxford Diary*, n.p.
13. PEM to CH, March 8, [1909], CHC.
14. Tanner, *Paul Elmer More*, 8.
15. Ibid., 1.
16. Quoted in Dakin, *Paul Elmer More*, 278.
17. Quoted in Tanner, *Paul Elmer More*, 4.
18. Ibid., 1; Dakin, *Paul Elmer More*, v.
19. PEM, *Pages from an Oxford Diary*, no. V.
20. Dakin, *Paul Elmer More*, v.
21. Ibid.

22. Aaron, *More's Shelburne Essays*, 10, 11. In a review of More's *A New England Group and Others*, Mencken wrote: "High above the blood-bathed battlements there is a tower, of ivory within and solid ferro-concrete without, and in its austere upper chamber he [More] sits undaunted, solemnly composing an elegy upon Jonathan Edwards, 'the greatest theologian and philosopher yet produced in this country.'" Quoted in Dakin, *Paul Elmer More*, 278.

23. Quoted in Dakin, *Paul Elmer More*, 20.

24. Aaron, *More's Shelburne Essays*, 9.

25. The Southern Agrarians with whom Harris shared many views were catalyzed into reaction by, among other causes, the New Humanism movement associated most directly with More. The difference between More's conservative values expressed in the New Humanism and those of the Southern Agrarians articulating southern conservative ideology can be found in Conkin, *The Southern Agrarians*, 52–53, 56, 74, 106; O'Brien, *Idea of the American South*, 19, 127, 144–47; and Stewart, *The Burden of Time*, 327–30. Feeling "threatened" by the erudition of the New Humanists, Agrarian Allen Tate "put more effort into [an] article" spelling out the distinctions between Agrarianism and the New Humanism "than any he had ever written," writes Conkin (*The Southern Agrarians*, 52). However, the two conservative movements turned out to be in many ways two sides of the same coin, or at least as "complementary" as they were "antagonistic" (Bingham and Underwood, *Southern Agrarians*, 23 n10). That the coexisting movements could be simultaneously antagonistic and complementary mirrors the way Harris could revere and admire More for his seeming self-possession and yet reject and expose as spiritually bankrupt his philosophy.

26. PEM, *On Being Human*, 10.

27. Ibid., 7–8, 117–43; CH and PEM, *JL*, 126; see also PEM, "The Pragmatism of William James," *Shelburne Essays*, 7th ser., 195–212; PEM, *Pages from an Oxford Diary*, no. XIII.

28. PEM, *On Being Human*, 164.

29. Alcoff, "Feminist Critique of Reason," 6. For feminist critiques of the Enlightenment see Alcoff and Potter, *Feminist Epistemologies*; Antony and Witt, *A Mind of One's Own*; Auslander, "Feminist Theory and Social History"; Benhabib, *Situating the Self*; Butler, *Gender Trouble*; Butler and Scott, *Feminists Theorize the Political*; Fraser and Bartky, *Revaluing French Feminism*; Garry and Pearsall, *Women, Knowledge, and Reality*; Hekman, *Gender and Knowledge*; Lloyd, "The 'Maleness' of Reason"; Nicholson, *Gender and History*.

30. For an account of the role of emotion in Western epistemology today see Jaggar, "Love and Knowledge."

31. Alcoff, "Feminist Critique of Reason," 6, 8.

32. PEM to Robert Shafer, September 13, 1931, quoted in Dakin, *Paul Elmer More*, 311–12.

33. PEM, *Aristocracy and Justice*, 174.

34. PEM to Alice More, March 12, 1894, quoted in Dakin, *Paul Elmer More*, 46.

35. CH and PEM, *JL*, 162.

36. Ibid., 162–65.

37. CH, *AWT*, 104.

38. CH and PEM, *JL*, 162–64.

39. CH, "What Men Know about Women," 379.

40. Ibid.

41. Quoted in Dakin, *Paul Elmer More*, 76.

42. PEM, "Oxford, Women, and God," in *A New England Group and Others*, 262–63, 287.

43. Dakin, *Paul Elmer More*. For More's remarks about Nettie, see Dakin, 110.

44. Ibid., 104. PEM to Professor Hall Frye, Oct. 16, 1907.

45. Ibid., 104. PEM to Louis T. More (Paul's brother), September 5, 1907.

46. PEM to Alice More, March 15, 1898, ibid., 61.

47. PEM to Alice More, October 7, 1909, ibid., 110.

48. CH and PEM, *JL*, 36.

49. PEM to Alice More, May 23, 1906, quoted in Dakin, *Paul Elmer More*, 98.

50. PEM to Alice More, August 6, 1910, ibid., 110.

51. CH to FHL, n.d., CHC. The date penciled in is 1910, but since Lundy died in September and Faith did not announce her marriage to Harry until after her father's death, the date is likely later.

52. CH to PEM, April 9, 1903, PEMP.

53. Singal, *The War Within*, 36.

54. Dakin, *Paul Elmer More*, 89; Shafer, *Paul Elmer More*, 103; Talmadge, *Corra Harris*, 34.

55. Princeton Library indexes seventy-two letters from Harris to More in the Paul Elmer More Collection. Hargrett Library indexes six letters from More to Harris from December 1906 to September 1911, but there were more. She refers to letters from him in her correspondence from 1901 to 1905, but early in her career she was not as diligent at keeping correspondence.

56. CH to PEM, January 15, 1905, PEMP.

57. Talmadge, *Corra Harris*, 35.

58. CH to PEM, November [10], 1901, PEMP.

59. Ibid.

60. CH, "A Southern Woman's View," 1354–55.

61. CH to PEM, July 1, 1906, PEMP.

62. CH to PEM, March 12, 1909, PEMP.

63. CH to PEM, April 15, August 24, 1903, PEMP.

64. CH to PEM, November 18, 1902, PEMP.

65. CH to PEM, May 28, 1902.

66. CH to PEM, January 14, 1902, PEMP.

67. CH to PEM, January 15, 1905, PEMP.

68. CH to PEM, October 29, 1903, PEMP.

69. CH to PEM, January 15, 1905, PEMP.

70. CH to PEM, March 3, 1902, PEMP.

71. CH to PEM, November [10], 1901, PEMP. Here Harris is quoting back to him his own words.

72. Ibid.

73. CH and PEM, *JL*, 178–79. More's influence on Harris's thinking about the differences between men's and women's nature showed up in Harris for the remainder of her life. She wrote, "The dual nature in man is more apparent than it is in woman." CH, "Editors."

74. CH and PEM, *JL*, 163–65; see CH, *MBH*, 221–22, for an example of Harris expressing this idea.

75. CH and PEM, *JL*, 179–80.

76. Ibid., 180.

77. Ibid., 121–22, 309, 311, 320, 325.

78. Ibid., 40, 93.

79. Ibid., 190.

80. Ibid., 95–96.

81. Ibid., 305–6.

82. Ibid., 182–83.

83. Ibid., 202–3.

84. CH to FHL, n.d., box 1, folder 14, CHC.

Chapter 4: "A Woman Takes a Look at Politics"

1. CH, *CCAJ*, August 17, 1932.

2. Haardt, "Southern Lady Says Grace," 57.

3. In *Gender and Jim Crow*, Glenda Gilmore writes about the ways black women used white middle-class standards of propriety to promote progress for African Americans in North Carolina.

4. Works on southern women in reform include Clinton, *Half Sisters of History*; Farnham, *Women of the American South*; Green, *Southern Strategies*; Gross, "Good Angels"; Hewitt and Lebsock, *Visible Women*; Hine et al., *"We Specialize in the Wholly Impossible"*; A. F. Scott, *Making the Invisible Woman Visible*; Wheeler, *New Women* and *One Woman, One Vote*; Whites, "Rebecca Latimer Felton."

5. CH, *AWT*, 101.

6. CH, "Obsolete Womanhood," 6.

7. CH, *AWT*, 104.

8. CH, "A Woman Takes a Look at Politics," 25, 128–33.

9. CH, *AWT*, 141.

10. CH, "Favorite Sons."

11. CH to Medora Perkerson, September 14, 1931, CHC.

12. Wheeler, *New Women*, 72–73.

13. Glasgow, *The Woman Within*, 187.

14. CH, "A Woman Takes a Look at Politics," 133.

15. CH, "Bartow."

16. The *Independent* titled the debate between Harris and Gilman "The Future of the Home." Gilman titled her contribution "Home-Worship" and Harris titled hers "The Monstrous Altruism," with a rebuttal by Gilman titled "Why Monstrous?" *Independent*,

October 4, 1906, 788–98. Although the editors prefaced the articles with the disclaimer "We do not say which gets the better of the argument," Hamilton Holt pointed out to Harris, "Every mail brings letters about it, slightly more of them approving of your position than hers." Having sat next to Gilman the night before at a "socialistic political banquet," Holt had firsthand news of her reaction. "She told Professor Giddings that you could write better than she, but she had the truth on her side. It is remarkable," Holt concluded, "how that debate has been reverberating." HH to CH, October 19, 1906, CHC; PEM to CH, December 17, 1906, PEMP.

17. CH to Adelaide Nealle, February 15, 1914, CHC. Jack London to CH, January 22, 1914. Letter to Robert Otis Haward of the Author's League on her resignation dated February 1914, though the day is not clear. HH to CH, February 11, 13, 1909, CHC; FH to Corra and Lundy Harris, January 17, 1909, CHC; CH to PEM, February 24, 1909, PEMP; Talmadge, *Corra Harris*, 32.

18. CH, "The Walking Delegate Novelist," 1213.

19. Ibid.

20. Jack London to CH, September 17, 1906, CHC. Harris likely was encouraged when Holt told her he thought she had "analyzed his [London's] character with great precision," in a letter to Holt, and agreed to read Harris and London's correspondence as she had asked. HH to CH, October 3, 1906, CHC.

21. Jack London to CH, January 22, 1914, CHC.

22. CH to Adelaide Nealle, February 15, 1914, CHC.

23. Ibid.

24. Ibid.

25. Ibid.

26. HH to CH, February 11, 13, 1909, CHC.

27. CH to PEM, December 13, 1906, PEMP. CH, "Upton Sinclair and Helicon Hall."

28. CH to PEM, February 24, 1909, PEMP.

29. Talmadge, *Corra Harris*, 32.

30. CH, "The Advance of Civilization in Fiction," 1167.

31. Upton Sinclair, "A Protest," *Independent*, January 9, 1909; CH to PEM, February 24, 1909, PEMP.

32. FH to CH and Lundy Harris, January 17, 1909, CHC.

33. CH to PEM, February 24, 1909, PEMP.

34. Ibid.

35. Thompson quoted in Flynt, *Dixie's Forgotten People*, 7.

36. CH, "If You Must Come to New York," 31.

37. CH, "The Valley—After New York," 65.

38. CH, "The Literary Spectrum of New York," 441.

39. Flynt, *Dixie's Forgotten People*, 64.

40. CH, *MBH*, 175; CH, *AWT*, 154.

41. CH, "If You Must Come to New York," 31.

42. Bartley, *Creation of Modern Georgia*, 127.

43. Ibid.

44. Danbom, "Romantic Agrarianism," 5. Even if "most women" found agrarian life "unappealing," Harris did not hesitate to romanticize it and offer it as a remedy for the evils born out of urban living.

45. CH, "If You Must Come to New York," 29.

46. CH, "Success."

47. Ibid.

48. CH, "To Restore Poverty's Good Name."

49. CH, "The Q.E.D. of Sentimentality."

50. CH, *My Son*, 97–100.

51. Cobb, "Georgia Odyssey," 39–40.

52. Quoted in CH, untitled "Candlelit" column, *Atlanta Journal*, November 14, 1934.

53. Talmadge, *Corra Harris*, 140.

54. CH, "Bartow."

55. CH, "A Woman Takes a Look at Politics."

56. CH, *AWT*, 40.

57. Harris's attitudes can be found in the titles of several of her "Candlelit" columns, such as "A Good and Glorious Poverty" and "To Restore Poverty's Good Name," and in the titles of essays she had difficulty getting published, such as "Robin Hood Roosevelt" and "Running a Welfare Racket." Indeed, editors during the depression had to censor her tone. Lorimer sent back "Running a Welfare Racket" and told her that if she had shown "in a constructive way what the individual who wants to help at this can do, instead of taking an ax to welfare workers and all their works," it might have been publishable (GHL to CH, April 16, 1933, CHC). Nor was John Paschall of the *Atlanta Journal* willing to publish that sort of thing. For a short time the reprimand worked. Harris claimed in a letter to John Paschall that she had learned that the welfare workers "are more sacred than the Sons of God" (CH to John Paschall, April 28, 1933, CHC). And in a "Candle" published in August 1933 titled "Sweetness and Light" she claimed to have "retired as a literary exponent of politics and other highly sensitized issues of the moment." But by 1934 she was back at it, likely reacting to the textile strikes sweeping the South, including Georgia, and Roosevelt's federalization of Georgia's relief operations. "This is a paternal government now, instead of a free country," she wrote in a "Candle," October 19, 1934. "The unemployed are the most fortunate people in it, idle, fed, clothed, happy and care-free." It simply was not "natural to love and feed the poor—other animals never do." In one place in "A Perfect Life" (CCAJ, October 19, 1934) she dismissed as "immoral [and] unethical" "sentimentality" all efforts to alleviate the economic effects of the depression. It would be "better to stain history red with the blood of battles than to make such a mistake as this," namely, practicing "mawkish sentimentality." CH, "Sweetness and Light"; CH, "A Perfect Life"; CH, "The Q.E.D. of Sentimentality"; CH, "Sober Reflections." Letters between CH and GHL, CH and Adelaide Nealle, and CH and John Paschall in April and May 1933 reveal the editors' concerns. See also GHL to CH, April 6, 1933, CHC; CH to John Paschall, April 28, 1933, CHC.

58. CH, "Sob Sister Citizens," 29, 105.

59. J. E. Blair to CH, July 15, 1925, CHC.

60. C. G. Fry to CH, September 12, 1925, CHC.

61. "Faithfully Ignoramus" to CH, December 13, 1934, CHC.

62. J. E. Wall to CH, January 28, 1934, CHC.

63. Dr. R. H. Main to CH, June 12, 1931, CHC.

64. CH to Warren Candler, October 29, 1899, WACP.

65. CH, "Fashions in Fiction," 1407; CH, "The Literary Spectrum of New York," 441.

66. CH, "Fiction, North and South," 275.

67. CH, "New York as Seen from a Georgia Valley," 97.

68. CH, "The Literary Spectrum of New York," 441.

69. CH, *AWT*, 70.

70. Ibid., 298.

71. CH, "Discussion on Evil."

72. CH, "The Pharisee's Lament," 83.

73. CH, "New York as Seen from a Georgia Valley," 97.

74. CH, "Price of Suffrage for American Women," 10.

75. Frank Daniel, "Corra Harris Gives Views on Woman Auto Drivers, Careers and Ruth Elder," *Atlanta Journal*, n.d., box 110, folder 30, CHC.

76. CH, "The Serpent and the Woman in Fiction," 1332–33.

77. CH, "Sob Sister Citizens," 29.

78. CH, "The Happy Day," 27.

79. Ibid.

80. CH, "Notes about Women."

81. CH, *AWT*, 171.

82. The quote comes from an address Harris gave to the American Club Woman in New York on May 27, 1916. Two newspaper clippings record the occasion and parts of the speech: "Corra Harris Addresses Club Women on 'Woman of Yesterday at the Biennial in New York'" and "Southern Tribute to Women of Yesterday."

83. Roth, *Matronage*, 104–5.

84. CH, "If You Must Come to New York," 31.

85. CH, "A Woman's Relation to the Two Sexes," 906.

86. Glasgow, "No Valid Reason," 25.

87. CH, "The Southern White Woman," 432.

88. CH, *AWT*, 140–41.

89. Glasgow, *The Woman Within*, 187.

90. HH, speech at dedication of memorial chapel, June 5, 1936, CHC.

91. Wheeler, *New Women*, 73.

92. Bibliography of published writings by Corra Harris on suffrage, in chronological order: "The Women and the Future"; "Price of Suffrage for American Women"; "Mrs. Harris Off to Farm"; "The New Militants"; "Was Eve a Feminist?"; "Demobilizing the American Women"; "Taking Over Our Problems"; "The Bonneted Hornets"; "Sob Sister Citizens"; "The Happy Day"; "The Synthetic Girl"; "Obsolete Womanhood"; "A Woman Takes a Look at Politics"; "A Southern Woman Author"; "Suffrage Means That Woman Will Have the Right"; "Mrs. Harris Off to Farm"; "Mrs. Corra Harris Discusses the Defeatt of the Anthony Amendment." See also CH to John Spurgean, July 3, 1922, and CH to FHL, n.d., box 7, folder 9, CHC.

93. CH, "Demobilizing the American Women," 127.

94. CH to Dr. Young, April 5, 1920, CHC.

95. CH, "The Other Forgotten Man"; CH, "Men and Women—And the 'Woman Question'"; M. M. Marshall, "Every Woman."

96. CH, "Suffrage Means That Woman Will Have the Right." Many years later, in "The Other Forgotten Man," Harris recalled that it was a "long-legged spinster" with a "militant feminine soul" who had stolen her title, "Co-Citizens," to publish an article about suffrage. The author shared with Harris on a chance encounter in New York that she was writing an article to be titled "Breaking Into the Human Race," so Harris shared that she herself was writing a serial for *Pictorial Review* to be titled "Co-Citizens." "Three weeks later," Harris wrote, this same author "published a sword-clashing article in *Collier's* entitled "Co-Citizens." "She was the first thief who paid me the compliment of stealing my stuff. I remember her with considerable poignance," Harris recalled.

97. CH, "Demobilizing the American Women," 127.

98. CH, "Mrs. Corra Harris Discusses the Defeatt of the Anthony Amendment"; CH, *AWT*, 100–101.

99. CH, "The New Militants," 3.

100. CH, "A Southern Woman Author."

101. CH, *MBH*, 306.

102. CH, "If You Must Come to New York," 31; CH, "Men and Women—And the 'Woman Question'"; M. M. Marshall, "Every Woman."

103. CH, *AWT*, 235–36.

104. Glasgow, *The Woman Within*, 163–64.

105. CH, "The Women and the Future," 1091.

106. Glasgow, "No Valid Reason," 19.

107. CH, "Letters of an Accomplished Lady."

108. CH, *AWT*, 104.

109. CH, *MBH*, 305.

110. CH, "Obsolete Womanhood," 6.

111. CH, *AWT*, 168.

112. This is not to suggest that all anti-suffragists thought the same. For works on the variety of positions, backgrounds, and histories of anti-suffragists, see Benjamin, *History of the Anti-Suffrage Movement*; Camhi, *Women against Women*; DuBois, "Radicalism of the Woman Suffrage Movement"; Graham, *Woman Suffrage*; Green, *Southern Strategies*; Jablonsky, *Home, Heaven, and Mother Party*; Kinnard, *Antifeminism in American Thought*; Kraditor, *Ideas of the Woman Suffrage Movement*; Marilley, *Woman Suffrage*; S. E. Marshall, *Splintered Sisterhood*; A. F. Scott and A. M. Scott, *One Half the People*; Thurner, "'Better Citizens without the Ballot'"; Wheeler, *New Women*.

113. A list of Harris's works that promote the domestic ideal would run for pages. For works that examine this approach see Coffing, "Corra Harris and the *SEP*" and "Southern Womanhood." An abbreviated list of works other than those in the *Saturday Evening Post* that promote Harris's brand of Victorian domesticity includes "A Woman's Relation to the Two Sexes"; "A Man's Relation to the Two Sexes"; "The Women and the Future"; "Ideal Husband"; "Men and Women—And the 'Woman Question'"; "Wife

Often to Blame If Husband Is Unfaithful"; "What Marriage Was and What It Is Not"; "The Happy Woman"; "On the Management of a Husband." A list of works that Harris wrote about marriage and its meaning to women, men, and society would also run for pages.

114. CH, "What Marriage Was and What It Is Not," 2. She wrote: "A mean husband can be a rather interesting diversion if you learn to regard him simply as a performance."

115. Faith Hathaway to CH, n.d., box 43, folder 14, CHC.

116. For examples of anti-suffragists' beliefs about women's antipathy to each other, see Howe, "An Anti-Suffrage Monologue"; Barr, "Discontented Women"; Adams, "In Opposition to Woman Suffrage"; Babcock, "Melancholia and the Silent Woman."

117. CH, "Price of Suffrage for American Women."

118. CH to PEM, October 8, 1903, PEMP.

119. For a recent work detailing the actively political nature of women anti-suffragists see S. E. Marshall, *Splintered Sisterhood.*

120. Harris, "The Women and the Future," 1092.

121. There was plenty of activism by women in the South, even in Georgia. In addition to the general works on suffrage in the South cited above, for general social activism by women in the club movement see Roth, *Matronage.* Lee Ann Whites writes about the suffrage activism of Georgian Rebecca Latimer Felton in "Rebecca Latimer Felton and the Problem of 'Protection'" and "Rebecca Latimer Felton and the Wife's Farm." See also A. Elizabeth Taylor's three articles on woman suffrage in Georgia.

122. CH, "Price of Suffrage for American Women," 56. Harris's prediction, of course, did not come true. The South remained as tradition-bound about sex as it did about race. All southern states except Arkansas, Tennessee, and Texas held out on woman suffrage until forced by federal amendment to grant the ballot to women.

123. Glasgow, "No Valid Reason."

124. CH, "A Southern Woman Author," 8.

125. CH, untitled speech, delivered, she says in one place, "nearly two years after" the publication of *Eve's Second Husband* (1910), and in another place "two years" after the publication of "Price of Suffrage for American Women" (October 1909), box 98, folder 17, CHC.

126. Felton, *The Romantic Story of Georgia's Women*, 38. See also Talmadge, *Rebecca Latimer Felton*, 141; and CH to Rebecca Latimer Felton, September 16, 1915, Rebecca Latimer Felton Collection, University of Georgia Library, Athens.

127. Frances M. Abbott of the New Hampshire Equal Suffrage Association to CH, October 1, 1915, and Mrs. J. D. Thomas of the Woman Suffrage Center in Philadelphia to CH, October 3, 1915, CHC. Harris had sent them both an autographed copy of the book. Interestingly, there are no copies of letters from southern suffrage associations in the Harris Collection.

128. Florence French Kelly, review of *Co-Citizens, Bookman*, November 1915, 325.

129. *Nation*, December 9, 1915, 690. Like Harris, this *Nation* reviewer also conflated the suffrage and feminist movements.

130. CH, *Co-Citizens*, 217.

131. Arthur Vance to CH, February 8, 1914.

132. Arthur Vance to CH, January 7, 1915.

133. Russell Doubleday to CH, December 7, 1915.

134. Sims, *The Power of Femininity in the New South*; Wheeler, *New Women*; Whites, "Stand by Your Man"; Gross, "Good Angels."

135. Hale, "'Some Women Have Never Been Reconstructed,'" 182.

136. Whites, "Rebecca Latimer Felton and the Problem of 'Protection' in the New South," 56.

137. Woloch, *Muller v. Oregon*.

138. Whites, "Stand by Your Man," 146.

139. Felton writes about Harris and Rutherford in *The Romantic Story of Georgia's Women*; on Harris, see 38–39; on Rutherford, 41.

140. The extent of the relationship between Harris and Felton is not clear from the two women's collected works, as there is little correspondence between the two women, and few references by either of them about the other in the existing correspondence. In a letter to Felton dated September 16, 1915, Harris acknowledges Felton's approval of *Co-Citizens*, and in a letter to Felton dated August 8, 1922, Harris declines Felton's offer to run a campaign for her as a candidate for the state legislature. Letters from editors to them both reveal that they had not met before Harris wrote and published *Co-Citizens*. See Harry E. Maule to CH, October 1, 1915, and Harry E. Maule to Rebecca Felton, December 29, 1915. Felton implies in *The Romantic Story of Georgia's Women* that she and Harris were friends and writes that she "was proud to discover . . . that she had made me the prototype of her book, 'Co-Citizens,' of which the heroine is a woman leader—a New Woman of the new century, who has thrown off the shackles of tradition and stepped into the political arena." Given Harris's antipathy toward ardent activists of Felton's type, her unsympathetic portrayal of Felton in the novel, and her benign reference to her in *My Book and Heart* (148–49), it is unlikely that they were close friends.

141. For Felton's racial politics see Whites, "Rebecca Latimer Felton and the Wife's Farm" and "Rebecca Latimer Felton and the Problem of 'Protection.'" For Rutherford's see Hale, "'Some Women Have Never Been Reconstructed.'"

142. Felton writes more generously about Harris than vice versa. In *The Romantic Story of Georgia's Women* she writes, "It has been my privilege to know her [Harris] intimately for many years, and her country place is but a few miles from my home in Cartersville" (38).

143. CH, "Notes about Women."

144. Talmadge, *Rebecca Latimer Felton*, 141.

145. In his biography of Felton, Talmadge writes about the potentially damaging effects of the novel on the memory of Felton's husband, Senator William H. Felton (ibid., 96–97).

146. CH, *MBH*, 148–49.

147. On the "reconstruction" of southern women see Harris, "The Southern White Woman"; on Rutherford see Hale, "'Some Women Have Never Been Reconstructed.'"

148. Whites, "Rebecca Latimer Felton and the Problem of 'Protection,'" 56.

149. Camhi, *Women against Women*, 177.

150. CH, "Men and Women—And the 'Woman Question,'" 164.

151. For Tarbell's position on suffrage see Camhi, *Women against Women*, 145–78; Jablonsky, *Home, Heaven, and Mother Party*, 142.

152. CH, "The Literary Spectrum of New York," 442.

153. CH, "Price of Suffrage for American Women," 56.

154. CH, "Old Texts Tried."

Chapter 5: The Woman of Yesterday versus the New Woman

1. CH, "Men."

2. CH, *AWT*, 247.

3. CH, "Robin Hood Roosevelt."

4. CH, "Memories of an Early Girlhood," 1071.

5. Charlotte Perkins Gilman devoted her writing career to debunking the biology-as-destiny myth. See *Women and Economics*; *The Home*; *The Man-Made World*; *His Religion and Hers*; and *The Living of Charlotte Perkins Gilman*. See also Calverton and Schmalhausen, *Sex in Civilization*; and articles in Leavitt, *Women and Health in America*.

6. Chapter 6 examines Gilman's thoughts on the ways it cost women, even those who knew better, to challenge convention.

7. CH, untitled "Candlelit" column, *Atlanta Journal*, November 14, 1934.

8. CH, "North and South: The Difference."

9. CH to PEM, July 13, 1901, PEMP.

10. CH, *AWT*, 253.

11. In a letter to George Lorimer she wrote, "You are a good business man and I am not, I am simply a hardworking man" (November 3, 1923, LP). In a letter to Faith she encouraged her daughter, who had "gentle graces," "patience," and "kindness," to write Lorimer because "I am not the man to push him, with a second letter! You do it! You are so engeniously [sic] gentle that he will not feel the shove, but I am, my beloved, a heavy body, long since past those gentle graces which for you insures patience and kindness" (April 9, 1918, CHC). The "brass knucks" she reputedly kept as a favorite paperweight are telling. Wylly Folk St. John, "Now Hollywood Has to Find a Circuit Rider's Wife," *Atlanta Journal Magazine*, April 27, 1947, 7.

12. CH to PEM, June 27, 1902, April 9, 1903, February 3, 1904, PEMP.

13. CH, *AWT*, 248.

14. CH, *MBH*, 223.

15. CH to John Paschall, n.d., box 54, folder 10, CHC. The letter is not dated, but its tone implies a familiarity that suggests it was written closer to the mid-1930s than the early 1930s.

16. CH, "The Feminine Vocabulary."

17. CH, "On Meeting a Princess." In a letter to a fan, Harris wrote, "I smoke cigarettes since my husband's death . . . but I think it is wrong for women to smoke. I do not know what God will do with me about this sin, but I doubt he will damn me." CH to Mrs. Strong, April 27, 1922, CHC.

18. Harris started smoking sometime in the 1910s. It was not something she tried to hide.

19. Harris wrote frequently to her daughter about developing the trait of indifference.

However, her earliest reflections on it show up in a letter to Paul More. CH to PEM, November [10], 1901.

20. CH to FHL, n.d., CHC, box 1, folder 14.

21. Ibid.

22. CH, "Early Recollections of Mortality."

23. CH, "Her Last Affair," 57.

24. CH to FHL, November 11, 1918, CHC.

25. CH, *MBH*, 310–11.

26. CH to PEM, November 18, 1902, PEMP.

27. CH to GHL, August 16, 1909, LP.

28. CH, "The Happy Woman," 33.

29. CH, *AWT*, 253.

30. CH, *MBH*, 311.

31. CH, *AWT*, 249.

32. CH, *MBH*, 90–91.

33. CH, "A Woman Who Likes Growing Old."

34. CH to John Paschall, December 16, 1934, CHC.

35. Jastrow, "The Implications of Sex," 130.

36. Ibid., 130, 131, 141.

37. Gilman, *Women and Economics*; *Concerning Children*; *The Home*; *Human Work*; *The Man-Made World*; *His Religion and Hers*; *The Living of Charlotte Perkins Gilman*.

38. Gilman, *The Man-Made World*, 20.

39. Ibid., 21.

40. Gilman, *His Religion and Hers*, 115. For an examination of how personal identity is formed according to the Western world's paradigm, see Benhabib, *Situating the Self*, 156–57.

41. Edwin E. Slosson to CH, July 13, 1909, CHC.

42. Will Harben to CH, November 10, 1908, CHC.

43. Al Harris to CH, December 30, 1922, CHC.

44. Ibid.

45. CH, *CRW*, 165–66.

46. CH, *MBH*, 222.

47. CH, "A Southern Woman Author."

48. CH, "Women Are Not Domestic."

49. CH, "Price of Suffrage for American Women," 11.

50. CH, "The Migration of Women." There is no date on the typescript, but parts of it appear in a speech by Selah Adams in *Co-Citizens*, 190–93.

51. CH, "Women Are Not Domestic."

52. CH, *AWT*, 241.

53. Ibid. Gerda Lerner hardly said it better when she wrote in *The Creation of Patriarchy*, "Men and women live on a stage, on which they act out their assigned roles, equal in importance. The play cannot go on without both kinds of performers. . . . But the stage set is conceived, painted, defined by men. Men have written the play, have directed the

show, interpreted the meanings of the action. They have assigned themselves the most interesting, most heroic parts, giving women the supporting roles" (6–7).

54. CH, "The Migration of Women."

55. CH, "The Synthetic Girl," 37.

56. Ibid.

57. A. F. Scott, "Women in the South," 26, 29.

58. Kerber and DeHart cite Frantz Fanon, a leader in the Algerian resistance against the French, and Christine de Pizan, a fourteenth-century professional writer, as articulating well the effects on a people of not knowing their history (*Women's America*, 1).

59. A. F. Scott, "Women in the South," 23.

60. CH, "Women Are Not Domestic."

61. CH, *AWT*, 240–41.

62. Ibid., 241.

63. CH, *MBH*, 222.

64. CH, *AWT*, 237.

65. CH, *MBH*, 222.

66. Ibid., 221.

67. CH, *AWT*, 247.

68. CH to John Paschall, July 23, 1933, CHC.

69. CH, "Wife Often to Blame If Husband Is Unfaithful."

70. CH, "These Husbands," 27.

71. Ibid.

72. Ibid.

73. CH, *MBH*, 104–5.

74. CH, "What Men Know about Women," 370; CH, "Men and Women—And the 'Woman Question,'" 165; CH, "A Woman Who Likes Growing Old"; M. M. Marshall, "Every Woman."

75. CH, "Reflections Upon Old Bachelors in New England," 1493.

76. CH, "Her Last Affair," 16.

77. CH to Mrs. Strong, April 27, 1922, CHC.

78. Relevant articles and books by Harris are listed here in chronological order: "A Woman's Relation to the Two Sexes"; "A Man's Relation to the Two Sexes"; "Reflections Upon Old Bachelors in New England"; "Superwoman"; "The Women and the Future"; "Price of Suffrage for American Women"; "Ideal Husband"; "Wife Often to Blame If Husband Is Unfaithful"; "The New Militants"; "What Men Know about Women"; "The Happy Woman"; *A Daughter of Adam*, 278–79, 287; *AWT*, 104; "These Husbands," 84.

79. CH, "On the Management of a Husband," 30.

80. CH, "A Woman's Relation to the Two Sexes," 906.

81. CH, "If You Must Come to New York," 31.

82. Dix, "Woman's Inhumanity to Woman," 633–35.

83. Ibid., 635.

84. CH, "A Woman's Relation to the Two Sexes," 906.

85. CH, "Ideal Husband."

86. Harris still believed jealousy the "worst" evil in 1930 when she was lecturing on evil at Rollins College. Interestingly, she gave it a much higher billing than sins of the flesh. "On Lecturing on Evil to College Students."

87. CH, "A Woman's Relation to the Two Sexes," 906.

88. Ibid.

89. CH to PEM, November [10], 1901, PEMP.

90. CH to PEM, February 3, 1904, PEMP. Harris disliked Edwin Slosson, who became literary editor at the *Independent* in 1903 largely because of his wife. At first Slosson had little tolerance for Harris's personal correspondence, but more insulting to Harris than Slosson himself was the fact that he turned her letters over to his wife, who also joined the staff there and happened to have a Ph.D. "I would not have been more distressed," Harris wrote, "if I had heard that there was a literary lady anoconda [*sic*] hibernating in the *Independent* office." Harris was convinced that Slosson and his wife not only did not like her personally but had no regard for her talent as a writer. She wrote More, who had by the time of this letter left the *Independent*, to ask him to help her find work if Slosson and Slosson kept refusing to print her reviews.

91. CH, "Be Sweet, Clever Maid," 1008.

92. Ibid.

93. CH to PEM, n.d., but it follows one dated "Saturday Night" and precedes one dated March 21, 1903, PEMP.

94. CH, *AWT*, 144.

95. CH to FHL, April 1919, CHC.

96. CH to John J. Spurgean, July 3, 1922, CHC.

97. CH to FHL, January 13, 1917, CHC.

98. CH to PEM, July 19, 1901, CHC.

99. Thurman, *A Strange Freedom*, 142.

100. CH to PEM, February 10, 1904, PEMP.

101. CH to Mrs. Strong, April 27, 1922, CHC.

102. CH, "A Woman Who Likes Growing Old."

103. CH to John J. Spurgean, July 3, 1922, CHC.

104. CH to PEM, June 17, September 14, 1901, PEMP.

105. For example, see her short story "Ideal Husband."

106. CH, *MBH*, 69–70. Growing old frightened Harris when she was approaching middle age. At thirty-eight she wrote More: "It frightens me, to think of the time when this great power to live dies in me with advancing years—to think of the polite indifference of the world to me, fading like a rose upon its breast.—For I have noticed that old people are not loved. We do our duty by them, we have a deep patient affection for them along with the [illegible] of our sense of obligation to them, but I do not think we love them with that immortal power of loving. Therefore the most earnest prayer I have prayed for many a day is that I may not live past this middle age that I am in now. I'd rather be in a green grave somewhere, forgotten, than an old lady in an armchair with whom my own grandchildren would have to learn to be patient." To be even more brutally candid, Harris wanted nothing to do with grandchildren. "Do you ever think of your grand children? I cannot bear mine. I cannot yield me to them, this weary heart,

nor confess [illegible] them! . . . The Good Lord preserve me from grand children!" CH to PEM, October 14, 1907, PEMP.

107. CH to FH, December 22, 1908, CHC. Faith mirrored her mother's sentiment on growing older. "Just think," she wrote her mother from college a few days before her Christmas Eve birthday, "nearly nineteen years old! It sounds pretty old but not as bad as twenty-one. I have a kind of feeling that I'm going to become positively sullen my twenty-first birthday" (December 20, 1906, CHC). She does not sound sullen around the time of her twenty-first birthday, but she was clearly thinking about aging when she wrote her father a few days afterward that she was "turning grey *rapidly*" (FH to Lundy Howard Harris, December 29, 1908, CHC).

108. CH, "A Woman's Relation to the Two Sexes," 907–8.

109. At the age of sixty-three, just two years before she died, Harris had apparently grown comfortable with aging and was vociferously defying "fashions founded on diet." In November 1933 she responded to a complaint made in the *Atlanta Journal* about the number of dresses women tried on in department stores. She would not apologize, she wrote, for the fact that she tried on "all the frocks of my size in the ready-to-wear department" and still found none that pleased her. Nor did she think it unreasonable to expect to find a fashion that made a "stout" woman such as herself look "slender," especially if that was the shape culture demanded. She saw the evils of the "fashion industrial complex" while it was in its infancy: "In a cultural period, where we spend more for style and for appearances than we do to preserve our morals or to educate our children, or to support the gospel or to save the heathen in the uttermost parts of the earth—indeed, more than we spend for all these things put together—I hold that my demand for 'slenderizing' effects in the frocks I wear is just and reasonable." CH, "Fashions Founded on Diet."

Chapter 6: Widows as the "Only Free Moral Agents"

1. CH, "The Southern White Woman," 430–32, and "A Southern Woman's View of Southern Women," 923–24.

2. CH and PEM, *JL*, 152.

3. Ibid., 121–22, 154–55, 309, 311, 314–19, 320, 325.

4. Both characters illustrate the doctrinal and theological debates going on in the southern Methodist Church at the time, particularly in Georgia and in Corra and Lundy Harris's own personal lives. See Owen, *Sacred Flame of Love*, 149–87.

5. Harris's questioning of the institutional church is found in *CRW*, 281, 290, 300, and in *RA*, 80.

6. CH, *CRW*, 182–83.

7. Ibid., 316.

8. Ibid., 314.

9. Ibid., 266–70, 276–77.

10. Ibid., 280.

11. Ibid., 284.

12. Ibid., 281.

13. Ibid., 283–84.

14. Ibid., 287.

15. Ibid., 289.
16. Ibid., 291, 301.
17. Ibid., 304–5.
18. Ibid., 305.
19. Ibid., 306, 309.
20. CH, *RA*, 273.
21. CH, *CRW*, 79. Love is described similarly in many places in this novel. See 22, 80, 220, 255, 273, 312, 317.
22. Ibid., 220.
23. Ibid.
24. Ibid., 314.
25. Ibid., 331.
26. Ibid., 332.
27. Ibid., 335–36.
28. CH, *RA*, 75.
29. Ibid., 62.
30. Ibid., 125.
31. Ibid., 115.
32. Ibid., 312.
33. Ibid., 117.
34. Ibid., 18.
35. Ibid., 79.
36. Ibid., 18.
37. Ibid.
38. Ibid., 21.
39. Ibid., 222.
40. Ibid., 20, 222.
41. Ibid., 20.
42. Ibid., 117.
43. Ibid., 214.
44. This same reasoning can be found in many of Harris's other works of fiction, including *Flapper Anne.*
45. CH, *RA*, 317.
46. Ibid., 214.
47. Harris believed the trait of indifference gave women power because of the ways it gave them control over men. It attracted and seduced some men while it intimidated and repulsed others, but at all times it kept them off guard. It was obviously not a feminine trait and hence often made women unattractive. But if a woman was willing to trade love for power, cultivating indifference was the key. "For men are certainly more easily attracted by the self-conscious woman, whether she is shrinkingly so or boldly so, than they are by one who sleeps soundly unmindful of them and who goes about her business the next day with no animated sense of them." *AWT*, 253.
48. CH, "The Widow Ambrose," 151–52.
49. Ibid., 7.

50. Ibid., 8.
51. Ibid., 9.
52. Ibid., 151.
53. Ibid.
54. Ibid., 9.
55. Ibid.
56. Ibid., 152.
57. Ibid.
58. Ibid.
59. Ibid., 8.
60. Ibid., 152.
61. Ibid.
62. CH, "Concerning Widows," 64.
63. CH, *AWT*, 243.
64. CH to FHL, August 22, 1913, CHC; CH, *HP*, 211–19.
65. CH, *AWT*, 183.
66. In addition to works already cited, see *MBH*, 309–10; "Concerning Widows"; Chapter XL, "Widowhood," in *AWT*; and her short story "The Pageant Widow."
67. CH, "Women Are Not Domestic."
68. CH, "The Synthetic Girl," 37.
69. Gilman, *The Man-Made World*, 176.
70. Gilman, *Women and Economics*, 260.

Chapter 7: "A Woman Who Writes Is Born to Trouble"

1. CH, "Editors."
2. CH, "Mature and Amateur Writers."
3. CH to FHL, February, 18, 1919, CHC.
4. GHL to CH, March 10, 1910, CHC.
5. H. J. Martin to CH, December 13, 1913, Henry Wamack to CH, March 23, 1912, Dr. George W. Carey to CH, March 12, 1912, and Dr. Mabel A. Geddes, September 9, 1925, CHC. For a further sampling see W. W. Ballew to CH, July 8, 1924, Joseph A. McCullough to CH, August 9, 1910, and July 23, 1924, R. O. Purdy to CH, October 20, 1916, J. F. Woodward to CH, July 3, 1924, Stovall Johnson to CH, January 1, 1911, Dr. J. F. Woodward to CH, July 3, 1924, Professor David Thomas to CH, October 22, 1916, Dr. George W. Carey to CH, March 12, 1912, John Byron Dame to CH, September 19, 1913, James N. Cox to CH, April 18, 1912, David Thomas to CH, October 22, 1916, and C. E. Kregloe to CH, October 27, 1916, CHC.
6. FH to CH, December 16, 1908, CHC. Harris's daughter wrote home to her mother from Woman's College of Baltimore that her economics professor, a Dr. Thomas, talked frequently about Harris's articles and that "the college is resounding with excited comment over your articles." At the time Harris was publishing primarily literary reviews and articles comparing North and South in the *Independent*.
7. Milton C. White to CH, May 5, 1933, CHC.
8. GHL and Adelaide Nealle of the *Saturday Evening Post* to CH, April 6, 14, and May

20, 1933, and CH to John Paschall, April 8, 28, and May 19, 1933, reveal Harris's difficulty toning down her political dogma opposing FDR's "welfare racket" as the reason she could not get published.

9. Wade H. Cooper to CH, 1919, and M. H. Gossett to CH, January 30, 1924, CHC.

10. GHL to CH, April 3, 1912, CHC.

11. Harris's writings ostensibly promoted traditional domesticity yet were written in the authority of a masculine voice. That they appealed especially to the business and banking sectors says as much about the conservative nature of the Progressive Era as it says about Harris. Known as a period of political and social reform, the first two decades of the twentieth century nonetheless harbored considerable reaction to progress, especially to gender reforms. The widespread acceptance of Harris's works suggests a more conservative than progressive reading public in American society during the Progressive Era. In "Corra Harris and the *SEP*," Karen Coffing illustrates Harris's commitment to the nineteenth-century traditional domestic ideal through an analysis of her works published in the *Saturday Evening Post*. Coffing was interested in Harris primarily as a "conveyor of southern domesticity to a national audience," or in her astute ability to discern and cater to what would have been "politically correct" in her day. Coffing shows that Harris's nostalgic themes were not reacting to but rather mirroring mainstream values in the era historians have deemed Progressive. Coffing's purpose, however, was more to demonstrate how the success of Harris's fiction proved it to be as much a reflection of the conservative values of middle-class white America in the 1920s, a time when America had theoretically grown progressive, as it was a reflection of Harris's values.

12. Jane B. Mundy titled her master's thesis "The Philosopher of the Heart: Corra White Harris, the Circuit Rider's Wife's Philosophy of Man."

13. HH, speech at dedication of memorial chapel, June 5, 1936, CHC.

14. CH to Adelaide Nealle, April 26, 1922, CHC; Bettie Rains Upshaw to Marjorie McClain, November 21, 1932, CWHP.

15. HH to CH, January 10, 1934, CHC.

16. HH, speech at dedication of memorial chapel, June 5, 1936, CHC.

17. CH, "Editors."

18. CH, "The South," 180.

19. Overton, *The Women Who Make Our Novels*, 154; Milton C. White to CH, May 5, 1933, CHC.

20. Both declined because of the prohibitive costs of upkeep. Talmadge, *Corra Harris*, 149.

21. Tate, "A Neighbor's Recollections," 3. Harris's faith in herself grew out of the experience in 1899 that she wrote about in many places, most dramatically and popularly in *CRW*. There is also a letter from her to Paul More that captures the way learning the art and skill of reviewing books nurtured that conviction until it became the cornerstone of her identity, and an urgent compulsion to know what it meant to be free in every sense of the word possible. CH to PEM, July 2 [or 12], 1901, PEMP.

22. Blackstock, "Corra Harris," 68. Others who have critiqued Harris's works include Ayers, *Promise of the New South*, 105, 168, 173, 335; Mixon, "'Traditionalist and Iconoclast'";

P. Schmidt, "Harris's *The Recording Angel*"; and Simms, "Corra Harris on the Decline of Southern Writing," "Corra Harris, William Peterfield Trent, and Southern Writing," and "Corra Harris on 'Literalism' in Fiction."

23. A. G. Jones, *Tomorrow Is Another Day*, 307.

24. Mixon, "Traditionalist and Iconoclast," 241.

25. Blackstock, "Corra Harris," 91–92.

26. Mixon, "Traditionalist and Iconoclast," 241. Mixon regards Harris's early critical essays and fiction, especially the Brasstown stories published in the first decade of the century in the *Independent* and *American Illustrated Magazine*, to be her best work.

27. Mixon, "Traditionalist and Iconoclast," 242. For more recent critiques of Harris's works see Coffing, "Corra Harris and the *SEP*" and "Southern Womanhood Preached to a National Audience"; Ayers, *Promise of the New South*; P. Schmidt, "Harris's *The Recording Angel*."

28. Gifford, "Women in Social Reform Movements," 296.

29. CH to GHL, November 11, 1916, LP.

30. CH to FHL, August 27, 1918.

31. Bettie Rains to "Aunt Sarah," December 22, 1934, CHC.

32. CH, "Answers to Correspondents," *Atlanta Journal*, January 5, 1934. "Nothing could be farther from my plans than to become a writer," Harris wrote in *AWT*, 116; see also *MBH*, 251.

33. CH to FHL, November 30, 1916. They were working together on the book they coauthored, *From Sun-up to Sun-down*, and were critiquing each other's work. Faith had criticized something in a passage of her mother's and was concerned that it might have offended her. Harris was trying to assure her that it had not but that she understood why Faith might have wondered about it. "I suppose it is natural that you should interpret me through your own more poignant sensibilities," Harris reasoned, "but it is a mistake." "For example, I was not discouraged. I did not brood over the criticism as you imagine." Later she wrote, "I think you would understand me better if you did not confuse yourself with me." CH to FHL, May 1, 1917, CHC.

34. CH to Fred Harris, June 23, 1933, CHC.

35. CH, *MBH*, 187.

36. CH to FHL, 1916, box 7, folder 9, CHC; CH to FHL, October 11, November 7, 1916, CHC.

37. CH, *MBH*, 253. The depressive episode described in *MBH* occurred after Lundy sided with the trustees at Vanderbilt University and they lost to the Methodist Church in their bid to control the university.

38. CH to FH, March 22, 1909, CHC.

39. Reference to "hack work" from CH to PEM, February 24, 1909, PEMP.

40. CH to FH, March 22, 1909, CHC. Since 1910, the book was re-released in 1933 by Houghton Mifflin and again in 1998 as a Brown Thrasher Book by the University of Georgia Press. The novel had apparently taken firm root in Harris's mind and was less subject to being lost from neglect than she supposed. She claimed in *MBH* to have written the novel in less than thirty days (264). When it was re-released in 1933, Houghton

Mifflin claimed the book was so successful in bringing about changes in the Methodist Church that "few missionaries served their cause more valiantly." "Book News," Houghton Mifflin Company, August 3, 1933.

41. CH to FHL, June 26, August 4, 1913.

42. CH, *AWT*, 220.

43. John Paschall, speech at dedication of memorial chapel, June 5, 1936, CHC.

44. CH to Medora Perkerson, July 23, 1933, CHC.

45. CH, "Half a Day in 'A Perfect Life.'"

46. CH to FHL, n.d. [probably 1910], box 1, folder 14, CHC.

47. CH to FHL, 1916, box 7, folder 9, CHC.

48. CH, *MBH*, 274.

49. Ennis, "Circuit Rider's Wife"; Mixon, "Traditionalist and Iconoclast"; P. Schmidt, "Harris's *The Recording Angel*"; Simms, "Corra Harris on the Decline of Southern Writing," "Corra Harris, William Peterfield Trent, and Southern Writing," and "Corra Harris on 'Literalism' in Fiction."

50. Wallerstein, "Southern Culture," 6.

51. O'Brien, *Idea of the American South*, 10.

52. Talmadge, *Corra Harris*, 30.

53. Simms, "Corra Harris, William Peterfield Trent, and Southern Writing."

54. Mixon, "Traditionalist and Iconoclast"; Simms, "Corra Harris on the Decline of Southern Writing" and "Corra Harris on 'Literalism' in Fiction."

55. See the following works by Harris: "Fiction, North and South"; "Neurotic Symptoms in Recent Fiction"; "Our Novelists"; "The Walking Delegate Novelist"; "The Rise and Fall of Popular Novels during 1906"; "Advice to Literary Aspirants"; "To License Novelists"; "The Advance of Civilization in Fiction"; "The Year's Curriculum in Fiction."

56. Simms, "Corra Harris, William Peterfield Trent, and Southern Writing," 642.

57. Harris writes about the experience in "Patriotic Criticism in the South" and "Southern Writers."

58. CH, "The Walking Delegate Novelist," 1213. Granted, here Harris follows with her chief purpose in referring to Stowe's novel, namely, to compare its effects with that of the socialist novelists. Granting credence to Lincoln's reputed quip that Harriet Beecher Stowe was responsible for starting the Civil War, *Uncle Tom's Cabin*, Harris wrote, "sowed seeds of bitterness between" whites of the North and the South, while socialists were stirring "lasting hatreds between the masses and the classes."

59. CH, *AWT*, 63.

60. Bartley, *Creation of Modern Georgia*, 107.

61. Edward A. Pollard in *The Lost Cause* (1866), 174. See Wilson, *Baptized in Blood*, for the moral fervor behind the cause.

62. CH, "Patriotic Criticism in the South," 550.

63. CH, "Fiction, North and South" and "Heroes and Heroines in Recent Fiction."

64. CH, "Fiction, North and South," 275.

65. Simms, "Corra Harris on the Decline of Southern Writing," 247.

66. CH, "The Literary Spectrum of New York," 441.

67. CH, "Fiction, North and South," 274.

68. Talmadge, *Corra Harris*, 31.

69. Ibid., 275.

70. CH, "Neurotic Symptoms in Recent Fiction," 2727.

71. On the origins of the United Daughters of the Confederacy see Cox, "Rise."

72. CH, "Patriotic Criticism in the South," 548.

73. Ibid., 549.

74. CH, "Advice to Literary Aspirants," 83.

75. CH in Simms, "Corra Harris, William Peterfield Trent, and Southern Writing," 644, 645, 646.

76. Ibid., 648.

77. Ibid., 647.

78. Ibid., 648.

79. CH, "The Year's Curriculum in Fiction," 1150.

80. CH, "Neurotic Symptoms in Recent Fiction," 2727.

81. CH, "Authors and Their Works"; CH, "Answers to Correspondents," *Atlanta Journal*, April 18, 1934.

82. CH, "The Rise and Fall of Popular Novels during 1906," 546; CH, "The Walking Delegate Novelist," 1216.

83. CH, "Fiction, North and South," 274; CH, "Patriotic Criticism in the South," 549; CH, "Neurotic Symptoms in Recent Fiction"; CH, "Our Novelists"; CH, "The Rise and Fall of Popular Novels during 1906," 544.

84. CH, "The Advance of Civilization in Fiction," 1172; CH in Simms, "Corra Harris, William Peterfield Trent, and Southern Writing," 650.

85. CH, "Southern Writers," quoted in Simms, "Corra Harris, William Peterfield Trent, and Southern Writing," 649–50.

86. CH, "Our Novelists," 1171. Harris's family's financial necessity likely explains why she catered to the demands of the market in several nonfiction essays published over the next two decades in which she romanticized southern identity, if not the past upon which it was based. In the essays she portrayed southern women obsequiously as long-suffering, "sad-eyed Madonnas" who were passive by nature and who lived to please. See CH, "The Southern White Woman" and "A Southern Woman's View of Southern Women." She wrote Paul More about southern women; see esp. CH to PEM, July 13, 1901, PEMP.

Harris portrayed southern men much as Wilbur Cash did. However, she mostly romanticized and celebrated the traits Cash critiqued, interpreted, and found regressive. Four decades earlier than Cash, Harris described, though she did not interpret, the contradiction between southern white men's obsession with individuality—their belief that they were entirely independent, the authors of their own fate—and their reverence toward authority. They were democratic in their feelings and yet "monarchical" in their respect for authority. CH, "The White Man in the South," 3475, 3477; CH, "The Confederate Veteran"; CH, "Fiction, North and South"; CH, "North and South: The Difference," 1349; CH, "The Cheerful Life in the South," 137; and CH, "The South's Way."

87. CH, "The Advance of Civilization in Fiction," 1171–72.

88. Although Harris moved on from literary critic to writing fiction, in 1929 the *Atlanta Journal* solicited from her a critique of "the South's Literary Revival," primarily a "revival of the negro in southern literature." An exposition of southern books occasioned the review. Harris was relieved to report that southern writers and the southern reading public had finally begun to move forward. She praised her old friend (then deceased) Joel Chandler Harris, whose works were being reissued. She believed he had been the only writer to capture authentic "negro dialect" in his stories until very recently. She reiterated the limits of Thomas Nelson Page on the genre. She praised Dubose Heyward, Julia Peterkin, and especially Roark Bradford as the most recently accomplished writers in the revival of "negro dialect." Obvious by omission are writers typically associated with the Southern Renaissance and who had published at the time: William Faulkner (whose fiction had not yet made him synonymous with the revival), Ellen Glasgow, Elizabeth Maddox Roberts, Isa Glenn, and Stark Young. CH, "Corra Harris Discusses Writers," 4. A typed copy of this article is found in CHC with the title "The Revival of the Negro in Southern Literature," box 81, folder 3.

89. Notwithstanding her doubts in *AWT* suggesting the contrary.

90. CH, *AWT*, 183.

91. CH to PEM, July 25, 1901, PEMP.

92. CH to John Paschall, October 6, 1934, CHC.

93. CH, *HP*, 12.

94. CH, *AWT*, 183–84.

95. CH to FHL, February 23, 1919, CHC.

96. CH to FHL, October 13, 1917, CHC.

97. CH to FHL, March 19, 1917, CHC.

98. CH to FHL, 1916, box 7, folder 9, CHC.

99. CH, *MBH*, 302.

100. CH, "Writing and Living."

101. CH, *AWT*, 143.

102. CH, *MBH*, 274.

103. CH, *AWT*, 144.

104. Ibid.

105. CH to John Paschall, October 6, 1934, CHC.

106. CH to PEM, March 23, 1903, PEMP.

107. CH to PEM, November 18, 1902, CHC.

108. CH to FHL, August 22, 1913, CHC.

109. CH to GHL, March 2, 1923, LP.

110. CH to PEM, February 14, 1902, PEMP.

111. CH to PEM, November 18, 1902, PEMP.

112. CH to Medora Perkerson, November 21, 1931, CHC.

113. CH to John Paschall, March 21, 1934, CHC.

114. CH, *MBH*, 180.

115. CH to GHL, October 12, 1912, LP.

116. CH to John Paschall, "Thawed Wednesday" [likely sometime in December 1933], box 54, folder 6, CHC.

117. John Paschall, speech at dedication of memorial chapel, June 5, 1936, CHC.

118. CH, "Editors."

119. Ibid.

120. Quoted in John Paschall's speech at dedication of memorial chapel, June 5, 1936, CHC.

121. Ibid.

122. Talmadge, *Corra Harris*, 33.

123. CH to PEM, February 3, 1904, PEMP.

124. CH to PEM, July 2 [or 12], 1901, PEMP.

125. CH to PEM, November [10], 1901, PEMP.

126. CH, "Editors."

127. CH to GHL, March 17, 1929, CHC.

128. CH to PEM, November 20, 1902, PEMP.

129. CH to PEM, March 21, 1903, PEMP.

130. CH to PEM, November 20, 1902, PEMP.

131. CH to PEM, December 2, 1903, PEMP.

132. John Phillips to CH, August 18, 1906, CHC.

133. John Phillips to CH, October 12, 1906, CHC.

134. HH to CH, November 28, 1906, CHC.

135. Russell Doubleday to CH, May 18, 1916, CHC.

136. Arthur Vance to CH, January 30, 1917, CHC.

137. Arthur T. Vance to CH, May 4, 1921, CHC.

138. Arthur Vance to CH, March 29, 1917, CHC.

139. Medora Perkerson to CH, June 27, 1931, CHC.

140. John Paschall to CH, March 20, 1934, CHC.

141. CH to John Paschall, January 1, 1935, CHC.

142. CH to John Paschall, "Thawed Wednesday," box 54, folder 6, CHC.

143. CH to Medora Perkerson, November 21, 1931, CHC.

144. CH to John Paschall, "Thawed Wednesday," box 54, folder 6, CHC.

145. John Paschall to CH, March 20, 1934, CHC.

146. CH to John Paschall, October 6, 1934, CHC.

147. John Paschall, speech at dedication of memorial chapel, June 5, 1936, CHC.

Chapter 8: From Circuit Rider's Wife to Spiritual Pundit

1. Ellsworth Hall to CH, July 28, 1933, CHC.

2. Overton, 154; Milton C. White to CH, May 5, 1933, CHC.

3. Lyerly, "Women and Southern Religion," 248; CH to Fred Harris, August 14, 1933, CHC.

4. CH to PEM, July 2 [or 12], 1901.

5. CH, "Answers to Correspondents." Periodically [at unspecified intervals] over the years Corra Harris published the Candlelit Columns. Harris responded through the column to readers' letters. There are nine published "Candles" titled "Answers to Correspondents" in the Corra Harris Collection. They can be found in box 84, folders 16–24; CH, "He Restoreth My Soul." Harris's attitude toward having the Bible taught in schools

was common in Georgia. Mixon explains, "Yet partly out of the fear of the forces of modernity, Georgia, as of the early 1920s, was one of only six states in the nation to require that the Bible be read daily in public schools." "Georgia," 94.

6. Harris attacked liberal theology and biblical higher criticism in many of her works, but it was a clear subtext in her autobiographical novels: *A Circuit Rider's Wife* (1910), *A Circuit Rider's Widow* (1916), and *My Son* (1921).

7. Dobbins, "Corra Harris," 76.

8. CH to GHL, January 8, 1925, LP; CH, "Answers to Correspondents," *Atlanta Journal*, December 28, 1934.

9. CH, *AWT*, 176; CH, "A Retired Methodist."

10. CH, "An Eruption of Saints."

11. CH, "Answers to Correspondents," *Atlanta Journal*, August 29, 1934.

12. CH, *HP*, 309.

13. CH, "Miracles."

14. CH to Charles Dobbins, November 30, 1930, quoted in Dobbins, "Corra Harris," 77–78; CH, "Not to See through a Glass Darkly."

15. CH, *AWT*, 95; CH, *MBH*, 309.

16. Reasons why Harris was not more strongly criticized, condemned, or censored for her published "heresy" but was rather tolerated or even indulged are varied. One is that however unorthodox her religious views were, she never openly challenged white supremacy. In a region where "Christ and culture"—or, in this case, religion and racial hierarchy—overlapped, Joel Martin explains, "This dual focus produced an interesting situation. It allowed lapsed Protestants and even non-Christians to gain respectability by defending Dixie and her values. Shared culture, language, and memory tied 'sinner' and 'saint' together into one big white Southern gemeinschaft. Indeed, in the old order, it was probably worse to show signs of being a traitor to Dixie and its dominant values, especially those regarding race, than to skip church or indulge agnosticism. Case in point: George Washington Cable ended up in exile; William Faulkner did not" ("All That Is Solid," www.jsr.fsu.edu).

17. Professor Jones to CH, August 18, 1933, CHC.

18. Mathews, "Lynching," 183. See the following monographs for the pervasive influence of religion on southern culture: Heyrman, *Southern Cross*; Hill, *The South and the North*; Owen, *Sacred Flame of Love*; Wilson, *Baptized in Blood*. Essays from the following are also helpful: Hill, *Religion and the Solid South* and *Religion in the Southern States*; Schweiger and Mathews, *Religion in the American South*.

19. CH, *MBH*, 193.

20. CH, "The Pharisee's Lament," 83.

21. CH, "A Foreigner in the Kingdom of Heaven."

22. CH, "A Woman Takes a Look at Politics," 128; CH, *AWT*, 243.

23. Harvey, "God and Negroes," 313.

24. CH to FHL, February 7, 1917, CHC.

25. Harvey, "God and Negroes," 283.

26. Mims, *The Advancing South*, 204.

27. CH, "Address at Rich's."

28. CH, *AWT*, 176–77. She spent "her real Christian charity on a family of Hardshell Baptists who are in graver need of help than a rich and prosperous church."

29. A. F. Scott, "Women, Religion, and Social Change," 95.

30. CH, "Address at Rich's."

31. CH, *AWT*, 91.

32. Mathews, "Lynching," 183.

33. Lyerly, "Women and Southern Religion," 249.

34. On this point Talmadge was off the mark when he wrote, "Like many people Mrs. Harris was more conscious of her admirable traits than of her dubious ones" (*Corra Harris*, 47). She wrote frequently and candidly about her temper, her prejudices, and her ego, neither making excuses nor breast-beating.

35. John Paschall, speech at dedication of memorial chapel, June 5, 1936, CHC.

36. To maintain that the tenets survived the war and remained fundamental to the churches of the New South is not to suggest that they were fixed and impervious to human agency. As Christine Heyrman writes in *Southern Cross*, southern evangelicalism "has never been a static, monolithic structure of belief and . . . its adherents have never been an undifferentiated mass" (254).

37. A. F. Scott, "Women, Religion, and Social Change," 95.

38. Mathews, "Lynching," 155.

39. Mathews, "Southern Rite," www.jsr.fsu.edu. Mathews is writing here about the insight of U.S. Commissioner of Education A. D. Mayo, also a Unitarian minister, on southern religion.

40. McLoughlin, *Revivals, Awakening, and Reform.*

41. Hill, *The South and the North*, 121.

42. A. F. Scott, "Women, Religion, and Social Change," 116. The fact that "the amount of social visiting" diminished during and after the war also contributed to women's re-channeling their energies.

43. Cox, *Dixie's Daughters*; Wilson, *Baptized in Blood.*

44. Harvey, "God and Negroes," 287.

45. Mathews, "Southern Rite," 5.

46. Mathews, "Lynching," 159.

47. Hill, "The South's Two Cultures," 31.

48. Reinhold Niebuhr in *The Irony of American History* and Edmund S. Morgan in *American Slavery, American Freedom* capture the element of irony in American history. See Cobb, "Does 'Mind' Still Matter?"

49. Lyerly, "Women and Southern Religion," 269.

50. Carter, *Spiritual Crisis.*

51. CH, "Patriotic Criticism in the South," 548.

52. Mathews, "'We Have Left Undone,'" 305. Mathews writes that it was likely during the 1920s that religion became "one of the most distinguishing marks of the American South."

53. Hill, *The South and the North*, 124.

54. Ibid., 125.

55. Hunter Dickinson Farish quoted in ibid., 125.

56. CH, "Letter to Home on Religion" and "The Communion of Saints."

57. CH, "The Communion of Saints."

58. Hill, *The South and the North*, 125–26.

59. Hudson, "Structure," 138.

60. Mixon, "Georgia," 95.

61. Hill, *The South and the North*, 128.

62. Hill, "The South's Two Cultures," 27.

63. A. F. Scott, "Women, Religion, and Social Change," 108. In *Personal Politics*, Sara Evans draws a similar conclusion about the relationship between white women in the Methodist Church and the civil rights movement.

64. CH to PEM, May 23, 1901, PEMP.

65. CH to Warren Candler, October 29, 1899, CWHP.

66. CH to PEM, October 10, 1901, PEMP.

67. CH to PEM, May 19, 1902, PEMP.

68. See, e.g., CH, "He Restoreth My Soul." Harris wrote often of attending the bedside of dying neighbors. The story she tells in this "Candle" reveals ways she may have counseled many a dissenter, unchurched and outside the fold of southern evangelicalism.

69. CH, "How Old?"

70. CH to Miss Douglas, November 8, 1930, CHC.

71. CH, "The Year's Curriculum in Fiction," 1152.

72. CH, "Negro Womanhood," 1688.

73. CH, "Our Novelists," 1175.

74. CH, "The Year's Curriculum in Fiction," 1154; see also CH, "Black and White."

75. Mathews, 182–83. In "Lynching," Mathews explores ways African Americans in the New South living under the constant threat of lynching turned to religion not as escape but as empowerment. Through their own interpretation of Christianity, they saw in "the death of Christ a sacrifice through which to transcend the terror inflicted upon them. All that Christ experienced demonstrated his oneness with African Americans. The Christian religion of black southerners could encourage them to believe ultimately that they would overcome all things. As believers, they saw that God was not a God of white purity, as segregation implied and as lynchers insisted, but of black sacrifice and eventual resurrection" (182).

76. Mathews, "Southern Rite," 6.

77. Ibid., 5.

78. CH, "Jeff," 716.

79. Ibid., 724.

80. Ibid., 717.

81. Ibid., 722.

82. The term *moral contamination* comes from Mathews, "Southern Rite," citing Virginia historian Philip Alexander Bruce writing in 1911. See also Gilmore's *Gender and Jim Crow*, especially chapter 3 ("Race and Manhood"), for a treatment what the term *best men* meant to middle-class African Americans at the time.

83. Harvey, "God and Negroes," 285.

84. In 1914 a book with a similar title was far more forthright about racial injustice in the South. Ann Scott writes about Lily Hardy Hammond, who helped establish and served as superintendent of a Bureau of Social Service. In *In Black and White*, Hammond used Christianity to challenge Jim Crow and other forms of institutionalized racism in the South. A. F. Scott, "Women, Religion, and Social Change," 108. See also Lyerly, "Women and Southern Religion," 257–58; Harvey, "God and Negroes," 313.

85. CH, "Black and White," 102. For an example of a black intellectual's thoughts on the subject, see Schuyler, "Our White Folks."

86. A. F. Scott, "Women in the South," 31.

87. CH, "Corra Harris Discusses Writers," 4.

88. In *Making Whiteness*, Grace Hale writes that many middle-class white women of Harris's generation, such as Rutherford and Felton, helped promote "mammy lore," or the belief that mammies loved the white children over whom they watched as much as or more than their own children, with an implicit message in some of their writings that mammies' love "went beyond 'love' for individual whites to support white supremacy itself" (102).

89. Some of the quotes are taken from a typed copy of "Black and White" found in box 74, folder 12, CHC. Responses to "Black and White" are interesting for what they reveal about perceptions by both races about race as an ontological subject at the time. Letters of praise came from as far away as Mondsee, Salzkammergut, Austria. Mr. J. M. Swanson, a "white collar workin' man" from Indiana, appreciated the distinction Harris made in the article between "immoral" and "un-moral." To Mr. Swanson, crediting the African race with the latter rather than blaming them for the former (as she had done in earlier works) "breeds a tolerance in our hearts that makes us broader and finer citizens." J. M. Swanson to CH, December 19, 1930, CHC.

Responses from two black male readers are even more telling of the level of awareness of the implications of her message. Gerald Hamilton of New York thanked her for shedding light on "the conflict which is so baffling to my people today." He praised the article for its "beauty of truth," compared it favorably with Walter Lippmann's "A Preface to Morals," and told her he sent copies to all his people "interested in our efforts to see clearly the realities of life." Gerald Hamilton to CH, December 5, 1930, CHC. James F. Lawson, M.D., from Chicago wrote that he had "never read such a profound exposition of truth from a Nordic," namely, that his people had a dynastic history. Thanks to her, he was "enjoying again the luxury of my throne." It is unlikely that Harris was moved one way or the other by the praise of two educated black men. James F. Lawson to CH, December 9, 1930, CHC.

90. All excerpts from CH, "Turkey Trot"—the first on p. 49 and the next three on p. 11.

91. CH, "The Abomination of Cities," 130.

92. Ibid., 129.

93. CH, "Politics and Prayers in the Valley," 156.

94. Angered after 1906 when the church hierarchy failed to consult them about the merger of the home and foreign missions, women in the Methodist Church began to agitate for voting rights in 1910. They finally gained them in 1922. Lyerly, "Women and

Southern Religion," 265; J. M. Schmidt, *Grace Sufficient*; A. F. Scott, "Women, Religion, and Social Change," 110.

95. CH, "The Methodist Conference as Viewed by Corra Harris."

96. Ibid. Harris was wrong, however. Laity rights for women were "achieved handily" when the conferences voted 270 to 50 in favor of the reform. J. M. Schmidt, *Grace Sufficient*, 230.

97. Talmadge, *Corra Harris*, 42.

98. Ibid., 102.

99. CH to GHL, May 18, 1919, LP.

100. Ibid.

101. CH, *AWT*, 243.

102. The letter is incomplete and the first page is missing, so neither the date nor the recipient is clear, but it was likely to Marjorie McClain sometime in the late 1920s. Box 54, folder 10, CHC.

103. CH, "The Advance of Civilization in Fiction," 1169.

104. CH, "The Willipus-Wallipus in Tennessee Politics," 626.

105. CH to GHL, January 8, 1925, LP.

106. CH, *HP*, 192–93.

107. Ibid., 195.

108. Ibid., 35, 53.

109. Ibid., 276.

110. Dobbins, "Corra Harris," 76.

111. CH, *HP*, 180.

112. Ibid., 28.

113. Ibid., 18.

114. CH to GHL, January 8, 1925, LP.

115. CH, "Women Again."

116. CH to GHL, January 8, 1925, LP.

117. CH, "On Lecturing on Evil to College Students"; and see box 110, folder 6, CHC.

118. CH, *MBH*, 193.

119. Ibid., 91.

120. CH, "Spiritual Speed."

121. CH, *AWT*, 29.

122. Ibid.

123. Ibid., 233.

124. CH, *HP*, 98.

125. CH, *MBH*, 289.

126. CH, *AWT*, 233.

127. CH, "Miracles."

128. Loose pages of diary of Alma McLain Coleman Brown, 1919, box 101, folder 13, CHC.

129. CH to John Paschall, "Thawed Wednesday" [likely sometime in December 1933], box 54, folder 6, CHC.

130. Letter quoted in Al Harris, speech at dedication of memorial chapel, June 5, 1936, CHC.

131. Ibid.

132. Ibid.

133. CH, "Out of Balance."

134. CH to John Paschall, September 6, 1933, CHC.

135. CH to GHL, January 8, 1925, LP; CH to John Paschall, n.d., "Thawed Wednesday," box 54, folder 6, CHC; CH, *HP*, 28, 48, 50, 222.

136. CH to GHL, October 9, 1910, LP.

137. CH, "The Feminine Vocabulary."

138. CH, "What Religion Means to Me"; "Editors"; CH to GHL, October 12, 1912, LP; "Flickering Reflections"; "Oratorical Faith"; "Religion for Secular Souls"; "Let Us Pray"; "Letter to a Beloved Atheist"; "Faith in This World"; "Critics and Cavaliers in Literature"; "Letter to Home on Religion"; "What Shall It Profit a Man"; "Spiritual Inebriates"; "Old Texts Tried"; "Sober Reflections"; untitled "Candlelit" column, *Atlanta Journal*, November 14, 1934.

139. CH, "On the Use of Enemies."

140. Anne Firor Scott identifies Jeremiah 17:9 as antebellum women's most often-quoted verse (*The Southern Lady*, 11). Harris's references to Psalm 51:10 are too numerous to count. Regarding her privileging this verse as a rule of life, see CH, "What Religion Means to Me"; Dobbins, "Corra Harris," 76–78.

141. CH, "He Restoreth My Soul" and "Alone with God."

142. CH, "On the Use of Enemies."

143. Harris expresses in "An Eruption of Saints" her belief that "eternal damnation" is "one of the most devastating of all religious doctrines." See also her "Letter to a Beloved Atheist."

144. CH to Mrs. Strong, April 27, 1922, CHC; Talmadge, *Corra Harris*, 63.

145. CH, "How to Escape the Sense of Time."

146. Ibid.

147. CH to John Paschall, n.d.; his letter to her dated March 20, 1934, CHC, indicates that it was just before that time. She expressed the sentiment in a number of "Candles," including "How to Escape the Sense of Time" and "The Generations of the Earth."

148. CH, "Letter to Home on Religion."

149. CH, "How Old?"

150. Ibid.

151. CH to John Paschall, January 29, 1935, CHC.

152. CH, *HP*, 76. In a letter to Paschall, Harris wrote in jest as well as truth how jealous she was that he had referred to some other woman, a longtime family friend, as "precious." All her life, she said, she had wanted someone to use that word to describe her, but no one had. CH to John Paschall, August 5, 1933, CHC.

153. CH, "Doubtful Heroines and Morbid Egotists."

154. CH, "Little Children . . . Love One Another."

155. Ibid.

156. CH to FHL, November 11, 1918, CHC; CH, "Sober Reflections."
157. CH, "Editors."
158. CH, "Alone with God."
159. CH, "The Oldest Altar."
160. CH, "Religion for Secular Souls."
161. CH, "Alone with God."
162. CH, "Spiritual Inebriates."
163. CH, "Out of Balance."
164. Ibid.
165. CH, "Critics."
166. CH, "On Coming of Age."
167. CH, *HP*, 7.
168. CH, "Not to See through a Glass Darkly."
169. CH to GHL, June 1, November 3, 1923, LP.
170. CH to Marjorie McClain, November 24, December 18, 1934, CWHP.
171. CH to John Paschall, March 8, 1934, CHC.
172. CH to Marjorie McClain, November 24, 1934, CWHP.
173. CH to Marjorie McClain, October 29, 1934, CWHP.
174. John Paschall, speech at dedication of memorial chapel, June 5, 1936, CHC.
175. Talmadge, *Corra Harris*, 149–50.
176. Senate Resolution 45EX2 of the Georgia General Assembly.

Bibliography

Abbreviations

CCAJ   "Candlelit" column in *Atlanta Journal*
CHC   Corra Harris Collection. Hargrett Rare Book and Manuscript Library, University of Georgia Library, Athens
LHJ   *Ladies Home Journal*
SEP   *Saturday Evening Post*

Books by Corra White Harris

As a Woman Thinks. Boston: Houghton Mifflin, 1925. Serial in *SEP*, August 15, 22, 29, September 5, 12, 19, 26, October 3, 10, 1925.

A Circuit Rider's Widow. Garden City, N.J.: Grosset and Dunlap, 1916. Serial in *SEP*, September 2, 9, 16, 23, 30, October 7, 14, 21, 1916.

A Circuit Rider's Wife. Athens: University of Georgia Press, 1998, 1988, 1933, 1910. Serial in *SEP*, January 22, 29, February 5, 12, 19, 26, 1910.

Co-Citizens. New York: Grosset and Dunlap, 1915.

A Daughter of Adam. New York: George H. Doran, 1923.

Eve's Second Husband. Philadelphia: Henry Altemus Company, 1911. Serial in *SEP*, December 3, 10, 17, 24, 31, 1910, January 7, 14, 21, 1911.

The Eyes of Love. New York: George H. Doran, 1922.

Flapper Ann. Boston: Houghton Mifflin, 1926. Serial in *LHJ*, September, October, November, December 1925.

From Sun-up to Sun-down. With Faith Harris Leech. Garden City, N.J.: Grosset and Dunlap, 1919. Serial in *Country Gentleman*, March 16, 23, 30, April 6, 13, 20, May 4, 18, August 31, September 21, October 12, November 9, 1918.

Happily Married. New York: George H. Doran, 1920.

The Happy Pilgrimage. New York: Houghton Mifflin, 1927. Serial in *SEP*, December 4, 11, 18, 25, 1926, January 1, 8, 15, 29, 1927.

House of Helen. New York: George H. Doran, 1923.

In Search of a Husband. Toronto: Copp Clark, 1995, 1919.

The Jessica Letters. With Paul Elmer More. New York: Putnam, 1904. Serial in *The Critic*, October, November, December 1903, February, April 1904.

Justice. New York: Hearst International Library, 1915.

Making Her His Wife. Garden City, N.J.: Doubleday, Page, 1918.

My Book and Heart. Boston: Houghton Mifflin, 1924. Serial in *SEP*, September 1, 8, 15, 22, October 6, 13, 20, 27, 1923.

My Son. New York: George H. Doran, 1921. Serial in *Pictorial Review*, December 11, 18, 25, 1920, January 1, 8, 1921.

The Recording Angel. Garden City, N.J.: Doubleday, Page, 1926, 1912. Serial in *SEP*, February 17, 24, March 2, 9, 16, 23, 30, 1912.

A Town That Became a University. Winter Park, Fla.: Privately printed, 1930.

Articles and Stories by Corra White Harris

Newspaper clippings were photocopied from the CHC. All newspaper clippings in this collection can be found in boxes 108–112. In some cases, the person photocopying noted the particular box and folder. In others they noted only the date.

"The Abomination of Cities." *Independent*, January 26, 1914, 129–31.

"Address at Rich's." Unpublished speech, n.d. but likely 1934, box 98, folders 1, 14, CHC.

"The Advance of Civilization in Fiction." *Independent*, November 19, 1908, 1166–72.

"Advice to Literary Aspirants." *Independent*, January 10, 1907, 79–84.

"Alone with God." *CCAJ*, July 3, 1932.

"Authors and Their Works." Unpublished manuscript, n.d., box 98, folder 2, CHC.

"Autobiography of a Mother-in-Law." *SEP*, March 8, 1913, 8–10, 45.

"Bartow." *CCAJ*, July 27, 1932.

"Be Sweet, Clever Maid." *Independent*, May 11, 1911, 1007–9.

"Black and White." *SEP*, November 21, 1930, 100–102.

"The Bonneted Hornets." *LHJ*, October 1923, 18, 134–35.

"A Change for the Better." *SEP*, September 12, 1931, 25, 63.

"The Cheerful Life in the South." *Independent*, July 20, 1905, 137–39.

"Communion of Saints." *CCAJ*, August 13, 1933.

"Concerning Widows, or How to Be a Widow." *LHJ*, September 1920, 13, 64.

"The Confederate Veteran." *Independent*, October 23, 1901, 2357–58.

"Corra Harris Addresses Club Women on 'Woman of Yesterday at the Biennial in New York.'" *Atlanta Constitution*, n.d., box 110, folder 30, CHC.

"Corra Harris Discusses Writers." *Atlanta Journal*, March 31, 1929.

"Critics." *CCAJ*, September 18, 1932.

"Critics and Cavaliers in Literature." *CCAJ*, November 22, 1933.

"Demobilizing the American Women." *SEP*, April 26, 1919, 9, 127–34.

"Discussion on Evil." Typed transcript, box 98, folder 4, CHC.

"Doubtful Heroines and Morbid Egotists." *CCAJ*, November 18, 1934.

"Do Women Miss Happiness? Modern Life as Seen through Grandmother's Eyes." *Evening Standard*, December 5, 1928.

"Early Recollections of Mortality." Notebook, CHC.

"Editors." *Atlanta Journal*, February 10, 1933.

"An Eruption of Saints." *CCAJ*, October 7, 1932.

"Faith in This World." *CCAJ*, June 3, 1932.

"Fashions Founded on Diet." *CCAJ*, November 15, 1933.

"Fashions in Fiction." *Independent*, June 22, 1905, 1407–11.

"Favorite Sons." *CCAJ*, May 4, 1932.

"The Feminine Vocabulary." *CCAJ*, April 3, 1932.

"Fiction, North and South." *The Critic*, September 1903, 273–75.
"Flickering Reflections." *CCAJ*, December 10, 1933.
"A Foreigner in the Kingdom of Heaven." *CCAJ*, August 26, 1934.
"From the Peace Zone in the Valley." *Independent*, May 3, 1915, 190–92.
"The Generations of the Earth." *CCAJ*, May 13, 1934.
"A Good and Glorious Poverty." *CCAJ*, May 22, 1932.
"The Great Kinship." *Independent*, April 23, 1908, 899–900.
"Half a Day in a Perfect Life." *CCAJ*, October 17, 1934.
"The Happy Day." *LHJ*, July 1925, 27, 78.
"The Happy Woman: Does the Dynamic Marvel of Today Gain Peace or Regret?" *LHJ*,
    November 1923, 33, 57.
"He Restoreth My Soul." *CCAJ*, July 23, 1933.
"Her Last Affair." *SEP*, September 1, 1917, 16–18, 57.
"Heroes and Heroines in Fiction." *Independent*, September 3, 1903, 2111–15.
"Hindering the Children." *Independent*, March 12, 1908, 582–83.
"How New York Appears to a Southern Woman." *Independent*, June 13, 1907, 1400–
    1402.
"How Old?" *CCAJ*, February 24, 1933.
"How to Escape the Sense of Time." *CCAJ*, January 3, 1932.
"Ideal Husband." *Harper's Weekly*, September 17, 1913.
"If You Must Come to New York." *Independent*, April 5, 1914, 29–32.
"In the Valley." *Independent*, July 24, 1916, 123–24.
"Jeff." *Independent*, September 26, 1912, 715–22.
"June Brides." *Independent*, June 5, 1916, 377.
"Letters of an Accomplished Lady." June 12, 1928. Unpublished manuscript, CHC.
"Letter to a Beloved Atheist." *CCAJ*, May 28, 1933.
"Letter to Home on Religion." Unpublished manuscript, box 55, folder 3, CHC.
"Letter to the Editor." *Independent*, July 18, 1912, 147–49.
"Let Us Pray." *CCAJ*, June 3, 1932.
"The Literary Spectrum of New York: New York as Seen from the Valley." *Independent*,
    March 30, 1914, 441–43.
"Little Children . . . Love One Another." *CCAJ*, September 9, 1934.
"Maneuvering toward the Kingdom of Heaven." *CCAJ*, November 10, 1933.
"A Man's Relation to the Two Sexes." *Independent*, May 26, 1904, 1188–90.
"Marriage—New Profession or Old Miracle?" *Independent*, February 16, 1914, 234–35.
"Marrying Off the American Army." *Independent*, February 22, 1919, 260–61.
"Mature and Amateur Writers." *CCAJ*, July 13, 1932.
"Memories of an Early Girlhood." *Independent*, May 7, 1903, 1071–75.
"Men." *CCAJ*, November 29, 1931.
"Men and Women—And the Woman Question." *Independent*, February 2, 1914, 164–65.
"The Methodist Conference as Viewed by Corra Harris." *Atlanta Constitution*, May 19,
    1918.
"The Migration of Women." Typescript, n.d., box 78, folder 23, CHC.

"Miracles." *CCAJ*, October 16, 1932.

"The Monstrous Altruism." *Independent*, October 4, 1906, 788–98.

"Mrs. Corra Harris Discusses the Defeatt [*sic*] of the Anthony Amendment." Montgomery, Alabama, February 17, 1919.

"Mrs. Harris Off to Farm." *Evening Post*, March 14, 1914, box 110, 31, CHC.

"The Negro Child." *Independent*, October 26, 1899, 2884–86.

"Negro Womanhood." *Independent*, June 22, 1899, 1687–89.

"Neurotic Symptoms in Recent Fiction." *Independent*, November 19, 1903, 2725–28.

"The New Militants." *SEP*, November 21, 1914, 3–5, 87.

"New Pigeon Holes for Novels." *Independent*, February 13, 1902, 94–96.

"New York as Seen from a Georgia Valley." *Independent*, January 19, 1914, 97–99.

"North and South: The Difference." *Independent*, June 15, 1905, 1348–50.

"Notes about Women." Unpublished manuscript, box 79, folder 11, CHC.

"Not to See through a Glass Darkly." *CCAJ*, November 26, 1933.

"Novels and Novelists." *Independent*, November 17, 1904, 1131–39.

"Obsolete Womanhood." *SEP*, August 24, 1929, 6–7, 98–101.

"The Oldest Altar." *CCAJ*, December 15, 1933.

"Old Texts Tried." *CCAJ*, August 20, 1933.

"On Coming of Age." *CCAJ*, January 22, 1932.

"On Lecturing on Evil to College Students: Corra Harris Describing Her Novel Experiment at Rollins University, Gives Sex a Minor Role in Dark Drama." *New York Evening Post*, February 22, 1930.

"On Meeting a Princess." *CCAJ*, February 26, 1933.

"On the Management of a Husband." *LHJ*, March 1925, 30.

"On the Use of Enemies." *CCAJ*, March 4, 1932.

"Oratorical Faith." *CCAJ*, January 28, 1934.

"The Other Forgotten Man." *CCAJ*, October 28, 1932.

"Our Novelists." *Independent*, November 16, 1905, 1171–75.

"Out of Balance." *CCAJ*, January 8, 1933.

"Parents and Children, Yesterday and Today." *SEP*, May 28, 1932, 24–25, 50.

"The Passing of Uncle Remus." *Independent*, July 23, 1908, 190–92.

"Patriotic Criticism in the South." *The Critic*, June 1904, 548–50.

"The Pendergrass Sanitarium for Curables." *SEP*, March 26, 1910, 9–11, 57.

"A Perfect Life." *CCAJ*, October 19, 1934.

"The Pharisee's Lament." *SEP*, December 19, 1931, 32, 83.

"Politics and Prayers in the Valley." *Independent*, July 31, 1916, 155–56.

"Posy." *Independent*, March 8, 1900, 594–96.

"Price of Suffrage for American Women." *SEP*, October 23, 1909, 10–11, 56.

"The Q.E.D. of Sentimentality." *CCAJ*, August 17, 1934.

"Reflections Upon Old Bachelors in New England." *Independent*, December 29, 1904, 1492–94.

"Religion for Secular Souls." *CCAJ*, June 24, 1934.

"A Retired Methodist." *CCAJ*, December 4, 1931.

"Revival of the Negro in Southern Literature." Unpublished manuscript, box 81, folder 3, CHC.

"The Rise and Fall of Popular Novels during 1906." *Independent*, March 7, 1907, 544–46.

"Robin Hood Roosevelt." Typescript, box 81, folder 16, CHC.

"Running a Welfare Racket." Typescript, box 81, folder 7, CHC.

"The Scarlet Flower." *Metropolitan*, June 1914, 10–12, 58–60.

"The Secret Marriage." *Independent*, June 5, 1920, 311, 342.

"The Serpent and the Woman in Fiction." *Independent*, December 7, 1905, 1332–33.

"Sober Reflections." *CCAJ*, October 12, 1934.

"Sob Sister Citizens." *LHJ*, February 1925, 29, 105.

"The South." *Forum*, February 1928, 177–80.

"Southern Tribute to Women of Yesterday." Birmingham, Alabama, newspaper, box 110, folder 30, CHC.

"The Southern White Woman." *Independent*, February 15, 1900, 430–32.

"A Southern Woman Author: Mrs. Corra Harris on the Problems of Her Sex." *The Sun*, June 3, 1911.

"A Southern Woman's View." *Independent*, May 18, 1899, 1354–55.

"A Southern Woman's View of Southern Women." *Independent*, April 17, 1902, 922–24.

"Southern Writers." *The Critic*, September 1905, 644–50.

"The South's Way." *Independent*, November 26, 1908, 1274–77.

"Spiritual Inebriates." *CCAJ*, September 16, 1932.

"Spiritual Speed." *CCAJ*, June 26, 1932.

"Spring Days in the Valley." *Independent*, May 8, 1920, 200.

"The Streets of the City." *Independent*, March 2, 1914, 306–8.

"Success." *CCAJ*, May 19, 1933.

"Suffrage Means That Woman Will Have the Right and the Awful Responsibility of Becoming a Partner in Life with Man." *Evening Sun*, September 25, 1915.

"Superwoman." *Independent*, February 21, 1907, 426–28.

"Sweetness and Light." *CCAJ*, May 26, 1933.

"The Synthetic Girl." *LHJ*, April 1928, 36–37, 73.

"Taking Over Our Problems." *SEP*, May 31, 1919, 10–11, 141–44.

"These Husbands." *LHJ*, June, 1925, 27, 84, 87.

"To License Novelists." *Independent*, November 14, 1907, 1247–50.

"To Restore Poverty's Good Name." *CCAJ*, December 12, 1934.

"Turkey Trot." *SEP*, June 14, 1913, 10–11, 49.

"The Unknown Great American Woman: Not a Singer, Nor a Writer, Nor a Musician, But a Simple Back-Country Mother." *LHJ*, January 1923, 25.

"Upton Sinclair and Helicon Hall." *Independent*, March 28, 1907, 711–13.

"The Valley—After New York." *Independent*, July 13, 1914, 63–65.

"The Walking Delegate Novelist." *Independent*, May 24, 1906, 1213–16.

"War and Brides in June." *Independent*, June 21, 1915, 506.

"War Time in the Valley." *Independent*, December 8, 1917, 471.

"Was Eve a Feminist?" *Independent*, March 8, 1919, 338.

"What Are We Fighting For." *Independent*, June 29, 1918, 502, 517–19.

"What Marriage Was and What It Is Not." *Pictorial Review*, January, 1923, 2.

"What Men Know about Women." *Independent*, March 13, 1916, 379.

"What Religion Means to Me." *CCAJ*, December 6, 1933.

"What Shall It Profit a Man." *CCAJ*, March 27, 1932.

"The White Man in the South." *Independent*, December 28, 1899, 3475–77.

"Who's Who—And Why: Serious and Frivolous Facts about the Great and the Near Great, Corra Harris Herself—by Herself." *SEP*, July 28, 1917, 23–24, 43.

"Why the [Single Woman's] 'Problem' Exists." *American Magazine*, August 1906, 426–27.

"The Widow Ambrose." *LHJ*, August 1920, 7–9, 151–52.

"Wife Often to Blame If Husband Is Unfaithful." *Omaha Daily News*, March 14, 1914.

"The Willipus-Wallipus in Tennessee Politics." *Independent*, February 25, 1909, 622–26.

"A Woman's Relation to the Two Sexes." *Independent*, April 21, 1904, 906–8.

"A Woman Who Likes Growing Old." Columbus (Ga.) *Enquirer*, March 21, 1929.

"A Woman Takes a Look at Politics." *SEP*, June 13, 1931.

"Women Again." *CCAJ*, December 20, 1931.

"The Women and the Future." *Independent*, May 14, 1908, 1090–92.

"Women Are Not Domestic." *Louisville Courier*, November 2, 1913.

"The Women of France." *SEP*, December 12, 1914, 11–12, 34–35.

"Writing and Living." *CCAJ*, April 7, 1933.

"The Year's Curriculum in Fiction." *Independent*, November 11, 1909, 1149–54.

"Yeast-Stirrers in New York City." *Independent*, April 18, 1907, 891–93.

Secondary Sources

Aaron, Daniel. *Paul Elmer More's Shelburne Essays on American Literature.* New York: Harcourt Brace, 1963.

Abrams, Richard M., and Lawrence W. Levine, eds. *The Shaping of Twentieth-Century America.* Boston: Little, Brown, 1971.

Adams, Mary Dean. "In Opposition to Woman Suffrage." *Pamphlets in American History* no. 265.

Alcoff, Linda Martin. "Is the Feminist Critique of Reason Rational?" *Philosophical Topics* 23, no. 2 (1994): 1–26.

———. *Real Knowing: New Versions of the Coherence Theory.* New York: Cornell University Press, 1996.

Alcoff, Linda Martin, and Elizabeth Potter, eds. *Feminist Epistemologies.* New York: Routledge, 1993.

Alexander, Maxine, ed. *Speaking for Ourselves: Women of the South.* New York: Pantheon Books, 1984.

Alpern, Sara, et al. *The Challenge of Feminist Biography: Writing the Lives of Modern American Women.* Urbana: University of Illinois Press, 1992.

Antony, Louise M., and Charlotte Witt, eds. *A Mind of One's Own: Feminist Essays on Reason and Objectivity.* Boulder, Co.: Westview Press, 1993.

Ascher, Carol, Louise DeSalvo, and Sara Ruddick, eds. *Between Women: Biographers, Novelists, Critics, Teachers and Artists Write about Their Work on Women.* New York: Routledge, 1993.

Auslander, Leora. "Feminist Theory and Social History: Explorations in the Politics of Identity." *Radical History Review* 54 (Fall 1992): 158–76.

Ayers, Edward L. *The Promise of the New South: Life after Reconstruction.* New York: Oxford University Press, 1992.

Babcock, Edwina Stanton. "Melancholia and the Silent Woman." *Outlook*, December 18, 1909, 868–74.

Bailey, Kenneth K. *Southern White Protestantism in the Twentieth Century.* New York: Harper and Row, 1964.

Barr, Amelia E. "Discontented Women." *North American Review* 162 (February 1896): 201–9.

Bartley, Numan. *The Creation of Modern Georgia.* Athens: University of Georgia Press, 1983.

Baym, Nina. *Woman's Fiction: A Guide to Novels by and about Women in America, 1820–70.* Urbana: University of Illinois Press, 1993.

Bederman, Gail. *Manliness and Civilization: A Cultural History of Gender and Race in the United States, 1880–1917.* Chicago: University of Chicago Press, 1995.

Belenky, Mary Field, et al., eds. *Women's Ways of Knowing: The Development of Self, Voice, and Mind.* New York: Basic Books, 1986.

Benhabib, Seyla. *Situating the Self: Gender, Community, and Postmodernism in Contemporary Ethics.* New York: Routledge, 1992.

Benjamin, Anne M. *A History of the Anti-Suffrage Movement in the United States from 1895 to 1920: Women against Equality.* Lewiston, N.Y.: Edwin Mellen Press, 1991.

Benn, Stanley I., and Gerald F. Gaus, eds. *Public and Private in Social Life.* New York: St. Martin's Press, 1983.

Bernhard, Virginia, et al. *Southern Women: Histories and Identities.* Columbia: University of Missouri Press, 1992.

Bingham, Emily, and Thomas A. Underwood, eds. *The Southern Agrarians and the New Deal: Essays after I'll Take My Stand.* Charlottesville: University Press of Virginia, 2001.

Bishop, Sharon, and Marjorie Weinzweig, eds. *Philosophy and Women.* Wadsworth Series in Social Philosophy, ed. Richard Wasserstrom. Belmont, Calif.: Wadsworth, 1979.

Blackstock, Walter. "Corra Harris: An Analytical Study of Her Novels." *Florida State University Studies* (Florida State University Press) (1955): 39–92.

Bleser, Carol. *In Joy and in Sorrow: Women, Family, and Marriage in the Victorian South, 1830–1900.* New York: Oxford University Press, 1991.

Boatwright, Eleanor Miot. *Status of Women in Georgia, 1783–1860.* In *Scholarship in Women's History: Rediscovered and New*, ed. Gerda Lerner. Brooklyn: Carlson, 1994.

Bradbury, John M. *Renaissance in the South: A Critical History of the Literature, 1920–1960.* Chapel Hill: University of North Carolina Press, 1963.

Brinkley, Alan. "The Problem of American Conservatism. *American Historical Review* 99, no. 2 (1994): 409–29.

Brundage, W. Fitzhugh. *Lynching in the New South: Georgia and Virginia, 1880–1930.* Urbana: University of Illinois Press, 1993.

Butcher, Patricia Smith. *Education for Equality: Women's Rights Periodicals and Women's Higher Education, 1849–1920.* New York: Greenwood Press, 1989.

Butler, Judith. *Gender Trouble: Feminism and the Subversion of Identity.* New York: Routledge, 1990.

Butler, Judith, and Joan W. Scott, eds. *Feminists Theorize the Political.* New York: Routledge, 1992.

Caldwell, Ellen M. "Ellen Glasgow and the Southern Agrarians." *American Literature* 56, no. 2 (1984): 203–13.

Calverton, Victor F., and Samuel Schmalhausen, eds. *Sex in Civilization.* Intro. Havelock Ellis. New York: Macaulay, 1929.

Camhi, Jane Jerome. *Women against Women: American Anti-Suffragism, 1880–1920. Scholarship in Women's History: Rediscovered and New.* Ed. Gerda Lerner. Brooklyn: Carlson, 1994.

Carby, Hazel. *Reconstructing Womanhood: The Emergence of the Afro-American Woman Novelist.* New York: Oxford University Press, 1987.

Carter, Paul A. *The Spiritual Crisis of the Gilded Age.* Dekalb: Northern Illinois University Press, 1971.

Carver, Thomas Nixon. *Essays in Social Justice.* Cambridge, Mass.: Harvard University Press, 1915.

Cash, Wilbur J. *The Mind of the South.* New York: Vintage Books, 1941.

Ceplair, Larry. *Charlotte Perkins: A Nonfiction Reader.* New York: Columbia University Press, 1991.

Chopin, Kate. *The Awakening.* In *The Complete Works of Kate Chopin,* ed. Per Seyersted. Baton Rouge: Louisiana State University Press, 1969.

Clinton, Catherine. "Bloody Terrain: Freedwomen, Sexuality, and Violence during Reconstruction." In *Half Sisters of History: Southern Women and the American Past,* ed. Catherine Clinton, 136–53. Durham: Duke University Press, 1994.

———, ed. *Half Sisters of History: Southern Women and the American Past.* Durham: Duke University Press, 1994.

Cobb, James C. *Away Down South: A History of Southern Identity.* New York: Oxford University Press, 2005.

———. "Does 'Mind' Still Matter? The South, the Nation, and *The Mind of the South,* 1941–1991." In James Cobb, *Redefining Southern Culture: Mind and Identity in the Modern South,* 44–77. Athens: University of Georgia Press, 1999.

———. "Georgia Odyssey." In *The New Georgia Guide,* 3–104. Athens: University of Georgia Press, 1996.

———. *Redefining Southern Culture: Mind and Identity in the Modern South.* Athens: University of Georgia Press, 1999.

Coffing, Karen. "Corra Harris and the *SEP*: Southern Domesticity Conveyed to a National Audience, 1900–1930. *Georgia Review* 79, no. 2 (1995): 367–93.

———. "Southern Womanhood Preached to a National Audience: The Writings of Corra Harris, Author and Novelist." Master's thesis, Kent State University, 1993.

Conkin, Paul K. *The Southern Agrarians*. Knoxville: University of Tennessee Press, 1988.

Conn, Peter J. *The Divided Mind: Ideology and Imagination in America, 1898–1917.* New York: Cambridge University Press, 1983.

Coser, Rose Laub. *In Defense of Modernity: Role Complexity and Individual Autonomy*. Stanford: Stanford University Press, 1991.

Cott, Nancy F. *The Grounding of Modern Feminism*. New Haven: Yale University Press, 1987.

Cox, Karen. *Dixie's Daughters: The United Daughters of the Confederacy and the Preservation of Confederate Culture*: Gainesville: University Press of Florida, 2003.

———. "The Rise of the United Daughters of the Confederacy, 1894–1914." In *"Lives Full of Struggle and Triumph": Southern Women, Their Institutions, and Their Communities*, ed. Bruce L. Clayton and John A. Salmond, 126–48. Gainesville: University Press of Florida, 2003.

Dakin, Arthur Hazard. *Paul Elmer More*. Princeton: Princeton University Press, 1960.

Danbom, David B. "Romantic Agrarianism in Twentieth-Century America." *Agricultural History* 65, no. 4 (1991): 1–12.

Dempsey, Elam Franklin. *Atticus Green Haygood*. Nashville: Parthenon Press, 1940.

Dillman, Caroline Matheny. *Southern Women*. New York: Hemisphere Publishing Corporation, 1988.

Dittmer, John. *Black Georgia in the Progressive Era: 1900–1920*. Urbana: University of Illinois Press, 1977.

Dix, Dorothea. "Woman's Inhumanity to Woman." *Everybody's Magazine*, May 1904, 633–35.

Dobbins, Charles. "Corra Harris, Life and Work." Master's thesis, Columbia University, 1931.

Douglas, Mary. *Implicit Meanings: Essays in Anthropology*. Boston: Routledge and Kegan Paul, 1975.

DuBois, Ellen. "The Radicalism of the Woman Suffrage Movement: Notes toward the Reconstruction of Nineteenth Century Feminism." *Feminist Studies* 3 (Fall 1975): 63–71.

Dumont, Louis. *Essays on Individualism: Modern Ideology in Anthropological Perspective*. Chicago: University of Chicago Press, 1986.

Edwards, Grace Toney. Foreword. *A Circuit Rider's Wife*. Reprint, Athens: University of Georgia Press, 1998.

Ennis, Stephen. "The Circuit Rider's Wife and the 'Hobo Novelist': The Corra Harris/Jack London Correspondence." *Resources for American Literary Study* 15 (Autumn 1985): 197–208.

Evans, Sara M. *Personal Politics: The Roots of Women's Liberation in the Civil Rights Movement and the New Left*. New York: Knopf, 1979.

Farnham, Christie Anne, ed. *Women of the American South: A Multicultural Reader*. New York: New York University Press, 1997.

Felton, Rebecca Latimer. *The Romantic Story of Georgia's Women.* Atlanta: The Atlanta Georgian and Sunday American, 1930.

Ferber, Marianne A., and Julie A. Nelson. *Beyond Economic Man: Feminist Theory and Economics.* Urbana-Champagne: University of Illinois Press, 1993.

Fitzhugh, George. *Sociology for the South, or the Failure of Free Society.* New York: Burt Franklin, 1854.

Flynt, Wayne. *Dixie's Forgotten People: The South's Poor Whites.* Bloomington: Indiana University Press, 1980, 1979.

Fought, Leigh. *Southern Womanhood and Slavery: A Biography of Louisa McCord, 1810–1879.* New York: Columbia University Press, 2003.

Frankenberg, Ruth. *White Women, Race Matters: The Social Construction of Whiteness.* Minneapolis: University of Minnesota Press, 1993.

Fraser, Nancy, and Sandra Lee Bartky, eds. *Revaluing French Feminism: Critical Essays on Difference, Agency, and Culture.* Bloomington: Indiana University Press, 1992.

———. *Unruly Practices: Power, Discourse, and Gender in Contemporary Social Theory.* Minneapolis: University of Minnesota Press, 1989.

Friedman, Jean E., et al. *Sex, Race, and the Role of Women in the South.* Jackson: University Press of Mississippi, 1983.

Garry, Ann, and Marilyn Pearsall, eds. *Women, Knowledge, and Reality: Explorations in Feminist Philosophy.* New York: Routledge, 1996.

Gates, Henry Louis Jr., ed. *Reading Black, Reading Feminist: A Critical Anthology.* New York: Meridian Books, 1990.

George, W. L. *The Intelligence of Woman.* Boston: Little, Brown, 1916.

Gifford, Carolyn DeSwarte. "Women in Social Reform Movements." In *Women and Religion in America,* ed. Rosemary Radford Ruether, 294–303. 1981. San Francisco: Harper and Row, 1986.

Gilman, Charlotte Perkins. *Concerning Children.* Boston: Small, Maynard, 1900.

———. *His Religion and Hers: A Study of the Faith of Our Fathers and the Work of Our Mothers.* Westport, Conn.: Hyperion Press, 1923.

———. *The Home: Its Work and Influence.* New York: McClure, Phillips, 1903.

———. *Human Work.* New York: McClure, Phillips and Co., 1904.

———. *The Living of Charlotte Perkins Gilman.* New York: Charlton, 1911.

———. *The Man-Made World or Our Androcentric Culture.* New York: Charlton, 1911.

———. *Women and Economics: A Study of the Economic Relation between Men and Women as a Factor in Social Evolution.* 1898. Berkeley: University of California Press, 1998.

Gilmore, Glenda Elizabeth. *Gender and Jim Crow: Women and the Politics of White Supremacy in North Carolina, 1896–1920.* Chapel Hill: University of North Carolina Press, 1996.

Glasgow, Ellen. *Barren Ground.* New York: Hill and Wang, 1957, 1933.

———. *The Freeman and Other Poems.* New York: Doubleday, 1902.

———. *Golden Thoughts on Mother, Home and Heaven from Poetic and Prose Literature of All Ages and Lands.* Intro. Rev. Theo. L. Cuyler, D.D. New York: E. B. Treat, 1882.

———. "No Valid Reason." In *Ellen Glasgow's Reasonable Doubts: A Collection of Her*

Writings, ed. Julius Rowan Raper, 19–26. Baton Rouge: Louisiana State University Press, 1988.

———. *The Woman Within.* New York: Harcourt Brace, 1954.

Graham, Sara Hunter. *Woman Suffrage and the New Democracy.* New Haven: Yale University Press, 1996.

Grammar, John M. "Reconstructing Southern Literature." *American Literary History* 1 (Spring 2001): 126–40.

Green, Elna C. *Southern Strategies: Southern Women and the Woman Suffrage Question.* Chapel Hill: University of North Carolina Press, 1997.

Gross, Jennifer Lynn. "Good Angels: Confederate Widowhood and the Reassurance of Patriarchy in the Postbellum South." Ph.D. diss., University of Georgia, 2001.

Guillaumin, Colette. *Racism, Sexism, Power, and Ideology.* New York: Routledge, 1995.

Haardt, Sara. "The Southern Lady Says Grace." *Reviewer*, October 1925, 57–63.

Hale, Grace Elizabeth. *Making Whiteness: The Culture of Segregation in the South, 1890–1940.* New York: Pantheon Books, 1998.

———. "'Some Women Have Never Been Reconstructed': Mildred Lewis Rutherford, Lucy M. Stanton, and the Radical Politics of White Southern Womanhood, 1900–1930." In *Georgia in Black and White: Explorations in the Race Relations of a Southern State, 1865-1950*, ed. John Inscoe, 173–201. Athens: University of Georgia Press, 1994.

Hall, Jacquelyn Dowd. *Revolt against Chivalry: Jessie Daniel Ames and the Women's Campaign against Lynching.* New York: Columbia University Press, 1979.

———. "Women Writers, the 'Southern Front,' and the Dialectical Imagination." *Journal of Southern History* 69 (February 2003): 3–38.

———. "'You Must Remember This': Autobiography as Social Critique." *Journal of Southern History* 64 (September 1998): 439–65.

Harvey, Paul. "God and Negroes and Jesus and Sin and Salvation: Racism, Racial Interchange, and Interracialism in Southern Religious History." In *Religion in the American South: Protestants and Others in History and Culture*, ed. Beth Barton Schweiger and Donald G. Mathews, 283–330. Chapel Hill: University of North Carolina Press, 2004.

Hauk, Gary S. *Legacy of Heart and Mind: Emory since 1836.* Atlanta: Bookhouse Group, 1999.

Hawley, Ellis W. *The Great War and the Search for a Modern Order: A History of the American People and Their Institutions, 1917-1933.* New York: St. Martin's Press, 1992.

Hayden, Dolores. *The Grand Domestic Revolution: A History of Feminist Designs for American Homes, Neighborhoods, and Cities.* Cambridge: MIT Press, 1981.

Hays, Samuel P. *The Response to Industrialism: 1885–1914.* Chicago: University of Chicago Press, 1957.

Hekman, Susan J. *Gender and Knowledge: Elements of a Postmodern Feminism.* Northeastern Series in Feminist Theory. Boston: Northeastern University Press, 1990.

———. *Moral Voices, Moral Selves: Carol Gilligan and Feminist Moral Theory.* University Park: Pennsylvania State University Press, 1995.

Hewitt, Nancy A., and Suzanne Lebsock, eds. *Visible Women: New Essays on American Activism.* Urbana: University of Illinois Press, 1993.

Heyrman, Christine Leigh. *Southern Cross: The Beginnings of the Bible Belt.* New York: Knopf, 1997.

Hill, Samuel S., ed. *Religion and the Solid South.* Nashville: Abingdon Press, 1972.

———, ed. *Religion in the Southern States.* Macon, Ga.: Mercer University Press, 1983.

———. *The South and the North in American Religion.* Athens: University of Georgia Press, 1980.

———. "The South's Two Cultures." In *Religion and the Solid South,* ed. Samuel S. Hill, 24–56. Nashville: Abingdon Press, 1972.

Hinding, Andrea. *Feminism: Opposing Viewpoints.* St. Paul, Minn.: Greenhaven Press, 1986.

Hine, Darlene Clark, et al. *"We Specialize in the Wholly Impossible": A Reader in Black Women's History.* Brooklyn: Carlson, 1995.

Hitchens, David Lee. "Peace, World Organization and the Editorial Philosophy of the Independent Magazine, 1899–1921." Master's thesis, University of Georgia, 1968.

Hodes, Martha. *White Women/Black Men: Illicit Sex in the Nineteenth Century.* New Haven: Yale University Press, 1997.

Hofstadter, Richard. *The Age of Reform: From Bryan to F.D.R.* New York: Knopf, 1955.

Holt, Hamilton. "A Circuit Rider's Wife in Literature." *Literary Digest International Book Review,* November 1924, 871–73.

Honnighausen, Lothar, and Valeria Gennaro Lerda, eds. *Rewriting the South: History and Fiction.* Tubingen: A. Francke Verlag, 1993.

hooks, bell. *Remembered Rapture: The Writer at Work.* New York: Henry Holt, 1999.

Howe, Marie Jennie. "An Anti-Suffrage Monologue." 1913. *Pamphlets in American History* no. 129.

Hudson, Charles. "The Structure of Fundamentalist Christian Belief System." In *Religion and the Solid South,* ed. Samuel S. Hill, 122–42. Nashville: Abingdon Press, 1972.

Hulme, Peter, and Ludmilla Jordanova. *The Enlightenment and Its Shadows.* London: Routledge, 1990.

Iles, Teresa, ed. *All Sides of the Subject: Women and Biography.* New York: Columbia University Press, 1992.

Inge, Thomas M. "The Fugitives and Agrarians: A Clarification." *American Literature* 62, no. 3 (1990): 486–93.

Jablonsky, Thomas J. *The Home, Heaven, and Mother Party: Female Anti-Suffragists in the United States, 1868–1920.* In *Scholarship in Women's History: Rediscovered and New.* Ed. Gerda Lerner. Brooklyn: Carlson, 1994.

Jaggar, Alison M. *Feminist Politics and Human Nature.* Sussex, U.K.: Harvester Press, 1983.

———. "Love and Knowledge: Emotion in Feminist Epistemology." In *Women, Knowledge, and Reality: Explorations in Feminist Philosophy,* ed. Ann Garry and Marilyn Pearsall, 166–90. New York: Routledge, 1996.

Jaggar, Alison M., and Susan R. Bordo, eds. *Gender/Body/Knowledge: Feminist Reconstructions of Being and Knowing.* New Brunswick, N.J.: Rutgers University Press, 1989.

Jastrow, Joseph. "The Implications of Sex." In *Sex in Civilization*, ed. V. F. Calverton and S. D. Schmalhausen, 127–42. New York: Macaulay, 1929.

Jones, Anne Goodwyn. *Tomorrow Is Another Day: The Woman Writer in the South, 1859–1936*. Baton Rouge: Louisiana State University Press, 1981.

———. "Women Writers and the Myths of Southern Womanhood." In *The History of Southern Women's Literature*, ed. Carolyn Perry and Mary Louise Weaks, 275–90. Baton Rouge: Louisiana State University Press, 2002.

Jones, Jacqueline. *Labor of Love, Labor of Sorrow: Black Women, Work, and the Family, From Slavery to the Present*. New York: Basic Books, 1985.

Josephson, Eric, and Mary Josephson. *Man Alone: Alienation and Modern Society*. New York: Dell, 1962.

Karlsen, Carol. *The Devil in the Shape of a Woman: Witchcraft in Colonial New England*. New York: Vintage Books, 1987.

Kaufman, Marjorie R. "Ellen Glasgow." In *Notable American Women, 1607–1950: A Biographical Dictionary*, ed. Edward T. James, 3:44–49. Cambridge, Mass.: Harvard University Press, 1971.

Kelley, Mary. *Private Woman, Public Stage: Literary Domesticity in Nineteenth-Century America*. New York: Oxford University Press, 1984.

Kelly, Joan. *Women, History, and Theory*. Chicago: University of Chicago Press, 1984.

Kerber, Linda, and Jane Sherron DeHart. *Women's America: Refocusing the Past*. New York: Oxford University Press, 2004.

Kessler-Harris, Alice. *Out to Work: A History of Wage-Earning Women*. New York, 1982.

King, Richard. *A Southern Renaissance: The Cultural Awakening of the South, 1930–1955*. New York: Oxford University Press, 1980.

Kinnard, Cynthia. *Antifeminism in American Thought: An Annotated Bibliography*. Boston: G. K. Hall, 1986.

Kolko, Gabriel. *The Triumph of Conservatism: A Reinterpretation of American History, 1900–1916*. New York: The Free Press, 1963.

Kraditor, Aileen S. *The Ideas of the Woman Suffrage Movement, 1890–1920*. 1965. New York: Norton, 1981.

Kreyling, Michael. *Inventing Southern Literature*. Jackson: University Press of Mississippi, 1998.

Lasch, Christopher. *The New Radicalism in America, 1889–1963: The Intellectual as a Social Type*. London: Chatto and Windus, 1966.

Lauretis, Teresa de, ed., *Feminist Studies/Critical Studies* Bloomington: Indiana University Press, 1986.

Lears, T. J. Jackson. *No Place of Grace: Antimodernism and the Transformation of American Culture 1880–1920*. Chicago: University of Chicago Press, 1983.

Leavitt, Judith Walzer, ed. *Women and Health in America: Historical Readings*. Madison: University of Wisconsin Press, 1984.

Lerner, Gerda. *The Creation of Patriarchy*. New York: Oxford University Press, 1986.

LeRoy-Frazier, Jill. "Saving Southern History in Caroline Gordon's *Penhally*." *Southern Literary Journal* 38 (Fall 2005): 62–75.

Litwack, Leon F. *Trouble in Mind: Black Southerners in the Age of Jim Crow.* New York: Knopf, 1998.

Lloyd, Genevieve. "Maleness, Metaphor, and the Crisis of Reason." In *Mind of One's Own: Feminist Essays on Reason and Objectivity*, ed. Charlotte Witt. 73–92. Boulder, Co.: Westview Press, 2001.

Lyerly, Lynn. "Women and Southern Religion." In *Religion in the American South: Protestants and Others in History and Culture*, ed. Beth Barton Schweiger and Donald G. Mathews, 247–83. Chapel Hill: University of North Carolina Press, 2004.

Lynd, Robert S., and Lynd, Helen Merrell. *Middletown: A Study in American Culture.* New York: Harcourt Brace, 1929.

MacCormack, Carol P., and Marilyn Strathern. *Nature, Culture, and Gender.* Cambridge: Harvard University Press, 1986.

Macpherson, C. B. *The Political Theory of Possessive Individualism, Hobbes to Locke.* Oxford: Clarendon Press, 1962.

Mama, Amina. *Beyond the Masks: Race, Gender, and Subjectivity.* New York: Routledge, 1995.

Mann, Harold W. *Atticus Greene Haygood, Methodist Bishop, Editor, and Educator.* Athens: University of Georgia Press, 1965.

Manning, Carol S. "Agrarianism, Female-Style." *Southern Quarterly* 30, nos. 2–3 (1992): 69–76.

———, ed. *The Female Tradition in Southern Literature.* Urbana: University of Illinois Press, 1993.

———. "The Real Beginning of the Southern Renaissance." In *The Female Tradition in Southern Literature*, ed. Carol S. Manning, 37–56. Urbana: University of Illinois Press, 1993.

———. "Southern Women Writers and the Beginning of the Renaissance." In *The History of Southern Women's Literature*, eds. Carolyn Perry and Mary Louise Weaks, 242–50. Baton Rouge: Louisiana State University, 2002.

Marilley, Suzanne M. *Woman Suffrage and the Origins of Liberal Feminism in the United States, 1820–1920.* Cambridge: Harvard University Press, 1996.

Marshall, Marguerite Mooers. "'Every Woman Is Born in Search of a Husband; Shop Girl Has Better Chance Than Rich Girl.'" *Evening World*, March 14, 1914.

Marshall, Susan E. *Splintered Sisterhood: Gender and Class in the Campaign against Woman Suffrage.* Milwaukee: University of Wisconsin Press, 1997.

Martin, Joel W. "All That Is Solid (and Southern) Melts into Air: A Response to Sam Hill's Fundamental Argument." *Journal of Southern Religion* 1 (1998) jsr.fsu.edu.

Mathews, Donald G. "Lynching Is Part of the Religion of Our People: Faith in the Christian South." In *Religion in the American South: Protestants and Others in History and Culture*, ed. Beth Barton Schweiger and Donald G. Mathews, 153–94. Chapel Hill: University of North Carolina Press, 2004.

———. "The Southern Rite of Human Sacrifice: Part II, Religion as Punishment." *Journal of Southern Religion* 3 (2000): 5.

———. "'We Have Left Undone Those Things Which We Ought to Have Done': Southern Religious History in Retrospect and Prospect." *Church History*, June 1998, 305–6.

McBlee, Kathleen. *Women of the Klan: Racism and Gender in the 1920s*. Berkeley: University of California Press, 1991.

McElroy, Wendy, ed. *Freedom, Feminism, and the State: An Overview of Individualist Feminism*. New York: Holmes and Meier, 1991.

McLoughlin, William G. *Revivals, Awakenings, and Reform: An Essay on Religion and Social Culture in America, 1697–1977.* Chicago: University of Chicago Press, 1978.

Meyers, Diana T. *Subjection and Subjectivity: Psychoanalytic Feminism and Moral Philosophy.* New York: Routledge, 1994.

Meyers, Diana T., and Eva Feder Kittay, eds. *Women and Moral Theory.* Totowa, N.J.: Rowman and Littlefield, 1987.

Mims, Edwin. *The Advancing South: Stories of Progress and Reaction.* New York: Doubleday, 1926.

———. Introduction to 1926 edition of *The Recording Angel.* Garden City: Doubleday, 1926.

Minoque, Kenneth R. *The Liberal Mind.* New York: Random House, 1963.

Mixon, Wayne. "Georgia." In *Religion in the Southern States*, ed. Samuel S. Hill, 77–100. Macon, Ga.: Mercer University Press, 1983.

———. *Southern Writers and the New South Movement, 1865–1913.* Chapel Hill: University of North Carolina Press, 1980.

———. "Traditionalist and Iconoclast: Corra Harris and Southern Writing 1900–1920." In *Developing Dixie: Modernization in a Traditional Society*, ed. Winfred B. Moore Jr. et al., 235–44. Westport, Conn.: Greenwood Press, 1988.

Moghadam, Valentine M. *Identity Politics and Women: Cultural Reassertions and Feminisms in International Perspective.* Boulder: Westview Press, 1994.

Mohanty, Chandra Talpade, et al. *Third World Women and the Politics of Feminism.* Bloomington: Indiana University Press, 1991.

Montagu, Ashley, and Floyd Matson. *The Dehumanization of Man.* New York: McGraw-Hill, 1983.

More, Paul Elmer. *Aristocracy and Justice. Shelburne Essays.* 9th ser. Boston: Houghton Mifflin, 1915.

———. *The Demon of the Absolute. New Shelburne Essays.* No. 1. Princeton: Princeton University Press, 1928.

———. *The Drift of Romanticism. Shelburne Essays.* 8th ser. Boston: Houghton Mifflin, 1913.

———. *A New England Group and Others. Shelburne Essays.* 11th ser. Boston: Houghton Mifflin, 1921.

———. *On Being Human. New Shelburne Essays.* No. 3. New York: Books for Libraries Press, 1936.

———. *Pages from an Oxford Diary.* Princeton: Princeton University Press, 1951.

———. *Shelburne Essays.* 7th ser. Boston: Houghton Mifflin, 1910.

Morgan, David. *Suffragists and Democrats: The Politics of Woman Suffrage in America.* East Lansing: Michigan State University Press, 1972.

Morgan, Edmund S. *American Slavery, American Freedom.* New York: Norton, 1975.

Moses, Norton H., comp. *Lynching and Vigilantism in the United States: An Annotated Bibliography.* Westport, Conn.: Greenwood Press, 1997.

Muller, Herbert J. *Issues of Freedom: Paradoxes and Promises.* New York: Harper, 1960.

Mundy, Jane B. "The Philosopher of the Heart: Corra White Harris, the Circuit Rider's Wife's Philosophy of Man." Master's thesis, University of South Carolina, 1963.

Nicholson, Linda J., ed. *Feminism/Postmodernism.* New York: Routledge, 1990.

———, ed. *Gender and History: The Limits of Social Theory in the Age of the Family.* New York: Columbia University Press, 1986.

Niebuhr, Reinhold. *The Irony of American History.* New York: Scribner, 1951.

Nye, David E. *The Invented Self: An Anti-biography, from Documents of Thomas A. Edison.* Odense, Denmark: Odense University Press, 1983.

O'Brien, Michael. *The Idea of the American South.* 1979. Baltimore: Johns Hopkins University Press, 1990.

O'Neill, William Lloyd. *Everyone Was Brave: The Rise and Fall of Feminism in America.* Chicago: Quadrangle Books, 1969.

Overton, Grant M. *The Women Who Make Our Novels.* New York: Moffat, Yard, 1918.

Owen, Christopher H. *The Sacred Flame of Love: Methodism and Society in Nineteenth-Century Georgia.* Athens: University of Georgia Press, 1998.

Ownby, Ted. *Subduing Satan: Religion, Recreation, and Manhood in the Rural South, 1865–1920.* Chapel Hill: University of North Carolina Press, 1990.

Painter, Nell Irvin. "Writing Biographies of Women." *Journal of Women's History* 9, no. 2 (1997): 154–63.

Papashvily, Helen Waite. *All the Happy Endings: A Study of the Domestic Novel in America, the Women Who Wrote It, the Women Who Read It, in the Nineteenth Century.* Port Washington, N.Y.: Kennikat Press, 1972.

Parini, Jay. "Biography Can Escape the Tyranny of Facts." *Chronicle of Higher Education,* February 4, 2000, A72.

Patterson, Orlando. *Freedom.* Vol. 1 of *Freedom in the Making.* New York: Basic Books, 1991.

Perry, Bliss. *The American Mind and American Idealism.* Boston: Houghton Mifflin, 1913.

Perry, Carolyn, and Mary Louise Weaks, eds. *The History of Southern Women's Literature.* Baton Rouge: Louisiana State University Press, 2002.

Plekhanov, G. V. *The Role of the Individual in History.* London: Lawrence and Wishart, 1976, 1941.

Pollard, Edward A. *The Lost Cause: A New Southern History of the War of the Confederates.* New York: E. B. Treat, 1866.

Pyle, Joseph Gilpin. "Christian Civilization in the Balance." Philadelphia: Pennsylvania Association Opposed to Woman Suffrage, [1900–1920].

Raper, Arthur F. *The Tragedy of Lynching.* Chapel Hill: University of North Carolina Press, 1933.

Raper, Julius Rowan. "Ellen Glasgow: Gaps in the Record." In *Regarding Ellen Glasgow:*

Essays for Contemporary Readers, ed. Welford Dunaway Taylor and George Longest, 127–39. Richmond: The Library of Virginia, 2001.

———, ed. *Ellen Glasgow's Reasonable Doubts: A Collection of Her Writings*. Baton Rouge: Louisiana State University Press, 1988.

Reeves, Ruby. "Corra Harris, Her Life and Works." Master's thesis, University of Georgia, 1937.

Roediger, David R. *The Wages of Whiteness: Race and the Making of the American Working Class*, 1991. New York: Verso, 1999.

Roth, Darlene Rebecca. *Matronage: Patterns in Women's Organizations, Atlanta, Georgia, 1890–1940*. In *Scholarship in Women's History: Rediscovered and New*. Ed. Gerda Lerner. Brooklyn: Carlson, 1994.

Schiebinger, Londa. *The Mind Has No Sex? Women in the Origins of Modern Science*. Cambridge: Harvard University Press, 1989.

Schmidt, Jean Miller. *Grace Sufficient: A History of Women in American Methodism, 1760–1939*. Nashville: Abingdon Press, 1999.

Schmidt, Peter. "Corra Harris's *The Recording Angel* (1912): Why Is One of the Best Comic Novels between *The Adventures of Huckleberry Finn* and *As I Lay Dying* Out of Print?" In *CrossRoads: A Southern Culture Annual*, ed. Ted Olson. 334–50. Macon, Ga.: Mercer University Press, 2005.

Schmitt, Richard. *Alienation and Class*. Cambridge, Mass.: Schenkman, 1983.

Schuyler, George S. "Our White Folks." *American Mercury*, December 1927, 385–92.

Schweiger, Beth Barton, and Donald G. Mathews, eds. *Religion in the American South: Protestants and Others in History and Culture*. Chapel Hill: University of North Carolina Press, 2004.

Scott, Anne Firor. *Making the Invisible Woman Visible*. Urbana: University of Illinois Press, 1984.

———. *Natural Allies: Women's Associations in American History*. Urbana: University of Illinois Press, 1993.

———. *The Southern Lady from Pedestal to Politics, 1830–1930*. Chicago: University of Chicago Press, 1970.

———, ed. *Unheard Voices: The First Historians of Southern Women*. Charlottesville: University of Virginia, 1993.

———. "Women in the South: History as Fiction, Fiction as History." In *Rewriting the South: History and Fiction*, ed. Lothar Honnighausen and Valeria Gennaro Lerda, 22–34. Tubingen: A. Francke Verlag, 1993.

———. "Women, Religion, and Social Change in the South, 1830–1930." In *Religion and the Solid South*, ed. Samuel S. Hill Jr., 92–121. New York: Abingdon Press, 1972.

Scott, Anne Firor, and Andrew M. Scott. *One Half the People: The Fight for Woman Suffrage*. In *The America's Alternatives Series*, ed. Harold M. Hyman. New York: Lippincott, 1975.

Scott, Joan W. "Deconstructing Equality-versus-Difference: or The Uses of Poststructuralist Theory of Feminism." *Feminist Studies* 14, no. 1 (1988): 32–50.

———, ed. *Feminism and History*. Oxford Readings in Feminism. New York: Oxford University Press, 1996.

———. *Gender and the Politics of History.* New York: Columbia University Press, 1988.

———. *Only Paradoxes to Offer: French Feminists and the Rights of Man.* Cambridge: Harvard University Press, 1996.

Scott-Maxwell, Florida. *Women and Sometimes Men.* New York: Knopf, 1957.

Shafer, Robert. *Paul Elmer More and American Criticism.* 1935. New York: AMS Press, 1977.

Simms, L. Moody Jr. "Corra Harris on 'Literalism' in Fiction." *Resources for American Literary Study* 9, no. 2 (1979): 213–17.

———. "Corra Harris on the Decline of Southern Writing." *Southern Studies: An Interdisciplinary Journal of the South* 18, no. 2 (1979): 247–50.

———. "Corra Harris, William Peterfield Trent, and Southern Writing." *Mississippi Quarterly* 32 (Fall 1979): 641–50.

Sims, Anastatia. *The Power of Femininity in the New South: Women's Organizations and Politics in North Carolina, 1880–1930.* Columbia: University of South Carolina Press, 1997.

Singal, Daniel Joseph. *The War Within: From Victorian to Modernist Thought in the South, 1919–1945.* Chapel Hill: University of North Carolina Press, 1982.

Skaggs, Merrill Maguire. "Ellen Glasgow." In *The History of Southern Women's Literature,* ed. Carolyn Perry and Mary Louise Weaks, 336–43. Baton Rouge: Louisiana State University Press, 2002.

Skevington, Suzanne, and Deborah Baker. *The Social Identity of Women.* London: Sage, 1989.

Solomon, Martha M. *A Voice of Their Own: The Woman Suffrage Press, 1840–1910.* Tuscaloosa: University of Alabama Press, 1991.

Spacks, Patricia Meyer. *The Female Imagination.* New York: Knopf, 1975.

Stanley, Liz. "Biography as Microscope or Kaleidoscope? The Case of 'Power' in Hannah Cullwick's Relationship with Arthur Munby." *Women's Studies International Forum* 10, no. 1 (1987): 19–31.

Steuter, Erin. "Women against Feminism: An Examination of Feminist Social Movements and Anti-feminist Countermovements." *Canadian Review of Sociology and Anthropology* 29 (August 1992): 288–307.

Stewart, John L. *The Burden of Time: The Fugitives and Agrarians.* Princeton, N.J.: Princeton University Press, 1965.

Suleiman, Susan R., ed. *The Female Body in Western Culture.* Cambridge: Harvard University Press, 1986.

Sumner, William Graham. *What Social Classes Owe to Each Other.* New York: Harper and Brothers, 1883.

Susman, Warren I. *Culture as History: The Transformation of American Society in the Twentieth Century.* New York: Pantheon Books, 1984.

Sykes, Gerald, ed. *Alienation: The Cultural Climate of Our Time.* New York: G. Braziller, 1964.

Talmadge, John E. *Corra Harris, Lady of Purpose.* Athens: University of Georgia Press, 1968.

———. *Rebecca Latimer Felton: Nine Stormy Decades.* Athens: University of Georgia Press, 1960.

Tanner, Stephen Lloyd. *Paul Elmer More: Literary Criticism as the History of Ideas.* New York: SUNY Press, 1987.

Tate, William. "A Neighbor's Recollections of Corra Harris." *Georgia Review* 5, no. 1 (1951): 1–12.

Taylor, A. Elizabeth. "The Last Phase of the Woman Suffrage Movement in Georgia." *Georgia Historical Quarterly* 43 (1959): 11–28.

———. "The Origin of the Woman Suffrage Movement in Georgia." *Georgia Historical Quarterly* 28 (1944): 63–80.

———. "Revival and Development of the Woman Suffrage Movement in Georgia." *Georgia Historical Quarterly* 42 (1958): 339–54.

Taylor, Welford Dunaway, and George C. Longest, eds., *Regarding Ellen Glasgow: Essays for Contemporary Readers.* Richmond: Library of Virginia, 2001.

Thurman, Howard. *A Strange Freedom: The Best of Howard Thurman on Religious Experience and Public Life.* Edited by Walter Earl Fluker and Catherine Tumber. Boston: Beacon Press, 1998.

Thurner, Manuela. "'Better Citizens without the Ballot': American Antisuffrage Women and Their Rationale during the Progressive Era." *Journal of Women's History* 5, no. 1 (1993): 33–60.

Tompkins, Jane P. *Sensational Designs: The Cultural Works of American Fiction, 1790–1860.* New York: Oxford University Press, 1986.

Tong, Rosemarie. *Feminist Thought: A Comprehensive Introduction.* 1989. Boulder: Westview Press, 1998.

Trachtenberg, Alan. "Home as Place and Center for Private and Family Life: Introduction." *Social Research* 58 (Spring 1991): 211–13.

Twain, Mark. *Autobiography [of] Mark Twain [Pseud.].* New York: Harper and Brothers, 1924.

Wade, Barbara Ann. *Frances Newman: Southern Satirist and Literary Rebel.* Tuscaloosa: University of Alabama Press, 1998.

Wallerstein, Immanuel. "What Can One Mean by Southern Culture." In *The Evolution of Southern Culture,* ed. Numan V. Bartley, 1–13. Athens: University of Georgia Press, 1988.

Ware, Vron. *Beyond the Pale: White Women, Racism, and History.* New York: Verso, 1992.

Warren, Joyce W. *The American Narcissus: Individualism and Women in Nineteenth-Century American Fiction.* New Brunswick, N.J.: Rutgers University Press, 1984.

Wheeler, Marjorie Spruill. *New Women of the New South: The Leaders of the Woman Suffrage Movement in the Southern States.* New York: Oxford University Press, 1993.

———. *One Woman, One Vote: Rediscovering the Woman Suffrage Movement.* Troutdale, Ore.: New Sage Press, 1995.

White, Cynthia L. *Women's Magazines, 1693–1968.* London: Joseph, 1970.

White, Deborah Gray. *Arn't I a Woman? Female Slaves in the Plantation South.* New York: Norton, 1985.

Whites, Lee Ann. *Gender Matters: Civil War, Reconstruction, and the Making of the New South.* New York: Palgrave Macmillan, 2005.

———. "Rebecca Latimer Felton and the Problem of 'Protection' in the New South." In *Visible Women: New Essays on American Activism*, ed. Nancy A. Hewitt and Suzanne Lebsock, 41–61. Urbana: University of Illinois Press, 1993.

———. "Rebecca Latimer Felton and the Wife's Farm: The Class and Racial Politics of Gender Reform." *Georgia Historical Quarterly* 72 (Summer 1992): 354–72.

———. "Stand by Your Man: The Ladies Memorial Association and the Reconstruction of Southern White Manhood." In *Women of the American South: A Multicultural Reader*, ed. Christie Anne Farnham, 133–49. New York: New York University Press, 1997.

Wiebe, Robert H. *The Search for Order, 1877–1920.* New York: Hill and Wang, 1957.

Williamson, Joel. *The Crucible of Race: Black-White Relations in the American South since Emancipation.* New York: Oxford University Press, 1984.

Wilson, Charles Reagan. *Baptized in Blood: The Religion of the Lost Cause, 1865–1920.* Athens: University of Georgia Press, 1980.

Woloch, Nancy. *Muller v. Oregon: A Brief History with Documents.* New York: St. Martin's Press, 1996.

Woodward, C. Vann. *Origins of the New South, 1877–1913.* Baton Rouge: Louisiana State University Press, 1951.

Yaeger, Patricia. *Dirt and Desire: Reconstructing Southern Women's Writing, 1930–1990.* Chicago: University Press of Chicago, 2000.

Young, Iris Marion. *Justice and the Politics of Difference.* Princeton, N.J.: Princeton University Press, 1990.

———. *Throwing Like a Girl and Other Essays in Feminist Philosophy and Social Theory.* Indianapolis: Indiana University Press, 1990.

Zinn, Maxine Baca, and Bonnie Thornton Dill, eds., *Women of Color in U.S. Society.* Philadelphia: Temple University Press, 1994.

Index

Catherine Oglesby is professor of history at Valdosta State University, where she teaches New South, U.S. women's history, and historiography. She received the E. Merton Coulter award in 2004 from the Georgia Historical Society for her article on Harris.